INSIGHT GUIDES

BaLI

Directed and Designed by Hans Johannes Hoefer
Text by Star Black and Willard A. Hanna
Photography by Werner Hahn
and Hans Johannes Hoefer

A P A
PUBLICATIONS

BALI

Fourteenth Edition (Reprint)

ABOUT THIS BOOK

Insight Guide: Bali holds a special position in the large library of Apa Publications. This is the volume, first published in 1970, in which founder-publisher **Hans Höfer** compounded the formula that has been used in each succeeding *Insight Guide*. Combining superb photographs, authoritative text, colorful printing and clean design, the book received a coveted ASTA/Popular Photography gold award for its use of photography to promote tourism and travel.

The Real Bali

Höfer, at that time a young West German native with diplomas in photography, printing and design, wanted to apply his Bauhaus principles to the literature of travel. He lived for three years in Bali, painting in a studio in Ubud and traveling the lovely island, mostly by bicycle. "I began to realise the popular projection of Bali then—the bare-breasted women—was misleading." Höfer recalled. "The tourist's expectations were being geared to something that existed, certainly, but which missed the whole point of what Bali was about ... its great cultural vitality ... I wanted to prepare visitors for the real Bali, so they wouldn't be disappointed in what they found, and so they would have an understanding of the island's soul."

Birth of Apa

The great success of *Insight Guide: Bali* led to the founding of Apa Publications in Singapore and the ensuing series of fine books that combine the same rich mixture of journalistic and artistic skills. In the beginning, however, Höfer had only a concept that he drafted into a layout that he took to **Siegfied Beil**, then manager of the Inter-Continental Hotel Bali Beach for P.T. Hotel Indonesia International. Overnight, Beil became a publisher; committees were formed to vet the book's accuracy with representatives from government, tourism organisations and religious affairs departments.

Höfer scoured the island with cameras shared by his friend, countryman, photographer and designer, **Werner Hahn**, who had been a partner in many of his earlier travels in Bali. For the text, **Star Black** was called in from Bangkok.

Black, California-born, with degrees in art and English literature from Wellesley, had spent many months in Bali, absorbing its richness, and was already known as a perceptive observer of the Asian scene from her base in Thailand. She has contributed to several *Insight Guides*.

Höfer, Hahn and Black turned the island upside down, exploring, evaluating and becoming involved in every aspect of its fascinating, colorful life.

Hahn

Black

Hanna

Bali: A Classic

The result, the first edition of *Guide to Bali*, was a classic almost from the day it left the presses. Now in its 12th edition, *Bali* has undergone various changes and revisions, though the essential editorial approach of the original has been retained.

This new edition of *Insight Guide: Bali* includes a fascinating historical overview of the island by **Dr. Willard A. Hanna**, condensed from his unprecedented *Bali Chronicles* also published by Apa Publications. Dr. Hanna has been exploring and writing about Asia since 1932 and has been a member of the American Universities Field Staff, Inc.

The current edition has been updated by **Made Wijaya**, with the assistance of **Eric Oey**. Wijaya, who put together the expanded and updated Travel Tips section, was born in Australia but has spent the past decade in Bali. He holds a degree in Environmental Science from Sydney University and writes a popular column, "Stranger in Paradise," for the *Sunday Bali Post*.

Oey, though an American, traces his roots to Indonesia itself; his father is an Indonesian-Chinese. Oey did graduate work in Indonesian literature and history and in Chinese studies at the University of California at Berkeley.

The rapid development of tourism in the island over the past few years has touched Sanur and Kuta in particular, and much of the content of this edition is a result of previous revision efforts of **David Stuart-Fox, Paul Zach, June Jacob, Sin Yoke Fund** and **Lai Kwok Kin**.

For having made this book possible in the first place, we are deeply indebted to Siegfied Beil for his faith and enthusiasm. Other friends and supporters include the Governor of Bali, **G.P. Rijasse**, P.T. Hotel Indonesia International, **I.B. Pt. Badra, Donald Friend, Ketut Ginarse, Njoman Oka, A.A.G. Rai, Wakid Basudewa, Drs I. Gst. Bg. N. Pandji, Wija Wawo Runtu, Djoti Mantjica, Arie Smit, Jimmy Pandy, Hans Snel, Warwick & Lisa Purser, Chris Carlisle, Sani Soemakno, Antonie Yazbeck, Ramond Khalife, Charles & Suarti Levine, Victor Mason, Annabelle Morgan, Suzanna Range, Mrs. Renata Meletzke** and especially, the people of Bali. For additional photographs we are grateful to **Brent Hesselyn** (cover) and **Leonard Lueras** (pages 86-87).

—Apa Publications

Fox

Zach

THE ISLAND

EXPLORING BALI

THE ARTS

Travel Tips

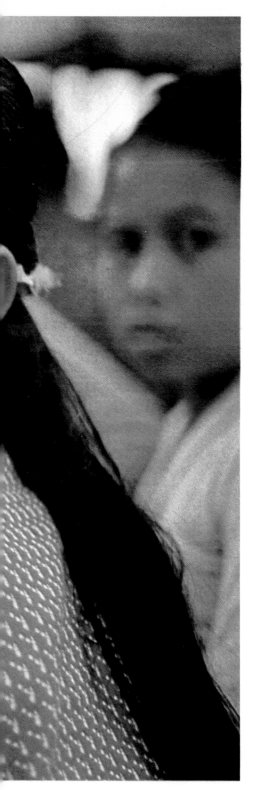

bali—a new look

Whether it be the charm of a young girl dressed for a festival or the mischief in the eyes of a comic storyteller, in Bali every new look is a surprise. For decades the island has startled the world with a fascinating and vibrant culture, born in deeply rooted cults of ancient magic and fostered by the guiding rituals of a strong religion. Ever since the fall of medieval empires when the spread of Islam drove nobles, priests and intelligentsia from Hindu Java to seek sanctuary in Bali, the island has been a haven for the arts, rituals and classics.

Through centuries of isolation, the people viewed the lofty volcano Gunung Agung as "Navel of the World" and nourished their philosophies in temples and palace courts of small kingdoms. The rule of native kings ended violently with the Dutch conquest of Bali early this century. After brief colonial rule and later liberation as part of a new country, Bali has emerged a lively, dynamic community, where past traditions are preserved, yet where styles are forever changing and new contrasts emerging. To understand the character of the people, one must see the island in its true perspective—as an oasis of undying ceremony and quiet beauty, yet as only one of over three thousand islands in Indonesia, fifth largest nation in the world and third richest in natural resources.

The earliest rumors of Indonesia to reach the West—rumors of jewels, mountains of gold, the white monkey and even the phoenix—arose from the distant realities of a huge archipelago surrounded by eight seas and two oceans. An immense region of six million square kilometers of land and sea, Indonesia is still growing. One fourth of its four hundred volcanoes (including two in Bali) are still active today, ever changing the country's contours to new scenes spectacular in their contrasts.

Preceding pages: a procession in Bona, the dance of "the revered angels"; the silhouettes of multi-roofed merus *at the Batur temple in Kintamani; and, a mythological creature known as* Barong *prances. Left, a girl receives a blessing of rice grains.*

19

Islands to the far east and west are remnants of two lost continents. Before the sea rose hundreds of meters during the last glacial period, Sumatra, Kalimantan (Borneo), Java and Bali were all linked to Asia; while in the east, Irian was joined to Australia. The treacherous strait that separates Bali from its neighboring island Lombok is an important landmark, believed to be the dividing line between Asia and Australia in geologic times. Contrasts between the two islands are obvious. Bali is lush, equatorial, smothered with the luxuriant vegetation of tropical Asia. Lombok is more wind-blown and dry like the Australian plain. Animals too are different. Rare marsupials, cockatoos, parrots and giant lizards that roam the arid regions of the eastern islands are nowhere to be found in Bali, where tigers, orangutans and pythons range the dense tropical forests.

The people of this varied land share in its diversity. The famous discovery of *Pithecanthropos erectus*, or Java Man, established Indonesia as home of one of the earliest races of mankind. Since then, migrations of many races have swept through the archipelago—aboriginal tribes of hunters which once occupied all Asia; primitive Negrito peoples who still inhabit the inland wilderness; and advanced Proto-Malays who brought from Yunan, in southwest China, refined implements of stone. The early Christian era brought sailors, warriors, priests and craftsmen from India in a sudden outburst of Hindu and Buddhist expansionism.

No wonder, then, that no Indonesian island, however small, has a population that is not racially mixed. Languages of the archipelago total about one hundred and seventy, with the national language *Bahasa Indonesia* bringing unity of expression to widely divergent cultures. Ninety percent of Indonesia's one hundred and twenty million people are Muslims, with minorities of Christians, Hindus and Buddhists. All people of different faiths have lived side by side in harmony. This tolerance has endowed Indonesia with a resilience to sustain centuries of foreign influences, and at last to incorporate them into her own society.

The first European to set foot in the country was none other than Marco Polo in 1292, while serving as an ambassador to the Great Khan of Mongolia. The first Europeans to alight in Bali were a group of Dutch sailors manning a small fleet headed by Cornelis de Houtman in 1597. The diifference of discoveries being that Marco Polo continued his voyage; the sailors just couldn't leave Bali. Their reaction was a natural one. The captain and all his men fell in love with the island and soon befriended the king, a jovial fat man who surrounded himself with dozens of wives, owned fifty dwarfs as retainers, and drove a chariot drawn by white buffaloes. After numerous postponements, Houtman set a date for his departure. But to the captain's chagrin, some of his men refused to go, and he was obliged to sail for Holland with only part of his crew. When news of discovering a new "paradise" reached Europe, it created such a sensation that the Dutch trader, Jacob van Heemskerck, was promptly sent to Bali with gifts for the king.

The rapport between voyager and islander remained. For the next two hundred years, Dutchmen and other Europeans continued to visit but not to stay. With the beginnings of Dutch colonization in the 19th century, scholars wrote the first monographs on the culture of Bali. It wasn't until the late 1920s that the remote little island made its debut in the Western world through a series of documentary films, inspiring an elite circle of world travelers and celebrities to adopt Bali as their isle at the rainbow's end and to build villas in Sanur and Ubud. During the thirties, a group of visiting artists, musicians and anthropologists devoted themselves to the study of the culture, leaving some memorable volumes and photographs behind them.

Nowadays Bali is the magic touch to world travel. Though many countrysides still linger where an automobile seems to disrupt the quiet solitude of the landscape, the island can now boast of an international jet airport, several luxurious international hotels (one of which is seen for kilometers around as being the first and only building over four stories high), and big plans for further developing beaches as holiday resorts. Yet the traveler to Bali is still the explorer, discovering untouched places and witnessing exotic rituals which have not diminished with the changing times.

From a world streaming beneath you at jet speed, you suddenly find yourself coasting by shaded roads bespeckled with sunlight. Relaxing is effortless. Off comes the tie for a sports shirt and city shoes for sandals. No heavy clothing is necessary to meet the weather, and no greeting formalities but a smile are needed to return a welcome. From your arrival, you are treated with the respect befitting a guest and the surprised delight in seeing someone new.

Bali is filled with nooks and corners, back roads and gateways into the heart of a people. When driving around the island, it is difficult to look straight ahead; there is always something eye-catching along the wayside. Take the road, for instance. It is a sidewalk, highway, playground, meeting place, cargo route and the path of ceremonial processions. Along its sides are countless temples, rustic shrines, *gamelan* rehearsals, markets and harvests. A turn-off may lead to a village of craftsmen who labor at a primitive style of woodcarving, or to royal tombs, half-hidden in the farmlands, that mirror the island's legendary past. Perhaps you stop at a hillside restaurant overlooking the mysterious Elephant Cave, or pause for tea at a local food stand shaded by an enormous banyan tree. Even the most secluded retreats provide cool refreshment, since it doesn't take long to find a climber eager to fulfill a personal order of one fresh coconut.

"Night life" in Bali is the question for many Orient travelers who have just emerged from Bangkok after dark or Hong Kong's torrent of evening entertainment. Night falls early over the island's country towns and farm villages, and among the Balinese 9 p.m. is late at night. However, the evenings of holy days, when temples hold their festivals, promise nightlong dramas of magic, romance plays and trance rituals—ending with good triumphing over evil in the first gray of dawn. For visitors, a respite on Sanur's coast is a pause from all the rush and traffic noise of the world's cities. With no garish city lights, night skies are magnificent, and few places bring you closer to Bali's romance than a calm seashore lit by the torches of night fishermen. Scattered along the beach are elegant hotels and restaurants where ambrosial buffets of Indonesian dishes, exotic *gamelan* music and the graceful, swaying dancers perfectly combine in starlit Bali dinners that capture the spirit of native festivity.

Many who truly enjoy being in Bali today wonder about the future now that tourism is a solidly established industry (in 1982 there were nearly 139 thousand visitors to Bali compared to 24 thousand a decade ago.) The concern many visitors have to safeguard the unique arts and ceremonies is a sign of respect to the people and a compliment to their culture. But just as Bali, seen and experienced today, is the accomplishment of past generations, so the island's future ultimately lies with the Balinese themselves. To wish for unconditional preservation of the culture is to put it behind glass and to deny Bali its identity as a key province in a developing nation.

Besides, the Balinese have a knack for mixing modernity with tradition. A fashionable young man these days hires a car to kidnap his bride—quicker and more convenient than carrying her off on his shoulders, as was the old custom. Streets by night in Denpasar are now a jubilee of neon lights, yet on every busy intersection stands a statue of a demon-giant to ward off evil spirits who might cause accidents. In many places where there is electricity, villagers may gather round a communal television set to watch "Hawaii Five-O" whilst, in the background, sounds of the *gamelan* practice waft gently across the fields from the *bale banjar*. Even far out in the country are touches of the modern world. Like a light bulb set on top of a temple shrine in a village without electricity. Why the bulb? The reason is simple, practical and typical: where function falls short, form takes over—in this case, the fine shape of glass serves as a good decoration.

In Bali, make no predictions. Each village has its own customs and every celebration its own style. You may journey to a distant village in hopes of seeing a traditional mask play performed in the courts of native kings four centuries ago, only to find at the same festival a master of ceremonies playing an Indonesian pop song or the latest hit from Boney M. Bali is at once a place of ceremony, ritual, fads and fashion. Where trucks carrying flesh-packed posters blaze through the town streets sounding rock 'n' roll records to announce the current film show entitled "Getting to Know the Sex", yet where village communities have long upheld a high standard of morality and where, by good manners, lovers never show affection in public.

The Balinese welcome a tourism beneficial to a country seeking to promote an understanding of its heritage. Villages which may expect guests attending their dramas are proud to present the community's orchestra and selection of dances. The nominal fees charged for seats to a drama or shadow play are collected as a contribution to maintain the community's dance properties, or as a fund for repairing the village temples. By supporting these activities as a visitor, you give the people an opportunity to improve their facilities without sacrificing the merit of their ritual.

With a growing international consciousness and imminent large-scale development, Bali is entering a period of transition. Many places on the island first introduced to the material comforts enjoyed automatically by the West have incorporated them into their style of life with a uniquely Balinese flavor. The cohesive bonds of religion, family ties and community life have given the people a sound basis from which they may meet the problems and challenges that face a young country. The Balinese have achieved a harmonious order to their environment without disrupting the beauty of nature, and have created a society that can contribute something of value to the world.

Storyteller re-enacts the glories of the past in today's entertainment: Topeng mask drama.

from the sacred volcanoes to the legendary elephant fish

Once a great Javanese priest was forced to banish his dissolute son to Bali which was then joined to Java by a very narrow isthmus. The despondent priest brought his son there and bade him to go. When the young man was lost to sight, the priest drew a line with his finger across the sands. The waters met and Bali became an island.

The legend points to a truth, for Bali was, indeed, once connected to Java. The strait, less than 3 kilometers wide between East Java and the western tip of Bali, reaches a depth of only 60 meters. To the east of the island, through the Lombok Strait, surge some of the deepest waters in the archipelago! Flanked by the Java Sea to the north and the Indonesian Ocean to the south, Bali is one of the smallest islands in Indonesia, with an area of 5,620 square kilometers. Just 8° south of the equator, it has the even and warm climate of the tropics. The only noticeable change in weather is between the rainy season, October through March, and the dry, balmy season during the remainder of the year.

A volcanic range dominates the landscape. According to Balinese mythology, the island was originally unstable. To stop it wobbling the gods set down upon it the mountain Mahameru, the holy mountain of Hinduism. The Balinese called it Gunung Agung ("The Great Mountain"), which was 3,140 meters high before the 1963 eruption. The other major mountains are: Batukau ("Stone Coconut-shell") at 2,278 meters; and in the center Batur at 1,717 meters and Abang at 2,152 meters. In the far south is the raised tableland of the Bukit Peninsula at only 220 meters.

Bali's volcanic chain, stretching from east to west, divides the island in half. The northern region of Buleleng, a narrow coastal strip which quickly merges into foothills, produces Bali's main exports: cattle, coffee, and copra. The northern fields clothe the highlands in patch-work quilts of peanut, cabbage, and

Preceding pages: boisterous schoolboys climb a banyan tree. At left, mists shroud the sacred volcanic peak of Mount Batur.

27

onion. Lofty prehistoric tree-ferns, elephant grass, and wild flowers hang from the steep cliffs which hug the roadside, while tall pines and cypress trees soar high above the lower embankments. The fecundity of the north extends down the mountain slopes to the densely populated plains of central Bali.

Despite the pressure of the island's population of nearly 3 million, lack of running water has kept the west in uninhabited desolation. One of the rarest birds in the world, Rothschild's Mynah, is found only in one such remote area of Bali. Crocodiles, jungle cocks, deer, and wild hogs prowl the low dusty brush of this hilly country the Balinese call *Pulaki*—the legendary home of the Invisible Ones who reside in a city condemned by the angered deities to sink into the earth. Another arid region is the limestone peninsula of Bukit, which rises in sheer cliffs from the deep pellucid waters off the south coast. The road through Bukit's dry fields ends at a long rock 75 m above the sea. Suspended on the precipice is Ulu Watu, one of the island's holiest temples whose rock foundation is believed to be the petrified ship of Dewi Danu, goddess of the waters.

Southeast of Bali lies the barren island of Nusa Penida, said to be the dwelling place of Gede Mecaling, the fanged giant who haunts the lonely beaches of South Bali. Nusa was once a penal colony used by the kings of Bali. Now the island is a county under the jurisdiction of the eastern district of Klungkung. The people of Nusa grow corn and coconut, but because the dry mountainous terrain does not permit an extensive irrigation system, many of the villages are impoverished. Nusa is famous among the Balinese for raising a certain breed of chicken particularly effective as an offering to drive off evil spirits. It is also renowned for its birds and is the northernmost breeding ground for the sulphur crested cockatoo.

The smaller island of Serangan across from Benoa Harbor is aptly nicknamed "The Turtle Island". Large sea turtles are caught and kept there in roofed palisades built in the shallow water until they are sold as a special dish for feasts. Serangan contains the old sea temple of Sakenan. Every 210 days thousands of Balinese cross the sand banks to pay homage.

Like the majority of Indonesians, the Balinese are a mixture of races. Primarily, they are descendants of the Malayo-Polynesians, ancient denizens of the archipelago. They also stem from central and eastern Javanese ancestors: Indonesians of a Hindu culture, perhaps with traces of Indian and Chinese blood. To this ethnic blend, Polynesian and Melanesian traces were added, resulting in a picturesque variety among the Balinese. While some people have sleek hair, high nose bridges and cream-yellow skin, others are dark and curly haired, like South Sea islanders.

Of the 7,000 foreigners living in Bali, the majority are Chinese, followed by Indian and Arabian citizens. Many other resident Chinese have become Indonesian citizens. Over 95 percent of the population practice the Bali-Hindu religion; the remainder are mostly Muslims, with some Buddhists and Christians.

When the Hindu Javanese established themselves in Bali many centuries ago, they introduced to the Balinese community two paramount social institutions: the Hindu caste system and the accompanying "language of courtesies". The caste system in Bali is relaxed and simple compared with that of India. Basically, there are four castes. The common villagers constitute the working class, the Sudras. The nobility is divided into three well-known groups: the Brahmanas, the highest caste with the male title of *Ida Bagus* (only a Brahmana may become a high priest); the Satrias, to which many of the former Balinese royalty belonged, with the male titles of *Anak Agung*, *Dewa*, and *Cokorda*; and the Wesias, the warrior class entitled *I Gusti*, who also became rulers of smaller principalities.

Although caste rules are largely restricted to the observance of established formulas of eti-

Left, irrigation canals and rivers bring precious water to the sawahs, the rich farmlands of central Bali.

quette, the full name of every Balinese includes the caste title, and in formal Balinese language one must be addressed accordingly. When two strangers meet, a man of low caste speaks to one of higher caste in high Balinese. The latter answers in low Balinese, the everyday tongue spoken in the villages. Undoubtedly, low Balinese is the oldest language of the island and belongs to ancient Malayo-Polynesian dialects, the aboriginal languages of the archipelago. High Balinese, largely Javanese in origin and using Sanskrit words (as does low Balinese), is a sub-language of about 600 words, especially connected with the person and bodily actions. There is also middle Balinese, the few words of which are used when caste is not stressed but politeness is still desired. In many parts of Bali today, high language is infrequently used in everyday intercourse.

Old Javanese (*Kawi*), the ancient language of poetry and classical literature, is still brought to life in certain forms of traditional drama and ritual. Sanskrit is the language of the high priest's mantras and hymns.

Multilingualism grows with the increasing importance of *Bahasa Indonesia*, the nation's official language. Simplified and free of caste rules, *Bahasa Indonesia* is widely spoken by the educated and in communities with mixed nationalities. And many young Balinese are adept linguists, who through the privilege of higher education, have mastered at least three languages, including English.

The island is one of twenty-six provinces constituting the Indonesian Republic. The provincial government, with its headquarters in Denpasar, is headed by the Governor who works directly under the Minister of Home Affairs in Jakarta. Bali is divided into eight districts called *kabupaten,* each headed by a government official, entitled the *bupati.* The most heavily populated districts are Badung in South Bali, containing the city of Denpasar, and Buleleng, on the north coast and the largest in area. Jembrana and Tabanan are west of Badung. Gianyar, Bangli, Klungkung, and Karangasem partition East Bali. Each of these districts is separated into smaller coun-

ties headed by a *camat*, the executive officer of the *bupati.* Under the *camat* are the village headmen, *perbekels*, who govern a village area consisting of several smaller communities. The smallest unit in the political system is the *banjar*, an individual community with two to three hundred male householders. The village of Sanur, for example, has twenty-two *banjars.*

Of Bali's four harbors, Benoa, located near the airport, is the main port for import-export. Singaraja, in the north, is the oldest harbor and once served Dutch navigation companies. Padangbai, to the east, handles traffic between Bali and Lombok; Gilimanuk, on the westernmost point of the island, receives cargo from East Java.

The Balinese are one of the few island peoples in the world who turn their eyes not outward to the waters, but upward to mountain peaks. The mountains with their lakes and rivers are holy, the source of the land's fertility. Water from the seashore, as from mountain streams and lakes, is used for purification; but the massive ocean extending far below the earth's surface, kingdom of giant fish and poisonous sea snakes, is considered dangerous and remains unfamiliar to most villagers. Only during low tide do small boys venture from the shore to catch tropical fish trapped in shallow tide pools. In the early hours shore-dwellers scan the beaches for coral used to make building lime. It is beautiful to see them wading about the reef, the sea breeze bearing their soulful chanting to the faraway shore. They retreat before the incoming tide because few of these people know how to swim and, although the sea teems with life, fishing is kept on a small scale. At sunset, bands of fishermen skim the still waters in quest of fish and turtle —the latter a banquet delicacy in the Denpasar area. The outrigger *prahu*s with triangular sails and forepeaks carved in the form of the mythical elephant-fish are swift and elegant craft.

A tourist-filled prahu cruises Sanur Beach, right. Following pages: rice terraces on the road to Kintamani, and a temple festival in Mas.

GENESIS

Beneath the cosmos there is a magnetic iron. From chaos, through meditation, the world serpent Antaboga created the turtle Bedawang, the stabilizer, on whom he coiled two serpents as the foundation of the world. On the world turtle there rests a lid, the Black Stone. There is no sun, nor moon nor light in the cave below the stone; this is the underworld whose god is Kala. Kala created the light and earth on which flows a layer of water. Above this are skies, high and low. One of mud, which dried to make the fields and mountains. Then the floating sky — the clouds enthroning Semara, god of love. Beyond lies the dark blue sky with the sun and moon, palace of the sun god Surya. Then the perfumed sky, beautiful and full of rare flowers where live the *awan* snakes, the falling stars. Still higher, a flaming heaven of ancestors; and above all the skies, live the divine guardians who keep watch over the heavenly nymphs.

— from the *Catur Yoga*

THE CHILDREN OF MYTH

When the world was ready for human habitation, the Great Teacher Batara Guru debated with his other self, Brahma, regarding the need for man and the nature of a human. The divine duality engaged in sporting competition, fashioning figures of clay. Each admitted that he worked on the basis of trial and error. Each ridiculed the other's efforts. When they experimented with baking the figures in an oven, the first came out in an underdone white finish, the next an overbaked black. The last batch of people came out just right, a golden brown — the

losophical, scientific, poetic, and quite characteristically Balinese. The concept of the evolution of the universe out of the void through the process of meditation is not far removed from faddish contemporary speculation, and the mention of magnetism throws it within the range of modern physics. The byplay between Batara Guru and Brahma is indicative of the spirit of inventiveness and earthiness with which the Balinese endow their drama. The catalogue of imported and indigenous deities, great and small; the invocation of magical names

Balinese. By meditation, Batara Guru and Brahma infused the creatures with life. They created dogs to keep men company and obey his orders. The first human figures were men. They required female counterparts that were duly provided. The first four couples of the Balinese world produced numerous children; to be precise, 117 boys and 118 girls. The extra female was regarded as somewhat excessive, but the total of 59¼ children per couple was hailed as a desirable target.

This Balinese account of the creation, with its curious echoes of the Sutras, the Bible, the Koran, and other sacred scriptures and the folklore of both East and West, is at once synoptic and syncretic, phi-

and mythical creatures, good and evil, the celebration of ancestors and of nature and of both sacred and profane deeds and thoughts; all these are key elements of the Balinese Genesis.

The Hinduization of Bali

While the mythical evolution of Bali is well-preserved in the island's inventive

Preceding pages: the rajas of all eight Balinese kingdoms about 1930, and an artist's conception of the island's cosmos. Above, etching on the prehistoric gong of Pejeng. Right, 11th Century gargoyles at Goa Gajah.

legends, its factual beginnings have faded from memory over the centuries. Stone Age Bali remains virtually a blank. No remains of early humans and only a few stone tools have been found. For tens of thousands of years, small bands must have hunted the jungles and gathered plants and the edible denizens of tidal pools. Bali was heavily-populated when the Metal Age began about 300 B.C. People lived in villages and buried the dead in pottery jars or stone sarcophagi together with bronze and iron implements and ornaments.

The early history of Bali is a matter of theoretical reconstruction of the precise origins of the population and the evolution of the society. The Balinese are clearly a blend of the various Mongoloid peoples who

ruler conducts himself in conformity with natural and divine law. Thus, every Balinese ruler had his monumental *kraton* or *puri*, a palace from which he exercised spiritual and temporal power through a hierarchy of courtiers and priests who not infrequently deposed an evil ruler and replaced him with a better one.

The conversion of primitive Bali into a Hinduized society was the result not of conquest and colonization but rather of the contagion of civilization. The rulers found in Indian culture the religious and administrative practices which exactly served their purposes, and the people responded with such enthusiasm as to prove the appropriateness of the choice. India provided the literary, the artistic, the social as well as the theolo-

moved through mainland Southeast Asia into the insular areas long before historic times. Their integrated society was the creation of an animistic, agricultural people inspired by vigorous priests and princes.

The first great outside influence upon the early Balinese was exercised by Indian or Indianized traders and travelers who brought their Hindu learning to Bali. Bali shared generously in the great wave of Indianizing influences which spread throughout most of Southeast Asia in the latter half of the first millennium. In politics and religion, the Indians introduced the key concept of the God-King, whose capital reflects the splendors and perfections of Heaven and whose people prosper only so long as the

gical and political model for an evolving Balinese society. The Balinese contrived creative adaptations while still retaining much of the Indian original.

The Hinduization of Bali was a process of many centuries. The most pervasive influence came out from distant India but from nearby Java which had been subject even earlier to an even more extensive Indianizing process. The documented history of Bali during this period is mainly a catalogue of names of obscure royal personages and imprecise references to forgotten events.

Modern archaeologists have reconstructed the approximate historical sequence from fragmentary incriptions in Sanskrit or classical Balinese on objects of stone and metal, most of them temple treasures.

The archaeological studies show that Hinduized rulers invoked certain Indian deities in commemorating the succession to the throne, in building or endowing a temple, in contracting a marriage, in winning a battle or in celebrating other events. By the year 1,001 (or perhaps 991), when the first reasonably well authenticated historic event occurred, Bali was extensively Hinduized and thoroughly steeped in such practices.

That year, presumably, was born Airlangga, the son of Balinese King Dharmmodayanawarmmadewa, also known as Udayana, and his Javanese queen, Gunapriyadharmapatni, also called Mahendradatta Airlangga was sent to the court of the Emperor of Java at an early age to be educated and eventually married. When the emperor was overthrown during civil wars, the victors invited Airlangga to take the throne.

Airlangga devoted himself to rebuilding the empire. In doing so, he added his home island of Bali to the Javanese domain and ruled it through a regent who was no doubt an uncle, brother or cousin. Airlangga thus inaugurated a period of close Javanese-Balinese political and cultural contacts which continued, to Bali's great advantage, for more than three centuries. The relationship was not without its conflicts, however. The Balinese occasionally asserted their autonomy and the Javanese Singasari emperors or their Majapahit successors as often reasserted their hegemony.

Balinese rulers, in whose veins flowed varying proportions of Balinese and Javanese blood, were always implicated in dynastic rivalries which the Majapahit Empire was often called upon to settle. For instance, the Javanese ruler, Kratanagara found it necessary to pacify and reunify Bali in either 1262 or 1284, as did the great General Gajah Mada in 1343. Majapahit imposed more and more of its own institutions upon its dependency and the Balinese proved to be far from unreceptive. When the Majapahit Empire collapsed in 1515, migrations of refugees from Java to Bali resulted in more massive cultural transfusions.

With the Majapahit period, Balinese history acquires clearer content and pattern. Still, much remains legendary. The visit of Gajah Mada, for instance, is associated with events which might seem to be excessively dramatic even by Balinese standards.

Bali's paramount ruler of the time, King Beda Ulu, was noted for trying to impress his subjects with his supernatural powers. Legends say he would even use a magical kris deftly to decapitate himself, then restore his head to its accustomed position and function — without pain or other associated discomforts. These royal seances eventually offended the god Siva, who deemed it unseemly for a mere mortal to behave in such fasion. So Siva seized the opportunity during Beda Ulu's next performance to cause the king to lose his grip upon the severed head. It fell into a swift flowing stream and was washed away. The king's quick-witted subjects amputated the head of a passing pig and handed it to their ruler as a substitute. After that King Beda Ulu became known as king Beda Muka, or the "king with the transposed face."

In order to spare himself rude stares, the king immediately decreed that everyone entering his presence must do so with head held deferentially low and must under no circumstances gaze into his face. But during a courtesy call, the curious General Gajah Mada decided to employ the ruse of raising his head to swallow a delectable but difficult morsel of food in order to confirm for himself the rumor about the king's oddly porcine features. So enraged was the king by this crafty but crude conduct and the necessity to condone it — custom forbade reprisals upon a guest — that he was consumed on the spot by the fires kindled within him. It was a Balinese cremation without precedent. On a moral level, the tale is recited by some Balinese as evidence of the vulgarity of the Javanese general and the ultra-refinement of the Balinese ruler, whose magnificent self-control proved to be his nemesis.

With Beda Ulu out of the way, Gajah Mada incorporated Bali as a province of the Majapahit Empire and appointed a Javanese nobleman named Kapakisan as governor. Balinese legends identify him as the offspring of a stone Buddha and a heavenly nymph. Kapakisan founded a line of princes who ruled Bali more as supporters than subordinates of the Javanese state. He and his successors sometimes used the Javanese title of Susuhunan meaning Great Sultan or Emperor. But more commonly they took the Balinese title Dewa Agung, or Great Deity, thus more than implying that they ruled independently and by divine rite. Kapakisan built his palace in Samprangan, near modern Gelgel, and ruled firmly but justly over the whole island.

A royal tomb near the Gunung Kawi of Tampaksiring, reputed to be the resting place of King Udayana, right. It dates back to the 11th Century.

THE GOLDEN AGE

Out of the rubble of the Majapahit Empire which fell in 1515, rose the new Javanese Empire of Mataram built out of small kingdoms newly reinspired and reinvigorated by the advent of powerful Islamic influences. Thousands of the Majapahit Empire's Hindu priests, nobles, soldiers, artists and artisans fled from Java to Bali to escape their Muslim conquerors. In Bali, they provided fresh impetus for the already strongly Hindu culture. In Java, the Hindu tradition was almost submerged under the Islamic overlay. Hindu Bali and Muslim

Batu Renggong welded together the various Balinese principalities into a strongly centralized kingdom. He conquered Blambangan and installed a vassal ruler. He also conquered and colonized the neighboring islands of Sumbawa and Lombok.

The political and military achievements of the reign of Batu Renggong were more than matched by a cultural renaissance. The Balinese molded the Majapahit influences to their own needs and in the process shaped the nucleus of contemporary Balinese culture. It was endowed with that

Java became implacable enemies. The little East Javanese state of Blambangan, separated from Bali by a mile-wide strait that was difficult and dangerous to cross, became a buffer region. The Balinese claimed and occasionally half-conquered Blambangan. Mataram as often threatened, but usually failed, to mount a counterinvasion. Balinese-Javanese relations remained explosive for centuries.

For Bali, the 16th Century marked the beginning of a golden age. Batu Renggong, inherited the title of Dewa Agung in 1550. He also inherited the still glittering legacy of the vanquished, vanished Majapahit Empire and from his remote court at Gelgel reigned in undreamed of splendor and authority.

special element of Balinese genius, the secret of eternal renewal of youth. The Balinese still share with the Javanese many common traditions of language, music, dance, sculpture and literature. But the gap between Hindu Bali and Muslim Java is almost as wide as the chasm that separates youth and old age. The older Balinese Majapahit culture, paradoxically preserved its freshness and animation, while the younger Javanese Mataram society grew both somber

A 17th Century European drawing of the Dewa Agung driving a chariot, right and a royal widow leaping upon her husband's funeral pyre in the rite of *suttee,* above.

and solemn. It is the riddle and the miracle of Bali that from the embers of Majapahit Java should have been ignited the fires which still burn bright in the neighboring isle.

The Coming of the Dutch

The 16th Century also marked Bali's first brush with the *orang putih*, the white men from distant Europe. The early Portuguese explorers, adventurers, merchants, missionaries and conquerors who reached Malacca in 1509 and the Moluccas in 1511, all but bypassed Bali in the eager rush to acquire riches, souls and empire. So did the Spaniards. The Magellan expedition of 1519-1522 sighted an island, probably Bali, which

ship from Malacca with soldiers and merchants, building materials and trade goods in an attempt to build a fort and open a trading post on the island. But the ship foundered on the reef off Bukit and most of the company drowned. The five survivors who managed to reach shore were impressed into the service of the Dewa Agung, who treated them quite kindly, gave them homes and wives, but refused to permit them to return to Malacca.

Twelve years later came the earliest Dutch explorer and trader in the East Indies, Cornelis de Houtman. He provided history with the first substantial body of information about Bali. Houtman was a braggart and scoundrel to whom the leadership of the expedition fell after the mysterious demise of

it identified as "Java Minor," but apparently no one went ashore. Fernando Mendez Pinto, the great Portuguese navigator and Munchausen-like narrator, may have visited Bali briefly in about the year 1546, but the evidence is not certain. Various other Portuguese and Spanish undoubtedly sighted Bali, if they did not actually explore it, and they made due notations of the island under various names including *Boly, Bale,* and *Bally*. Sir Francis Drake called briefly in 1580 and Thomas Cavendish may have visited Bali in 1585, but they left no written records.

The first *orang putih* to entertain any designs upon Balinese trade and territory were the Portuguese. In 1588, they dispatched a

several predecessors. But he and his crew conducted themselves in Bali in a reasonably respectable manner. In fact, Houtman was so moved by the beauty and wealth of the island that he indulged in an unaccustomed, but inappropriate, flight of poetic fantasy and christened Bali *Jonck Hollandt*, Young Holland. It was a description so evocative of misapprehension as to lead later Dutchmen to fancy that in introducing Dutch civilization and commerce they were guiding the islanders toward their manifest destiny.

In the Court of the Dewa Agung

The four members of the expeditions' shore party were treated as honored guests by the Balinese and the Dewa Agung, Raja Bekung, the son of Batu Renggong. The leader of the shore group, Arnouldt Lintgens, described the Dewa Agung as a tall, dark, stout, vigorous man of about 40, who possessed astounding wealth, power and magnificence. Lintgens said the Agung usually lived in a huge palace in the walled town of Gelgel, surrounded by a harem of 200 wives, a troupe of 50 dwarfs whose bodies were deliberately deformed to resemble the grotesque figures of *kris* hilts, and by many noblemen, who ruled in his name over a population of about 300,000. Lintgens said the state *kris* was particularly splendid, a two-pound dagger with jewels set in its intricately-wrought golden hilt. Equally showy was the handle of the state parasol, one of

Lintgens found the island itself equally fascinating. He was the apparent author of the following report on the expedition:

The Island of Baly lying at the East end of Iaua, is a verie fruitfull Island of Ryce, Hennes, Hogges, that are verie good and great store of cattle: but they are very drie and leane beastes. They haue many horses: the inhabitantes are heathens, and haue no religion, for some pray to Kine, other to the Sunne, and euerie man as hee thinketh good. When a man dyeth his wife burneth her selfe with him: there were some of their men aborde our shippes, that told vs, that when some man dyeth in that Countrey, that sometimes there are at the least fifty women that will burne themselves with him, and she that doth not so is

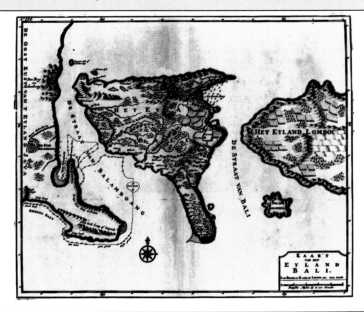

dozens of parasols, lances, vessels of gold and silver and other miscellaneous palace treasures that would be the envy of any king in Europe.

Lintgen said the Dewa Agung was accompanied by scores of lance and banner bearers whenever he ventured outside his palace. He rode in a procession either in a palanquin or in a cart drawn by two white oxen which he himself drove. According to this early Dutch observer, the Dewa Agung commanded the love and respect of his people and his courtiers and was famous for the clemency of his rule, having only recently spared certain conspirators who had plotted against his life by commuting their sentence from execution to exile on a nearby islet.

accounted for a dishonest woman: so that it is a common thing with them.

The Dewa Agung and his people were as curious about the Dutch as the Dutch were about the Balinese. He managed to extract detailed information about Holland from Lintgen's group as well as a number of gifts including a rifle and a much-coveted chart of the world. However, the Dutch declined an eager offer from the Dewa Agung to purchase their ships' cannon. Later the Dewa

The first known Western map of Bali believed prepared by cartographers with the Houtman expedition, above. Right, *The Crowned Lion*, a famous ship used during the early years of the Dutch East Indies Company.

Agung proposed to write a letter of appreciation to the Dutch king and to send him a *kris* and a dwarf as gifts, but there is no evidence that he actually did so.

Houtman himself made only one trip ashore only a few days before setting sail for Holland. The departure of the expedition made history. Lintgens was safely on board, but two other members of the shore party, Emanuel Roodenburg and Jacob Claaszoon, were mysteriously absent. They had jumped ship to enter the service of the Dewa Agung, perhaps of their own volition, perhaps not, but most probably quite willing to forego the rigors of the voyage back to cold, gloomy Holland for the pleasures of tropical Bali. Both men settled in Gelgel, took Balinese wives, learned the language, and served the

Heemskerck nor his successors proved reluctant to accept the Dewa Agung's far from naive consent to reciprocal trading conditions as a charter for one-way trade or his offhand endorsement of Dutch hopes for unity as acknowledgment of an alliance. Although nothing much came of the contact for more than two centuries, it was on the basis of the Heemskerck agreements that the Dutch assured themselves that they had special rights in the island.

The very skimpy records of Dutch contacts with Bali during the 17th and 18th centuries relate mainly to the opium runners, the acts of mutiny, piracy, and treachery which their activities provoked and the ineffectual efforts of the Netherlands East India Company (V.O.C.) to either ban or to

Dewa Agung. Roodenburg eventually returned to Holland, but Claaszoon apparently lived out his life in Bali.

The Decline of the Dewa Agung

The next Dutch expedition to Bali in 1601 was led by Jacob van Heemskerck, who brought a request from the King of Holland to open trade with the island. The Dewa Agung granted permission for trade links. He also presented van Heemskerck with a typical token of royal favor, a beautiful Balinese slave. Van Heemskerck seemed unaccountably indisposed to accept, until he was advised that it would be impolitic to decline the gift. However, neither Van

control and restrict the trade.

Meanwhile, the golden age of Gelgel flickered during the latter part of the reign of Raja Bekung, then died out altogether under his grandson Di Made. The Raja's ill-advised adventures in Blambangan provoked a full-scale invasion of Bali by Mataram in 1639. Bekung subsequently lost the respect of the other Balinese princes. Di Made not only lost Blambangan, but Sumbawa and Lombok as well. He also lost the allegiance of the other princes. His successor, Gusti Sideman, abandoned the *kraton* of Gelgel, which he deduced was clearly under a curse. He built a new palace in nearby Klungkung and sought to rule the office of Dewa Agung as grandly as had his predecessors. But it was already too late. Bali's silver age set in when Klungkung was founded. It marked the island-wide dissemination of the Gelgel culture, but Klungkung never matched Gelgel in glory.

The Dewa Agung and his court in Klungkung continued to symbolize Hindu imperial grandeur but never again imperial power. He became less prominent thereafter than some of his presumed vassals. The other princes became the Dewa Agung's rivals and even his enemies; their own *punggawa* (chiefs) at times presumed to virtual autonomy; the *pendada* (priests) sometimes assumed almost independent temporal power over villages and groups of villages which fell theoretically within the domain of the rajas. The ruling families, princely and

home.

If the Dutch refrained from intervening in the Balinese-Javanese wars, the English apparently did not. The Dutch believe that the English were providing the rajas with arms and were also selling opium and buying slaves; the northern Balinese port of Buleleng was rumored to be a hotbed of British-Balinese anti-Dutch intrigue.

The persistent intrusions of the English into Balinese waters caused the Dutch political and financial agony. They were convinced the English were seeking a new colony and would seize any opportunity which they themselves might overlook to establish some British monopoly in competition with the V.O.C. The Dutch lived with the suspicion that the predatory English would

priestly, were polygamously intermarried and easily provoked to blood feuds. Divination, prophecy, and mere superstition were factors of comparable significance to jealousy, intrigue and military conflict in conditioning personal and state affairs.

In the course of the 18th Century, there were frequent outbreaks of hostilities between the Dewa Agung and the Susuhunan, and both Bali and Mataram applied for Dutch assistance. The Dutch never obliged — at least not openly. But in the years 1717-18, when Balinese troops were roaming East Java and Madura, causing great destruction and dismay throughout the region, the Dutch launched little clean-up operations which helped to chase the intruders back

pounce upon one of the many islands that the Dutch regarded as the indisputable patrimony of the Netherlands; possibly Bali, a rich strategic little island which they had never yet really explored. Dutch and English rivalry over Bali eventually played a minor part in the world wide English-Dutch conflict and preceeded the actual opening of the island to massive Western impact. This latter eventuality somehow managed to postpone itself from the early 17th to the early 19th

Buleleng rose to power during Bali's golden age. Members of its royal court posed above about 1880. At right, a wife (left) and a nephew (right) of the Raja of Buleleng.

Century. During that interval, except for a few episodes, Bali enjoyed the priceless benefits of European neglect.

The Birth of Gianyar

As the domain and the authority of the Dewa Agung diminished, there emerged a dozen more or less clearly defined little independent rajadoms. Eight still survive as geographical and political entities now called administrative districts: Gianyar, Badung, Bangli, Tabanan and Klungkung in the south-central region and Buleleng, Karangasem and Negara (now Jembrana) in the north, the northeast and northwest respectively.

The history of these eight Balinese raja-

Gianyar, with frequent episodes involving more docile and obedient neighbors like Bangli and Mengwi, the aloof Badung and Tabanan and the remote Negara. It also involves the score or more of villages of which each of these rajadoms was composed. The *punggawa* who ruled these villages on behalf of the rajas quite frequently assumed the airs and even the titles of rajas, built themselves *puris* which amounted to little fortified castles and entered into alliances and conspiracies which characterized the relationships between the rajas themselves.

The founder of the Gianyar line was Dewa Manggis Kuning, now commonly referred to as Dewa Manggis I. The Dewa (divinity, a favorite given name) and Manggis (the name of the town in which he was born and the

doms of modern times is closely linked to that of Dutch colonial penetration. It is a story which remains as yet to be very accurately reconstructed from fragmentary and conflicting records. With present resources, it must suffice to identify the protagonists and to establish the progression by reference to rajas and rajadoms.

The new seat of the rajadom in Klungkung survived but did not flourish, for the Dewa Agung maintained little power and his kingdom was minute. In fact, little Gianyar came to rival Klungkung as a center of traditional Balinese culture and even presumed military might. The story of the decline of Klungkung merges with that of the rise, fall and, later, the revival of the House of

word for mangosteen, a fruit that became the family emblem) became the state title that was conferred upon the occasion of the solemn *Abiseka* ceremony. Kuning, the Indonesian word for yellow, referred to the deep golden glow of the child's skin. His father was Baginda Raja Sri Dalem-Saganing, the fourth Dewa Agung of Gelgel.

This handsome, adventuresome youth so pleased the Dewa Agung that he was sent to Badung to assist the raja there in administering that unruly kingdom. In Puri Badung, Dewa Manggis Kuning had an affair with the raja's most beautiful wife. Upon being discovered, and threatened with arrest and torture, he had to make a rather sudden and undignified exit. Wrapped in a woven mat like a bundle of charcoal, he was carried on the head of an old female servant through concentric rings of sentries who carelessly waved her onward. The fugitive prince eventually made his way northward and set up shelter in a forest of *bengkel* trees near present day Gianyar. Other settlers helped turn Bengkel into a thriving village.

Dewa Manggis Kuning emerged as a major figure upon the death of his father in 1667. He utilized a spear named Ki Baru-Alis and a *kris* called Ki Baru Kama essential items of the Gianyar royal regalia that became venerated *pusaka*, heirlooms endowed with magical properties. He was said to have used the spear to rebuke an attack from an army from Buleleng, unseating its raja from an elephant that Dewa Manggis caused to bolt and die with mere thrusts of Ki Baru-Alis.

One of the greatest of the Kuning's descendants, Dewa Manggis IV, built Puri Gianyar in 1771 and thus became the first actual raja of Gianyar. It became the most prosperous and powerful of the southern states under Dewa Manggis Disasteria (VII) the following century. But until the latter part of the 19th Century, Gianyar was never at the focus of Balinese events The Dewa Agung's military and political power passed first to Buleleng, the large northern state which was the first focus of foreign commerce and international competition; next to Karangasem, the large eastern state which came to dominate Lombok as well as Bali; and, eventually, to the Dutch. Buleleng and Karangasem, sometimes friends, sometimes enemies, long under the rule of members of the same royal family, were to become the two power factors in early modern Bali.

Buleleng and Karangasem

Gusti Pandji Sakti, who came to the throne at the end of the 17th Century, was primarily responsible for Buleleng's assertion of island hegemony. By skillful political and military maneuvers he extended his authority throughout most of Karangasem and Jembrana, exacted deferential treatment from the southern states and put an ally on the throne in Blambangan. The ruler of Mengwi, Gusti Agung Sakti, usurped the throne of his father-in-law Gusti Pandji Sakti in 1711 then consolidated Buleleng's power. The joint rajadom of Buleleng-Mengwi flourished for the better part of the 18th Century, but then separated again and forfeited power to Karangasem.

Karangasem began its rise to prominence by championing Balinese interests in Lombok at a time when Buleleng was preoccupied by exploits in Java. After intermittent efforts, Karangasem engineered control of Lombok by the middle of the 17th Century and parceled it out among four weak rajadoms, each ruled by a Balinese prince who owed allegiance to Karangasem.

At that time, the Raja of Karangasem was an ascetic sage of repulsive physical habits and appearance, generally so engrossed in meditation that he let his excrement drop where it might. During a visit to Klungkung, this raja shocked and outraged the Dewa Agung, who subsequently had the man ambushed and assassinated. Seeking vengeance, the Raja's three sons raised an army and marched into Klungkung. Some residue of respect for tradition deterred them from either killing or desposing the Dewa Augung or even depriving him of much of his realm. But they made a virtual declaration of independence and returned home without much further regard for the authority of the Dewa Agung. The eldest son succeeded his father as raja of Karangasem and soon conquered Buleleng. Gusti Gde Karangasem, as he was named, became the kingpin of a new coalition at the turn of the 19th Century and one of the famous figures of Balinese history. He appointed his brothers as rajas of Buleleng and Lombok, then seized Negara against the vigorous protests of Badung. He put rude pressures upon other states as well and stirred up widespread resentment and resistance.

By this time, the patterns of Balinese power and politics were becoming incomprehensible, even to the Balinese — as is further indicated by the sudden emergence of the state of Gianyar as a rival to Klungkung and a military threat to Mengwi and Bangli. Buleleng itself rebelled successfully against Karangasem in 1823. Raja Gusti Gde Nugurah Lanang fled to Lombok where he built a new *puri* and tried to impose his authority over the mutually jealous little Lombok rajadoms, which welcomed his defeat in Bali as an invitation to defiance of Karangasem; he sought at the same time to force his onetime vassals in Bali to again recognize him as ruler. Gusti Gde Ngurah Lanang thus did much to create the insular and inter-insular turbulence which the Dutch found conducive to the imposition of Western rule.

At right, the Raja of Karangasem and his grandson circa 1901.

50

THE DUTCH CAMPAIGNS

At the beginning of the 19th Century, Bali remained relatively unaffected by the Western influences which were already transforming much of the Indonesian archipelago. Bali's 16th Century Hindu civilization was still inviolate to any serious religious, commercial, or political infiltration either by Muslims or by Christians.

Dutch traders, agents and colonial officials failed to gain a foothold in Bali at first. By 1830, Dutch officials in The Hague, Amsterdam and Batavia, having engaged in a prolonged exchange of government and company papers formulating various policy alternatives with regard to Bali, decided to infiltrate traders, then assert sovereignty. The N.H.M., successor to the trading interests of the long since bankrupt and defunct V.O.C., was intimately involved in these intrigues.

A time-honored Balinese concept of ship salvage eventually provided the catalyst for Dutch military intervention. In accordance with their principle of reef rights, *tawan karang*, honoring the sea deity Batara Baruna, the rajas accepted as a gift of the gods whatever ship came to grief on the treacherous reefs which ringed their island. They took the ship, the cargo, the crew and the passengers as their personal property, naturally sharing with those who actually performed the act of salvage or rescue, but entertaining no doubts at all regarding the sanctity of the deed. From the Dutch point of view, it was bad enough if the Balinese exercised their so-called reef rights upon a Chinese, an Arab, a Bugis or a Javanese craft, many of which sailed under the Dutch flag and expected Dutch protection. It was quite intolerable if the ship in question was Dutch owned and operated.

A Sorry Shipwreck, a Defiant Pledge

By the end of the 1830s, all circumstances combined to prompt the Dutch to address themselves quite earnestly to discussion with the Balinese rajas of the delicate subjects of trade and politics, slavery and plunder. They tried to blanket these various topics with treaties of friendship and commerce, in fact, recognition of Dutch sovereignty and monopoly.

A famous Dutch colonial official known as a "*contractsluiter*" or contract-maker, H.J. van Huskus Koopman, was dispatched to

the island to try to coax the rajas into giving the Dutch virtual sovereignty over the island. His efforts met with little success. The Dutch finally decided to resort to force. As a pretext for invasion, they used the wreck of the Dutch frigate *Overijssel* on the Kuta reef — and the plunder of its cargo by Balinese exercising their reef rights. The sorry saga of the *Overijssel* began on July 19, 1841, when the vessel, on its maiden voyage from Plymouth to Surabaya with a valuable cargo of machinery, hit the Kuta reef and was promptly plundered. Subsequent Dutch outrage served in part to cloak humiliation that a large and heavily armed frigate was wrecked by reason of a flagrant navigational error. The captain had mistaken the coast of Bali for Java. The Dutch were equally embarrassed that the ship was looted despite the presumed vigilance of the ship's company against exactly that contingency.

As the furor over the incident increased in Holland, a Dutch mission was sent to Bali to protest continuing outrages and demand reconfirmation of earlier promises that the Balinese would give up the practice of salvaging ships that foundered off their shores. A new Dutch commissioner for Bali arrived with a new set of agreements scheduled to be formally ratified by the rajas and rigidly enforced by the Dutch. He landed at Buleleng to meet with its raja and council of state. It was on this occasion that the great hero of mid-19th Century Bali identified himself. He was Gusti Ktut Jelantik, a dramatic, dynamic young prince, the brother of the rajas of Buleleng and Karangasem. He defied the Dutch commissioner in the following apocryphal words:

Never while I live shall the state recognize the sovereignty of the Netherlands in the sense in which you interpret it. After my death, the Raja may do as he chooses. Not by a mere scrap of paper shall any man become the master of another's lands. Rather let the kris decide.

Preparations for War

The Dutch began preparations for an expeditionary force, which assembled at Be-

Preceding pages: Balinese choose the suicidal rite of *puputan* rather than surrender to the Dutch in this modern painting by Budi. At left, Balinese warriors in battle dress 1880s.

suki, to sail to Bali on the east monsoon of 1846. Jelantik began building fortifications, raising troops, and acquiring arms, relying, as the Dutch correctly surmised, upon certain enterprising merchants in the British colony of Singapore for large shipments of weapons. Balinese-Dutch relations were rapidly moving into a new and tragic phase.

Balinese military preparations centered upon the northern rajadom of Buleleng, ruled by Gusti Madya Karangasem, the elder brother of the Raja of Karangasem. Buleleng and Karangasem, the two most powerful rajadoms of the island but long-time rivals, were now closely allied in opposing the political and military aims of the Dutch. They had the blessing of the Dewa Agung of Klungkung, who was in no position to provide much more than that. The Raja of Badung in the south, who wished to preserve the profits of trade and was no friend of the turbulent northerners, sought to remain detached from the conflict and exercised his influence upon his friendly neighbor, the Raja of Tabanan to do likewise. The other states were allied rather tenuously with Klungkung but were attentive to Badung. They were not disposed to become involved.

Once the Dutch set themselves to subdue Bali, the outcome was never in doubt. But it took three campaigns to shatter the Balinese defenses and morale, campaigns in which the Dutch did not always by any means achieve either glory or victory.

The Punitive Expeditions, 1846-49

The First Dutch Military Expedition against Bali in 1846 seemed a formidable enough force to cope with any native impudence. The invasion fleet consisted of 58 vessels and nearly 3,000 men well-armed and equipped. The force anchored off Buleleng on June 22 and the Dutch sent ultimatums to the rajas ashore. The rajas ignored them and the Dutch attack began six days later. The Balinese put up a strong defense under the guiding hand of Jelantik, but the Dutch nevertheless won a swift victory, losing only 18 dead while the Balinese suffered severe losses of life and property. The Dutch victory was empty, however, unless they could enforce their will upon the rajas who were firmly entrenched in the nearby hills.

A flamboyant Danish trader who had set up a profitable enterprise in Kuta, Mads Lange, stepped into the stalemate. He helped negotiate a truce. But the Balinese rajas led by Jelantik failed to deliver on promises to pay reparations and to provision a Dutch garrison on the island.

A second military expedition against Bali was thus mounted in 1848. This time the Dutch sent even more men and ships. But the Balinese, boldly and brilliantly led by Jelantik, had installed 25 cannon and mustered 16,000 men, 1,500 equipped with firearms. They fought off three attacks inflicting severe casualties upon the Dutch, who retreated to plan and prepare an even more forceful assault.

The third expedition arrived off Buleleng in March 1849. This time the fleet numbered over 100 vessels, — heavily armed frigates, steamships, schooners, and scores of large and small auxiliary craft and manned by 3,000 sailors and 5,000 landing troops. They marched into Buleleng and Singaraja, where the Dutch general set up his headquarters in the raja's palace.

The final showdown occurred on April 4. The Dutch deployed their troops in full dress uniform. The Balinese troops were dressed in their most splendid costumes as if prepared not for battle but for the *baris* warrior dance. They carried themselves haughtily, struck theatrical stances, and fingered their weapons suggestively. The Raja and Jelantik were especially magnificent in brilliant red sarongs nattily gathered up to display short tight trousers, below and above which gleamed bare, bronze skin. Their waists were nipped in by golden girdles. At the back each displayed a huge jeweled kris, the ornate handles extending above shoulder height for quick dramatic draw. Their thick, flowing black hair was bound by white headclothes in which the raja wore a green sprig and Jelantik wore a crimson flower.

The encounter, which started as a triumph of Dutch and Balinese showmanship, deteriorated into a miserable failure of statesmanship. It ended without a fight or an agreement. Several weeks later, the Dutch attacked the Balinese fortifications at Jagaraga. They suffered 33 dead and 148 wounded. The Balinese lost thousands. Among the victims was the wife of Jelantik and a party of high-born ladies whom she led in the rite of the *puputan,* advancing in a state of near trance directly into the line of Dutch fire in a deliberate act of self-destruction.

Pitched battles continued well into the following year. The Dutch managed to gain allies and troops from Lombok. The Raja of Karangasem, despairing at the news, killed his family and himself. The Dutch battled their way to the gates of the Dewa Agung in Klungkung. But they were repelled.

The fluctuating fortunes of war were dramatically signalled by the commander of the

Lombok forces, who visited a Dutch colonel on shipboard and displayed to him three especially valuable and significant prizes. The first was the kris of the Raja of Karangasem, signifying his death and the fall of that kingdom; the second was the kris of the Raja of Buleleng; the third that of Gusti Ktut Jelantik. The Raja of Buleleng and Jelantik had been ambushed by the wily troops from Lombok. The Raja had been killed on the spot; Jelantik, seeing no escape, had taken poison.

With Jelantik and the two rajas dead, with the Dewa Agung and his surviving protectors deeply grieved and dismayed, the Balinese resistance was in a state of complete disarray. The Dutch, decimated though they were by tropical diseases, could

principalities to fall under Dutch administration. In 1855, the Dutch also assumed control over Jembrana. In each case, the Dutch adopted the administrative device they had found to be effective in Java. They appointed a member of the royal family as regent and assigned him a Dutch controleur who, as the title clearly implied, controlled both the regent and the kingdom. Thus, as of the mid-1850s, the Dutch actually began to acquire the sovereign power which they had long claimed, at least in northern and western Bali. Half a century later, they ruled the entire island.

The colonial administration in Bali remained centered in the port town of Buleleng and the adjoining royal capital of Singaraja. The first resident Dutch official

scarcely even have blundered into defeat.

Again, Mads Lange stepped in. He negotiated a new agreement between the Dutch and the Dewa Agung. It was a difficult task which involved the installation of new rulers, the redefinition of overlord-vassal relationships, and also, of course, a whole new Balinese-Dutch *modus vivendi*.

The Dutch Take the North

As a result of the military expeditions, the Dutch began to exercise rapidly increasing control over northern Bali and to interfere more frequently and vigorously in Balinese domestic affairs.

Buleleng became the first of the Balinese

was Heer P.L. van Bloemen Waanders, who like certain of his successors, was to become a serious and sympathetic student of Balinese life and customs. After the difficulties of the first few years were overcome and the Dutch and Balinese had made certain basic accommodations to each other, the latter part of the 19th Century was reasonably peaceful and saw satisfactory development for the northern states. But continuing strife between the warring factions in the states of the south resulted in several more Dutch

Above, Dutch soldiers board small craft as they prepare to land on Bali's Sanur Beach in 1906.

57

military campaigns.

Meanwhile, the Dutch under van Bloemen Waanders and his successor announced strict new regulations against slavery and undertook to improve economic conditions. They encouraged extension of the irrigation system to improve the rice harvest, the planting of coffee as a cash crop and by 1875, northern Bali was already a distinctly profitable colonial enterprise. The ever-increasing contact between Buleleng and the outside world resulted in an attempt to introduce Christian missions. But they met with little success. The colonial successes and failures produced a policy of benevolent paternalism which resulted in Bali in a relatively enlightened administration. Still, the darkest days of the Dutch colonial penetration lie ahead.

Disasteria enlisted the aid of Karangasem and Lombok and managed to shatter the Klungkung army in 1868.

After its victory, Gianyar enjoyed well over a decade of relative immunity from invasion and ever-increasing prosperity. In fact, a Dutch visitor to Bali, Dr. Julius Jacobs, reported in 1883 that Gianyar was by far the most pleasant and prosperous of the southern states.

The island of Lombok also played an integral part in the trilogy of tragedies that marked Bali's total takeover by the Dutch after the turn of the century. The trouble began when the Dutch sent a military expedition in 1894 to punish the Balinese rulers of Lombok for reported complaints of cruelty and discrimination toward Lombok's

Ambush in Lombok

The rajadom of Gianyar enjoyed its turn at the top during the middle of the 19th Century. Under Dewa Manggis Disasteria (VII), Gianyar became the most prosperous and powerful of the states of the south and he earned island-wide fame as a shrewd ruler. In the process, however, he made a host of enemies among other rajas by continually attempting to expand his kingdom by swallowing up villages in their areas.

The Dewa Agung even created a military coalition against Gianyar and he found a ready ally in the Raja of Bangli, whose sister was a favorite in the Klungkung harem. But

large contingent of Sassak Muslims.

The Dutch, led by Major-Generals J.A. Vetter and P.P.H. van Ham marched into the heart of the island without encountering any resistance. Just as it seemed they would win a bloodless victory, thousands of Balinese warriors staged a surprise attack on the Dutch camp in the town of Jakranegara. They fired their rifles with deadly aim and their battle cries proved as blood-curdling as their attack was furious as they massacred

Above, the Dutch staff of the Lombok expedition and Balinese royalty: front row (l to r), Raja Anak Agung Ktut, Generals van Ham and Vetter, and Gusti Jelantik. Right, Dutch guns on Sanur Beach.

Dutch soldiers who had no place to take cover. General van Ham himself was fatally wounded. In all, Dutch casualties totaled 98 dead and 272 injured. The Dutch government and people in Batavia and The Netherlands were outraged and the battle entered Dutch colonial history as "The Lombok Treachery."

The Wreck of the Sri Kumala

The Dutch quickly sent in reinforcements to revenge their stunning defeat in Lombok. They laid waste to the island. In Mataram, the Balinese defenders chose the rite of *puputan* over defeat or surrender to the Dutch. The island's raja later chose the same fate in another village. As the Dutch ad-

Balinese exercise of their right of salvage.

The vessel was a Chinese-owned schooner the *Sri Kumala*, out of Banjarmasin, Borneo. It struck the reef near Sanur not far from the Badung-Gianyar border. The area's people plundered the ship with the complicity, it was alleged, of the rajas. The Chinese owner of the craft gave an altogether implausible account of his misfortune and demanded fanciful indemnity for the cargo. To the original claim he added, as a curious afterthought, large quantities of gold and silver. The Dutch scaled down his claims and presented the bill to the Raja of Badung who flatly refused to pay. The Dewa Agung backed him in his defiance. So did the Raja of Tabanan who just then was also involved in a crisis over a recent ceremony of

vanced, men, women and children emerged from the village as if in a trance. If they did not die by the kris, they rushed headlong into the fire of the troops. By Dutch count, ten of the highest-ranking nobles of that kingdom perished. The Dutch got their victory — by default. The events in Lombok in 1894 left deep scars upon the Balinese soul and the Dutch conscience.

The events in Lombok also disturbed the Dewa Agung and other leaders in Bali. They grew increasingly uneasy about the Dutch presence in their island. It was widely assumed that some outrageous incident would launch yet another Dutch expeditionary force. That incident occurred on May 27, 1904. Again it involved a shipwreck and the

suttee which he had permitted despite Dutch protest. So in June of 1906 the Dutch blockaded the coasts of Badung and Tabanan while they drew up certain ultimatums and assembled a military expedition.

The Sixth Military Expedition to Bali, consisting of infantry, cavalry, artillery and naval support, arrived off the southern coast of Bali in September that year. They sent the Raja of Badung a final ultimatum. He rejected it. On September 14, the Dutch landed their troops on Sanur Beach.

Drums of the Puputan

Without meeting any significant resistance, the Dutch troops marched through

Kesiman toward Denpasar, expecting the action to be more of a dress parade than a pitched battle. Marching in orderly ranks along a roadway, walled on either side, which led to the royal palace, they found the town apparently deserted and smoke rising over the *puri*. The most disquieting factor was the sound of the wild beating of drums within the palace walls.

As the Dutch drew closer, they observed a strange, silent procession emerging from the main gate of the *puri*. It was led by the Raja, seated in his state palanquin carried by four bearers, dressed in white cremation garments but splendidly bejeweled and armed with a magnificent kris. The Raja was followed by officials of his court, armed guards, priests, wives, children and retainers, like-

To the scene of carnage was soon added the spectacle of looting as the soldiers stripped the valuables from the corpses and then set about sacking the palace ruins. It was a slaughter and self-slaughter of the innocents made all the more appalling by reason of its recurrence that same afternoon in nearby Pemacutan, a minor state of Badung. There the frail old Raja and his terrified court, having heard what had happened in Denpasar, elected the same fate. When the victorious Dutch troops marched from Denpasar to Pemacutan, the Raja and his retainers were ready to enact once again the grisly rites of *puputan*. This time the Dutch refrained from participation if not from profit.

The Dutch expeditionary force marched next upon Tabanan, where the wives of its

wise dressed in white, flowers in their hair, many of them almost as richly ornamented and as splendidy armed as was their ruler.

One hundred paces from the startled Dutch, the Raja halted his bearers, stepped from his palanquin, and gave a signal. A priest plunged his dagger into the Raja's breast. Others of the company also began turning their daggers upon themselves or upon one another. The Dutch troops, startled into action by a stray gunshot and reacting to attack by lance and spear, directed rifle and artillery fire into the surging crowd. Some of the women mockingly threw jewels and gold coins to the soldiers. More persons emerged from the palace gate. The mounds of corpses rose higher and higher.

venerable old Raja had earlier followed their husband in death by jumping into his cremation fire in the rite of *suttee* — against Dutch protests. The new Raja and Crown Prince fled from the *puri* when the Dutch advanced. They eventually gave themselves up to their adversaries. The Dutch informed them they would be exiled to Madura or Lombok. The Raja and Prince instead chose suicide in their Denpasar prison. For lack of a kris, the raja plunged a *sirih* knife into his

The aftermath of the 1906 Denpasar *puputan*: the bodies of Balinese victims piled outside the palace, above; and, the body of the Raja of Badung wrapped in a woven mat, right.

throat and the crown prince took poison — and Tabanan followed Badung into the Dutch sphere.

As a side excursion to their invasion of Klungkung, the Dutch made a show of force in Klungkung hoping to provoke a show of resistance by the Dewa Agung. But the Dewa Agung was either too cowed or too prudent to oblige and the Dutch withdrew.

Later, the Dutch presented the Dewa Agung with a whole new set of agreements almost indistinguishable from ultimatums. He accepted them virtually at sight. All knew that the next move would be Dutch imposition of an administrative system upon Klungkung. By 1908, disorders broke out in the area. In Gelgel, the *punggawa's* men intimidated and attacked some agents of the

The Dewa Agung ordered the gongs to sound the call to the *puputan*. He himself led a procession of some 200 persons who emerged from the *puri* to confront the Dutch soldiers. Clad all in white, he carried in one hand a ceremonial lance with a golden tip and in the other his ancestral kris. Pausing about 100 meters from the momentarily silent cannon, he bent over and with an imperious gesture thrust the kris blade into the ground. Thus, if the prophecy of his high priest came true, his magical kris would create a great chasm which would swallow up all of his enemies. As the Dewa Agung straightened up, he received a gunshot in the knee. Before he could even crumple, he was killed outright by another. Six of his wives knelt around him and solemnly drove their

opium monopoly. The Dutch landed a small party of troops to march into Gelgel to punish the *punggawa*. The *punggawa* mounted a counterattack. So many Dutch soldiers were injured that the detachment withdrew to the seacoast. The *punggawa* then sought shelter in Klungkung, where the Dewa Agung, correctly anticipating naval bombardment and land maneuvers, had already authorized certain measures of defense. The bombardment swiftly followed. It demolished Gelgel and destroyed parts of Klungkung. Then came the troops with their field pieces, which they deployed in the square in front of the *puri* at a distance no more than 200 meters from the main gate. The Dutch began firing admonitory salvos.

kris blades into their own hearts. The whole company — men, women and children alike — engaged in ritualistic self-immolation or sacrificed one another while murderous cannon and gunfire contributed to the mayhem.

There were very few royal or other survivors of the Klungkung *puputan*. The *puri* was razed, except for one gateway which led to a barracks and a prison. What little remained of Klungkung's ancient glory, had vanished, but the last bright blaze of martyrdom had burnt away many stains. On April 18, 1908, after 600 years of rule in Bali, the lineal descendants of the Majapahit emperors were decimated, the ritualistic victims of relentless Western intrusion.

BALI IN THE 20TH CENTURY

Although the punitive expeditions against Bali in the 1840s passed almost unnoticed in the outside world, the reports of the *puputan* of 1906 in Badung and in 1908 in Klungkung shocked private citizens, religious groups and governments from The Hague to London, Paris and New York. Protests poured into the colonial office condemning Dutch reprisals believed to be wildly disproportionate to any known Balinese offenses. Also under pressure with regard to their policies in Java, Sumatra and the eastern islands, the Dutch resolved to make amends. They introduced reforms which led to what they rather sanctimoniously announced and acclaimed as the Ethical Policy.

In 1914, The Dutch replaced their army with a police force. They also reorganized the government along the lines it had had under the rajas. The raja continued to reign in magnificence. But as regent, he ruled by consent of the Dutch resident and controleur. The latter prompted his important decisions and relieved him of much routine by controlling the *punggawa* as well. The controleur soon introduced the engineer who built the public works, the doctor who opened a clinic, the teacher who established a school, and eventually the military officer who recruited and trained a few soldiers. Visitors to Bali began to report that the island was just about the prettiest little exhibit in the whole of the Indies of Dutch efficiency and enlightenment.

Not the least of the evidences of ethical Dutch behavior and Balinese benefit was the absence of any conspicuous colony of Western residents. From the very beginning, the Residency opposed all efforts of Dutch big business firms to open up rubber or tea plantations or sugar or tobacco estates such as flourished in Java. Only a very few Dutch business interests therefore found it either expedient or profitable to open up offices in Bali; the few that appeared were to be found in Buleleng and Denpasar. The most conspicuous was K.P.M., the giant steamship line which linked Bali to Java and the eastern islands and began to experiment with tourism. The really important foreign enterprises in Bali were those of the Chinese, who acquired much urban property and a few coffee gardens and coconut groves. The Chinese generally held them in the name of a Balinese wife, but were rigorously excluded from acquiring other agricultural land. Protection of the Balinese farmers against the exploitation of foreign merchants and planters and protection of the Balinese culture against sudden and disruptive influences constituted the two great achievements of the Dutch colonial administration.

Early Tourism

The Dutch policy of cultural conservationism resulted in large part from the fact that in preparing themselves better to fulfill their functions, certain of the Dutch colonial officials became distinguished scholars and appreciative connoisseurs of many aspects of Balinese life. Diligent Dutch research even refreshed the Balinese memory with regard to traditions and customs which might otherwise have lapsed. Whether Dutch policy and practice did or did not have anything much to do with it, Balinese culture seems to have experienced a quickening influence which made the early part of the 20th Century an era of quite distinguished achievement in art and architecture and in all the ceremonial manifestations of Balinese life, which the greatly increased wealth of the rajas could more readily finance.

The Residency that sheltered Bali from missionaries and merchants also sought to shelter the island from world travelers. But foreign anthropologists, archaeologists, ethnologists, artists, musicians, dancers and actors and, eventually, sociologists, economists and political scientists inevitably and eagerly sought out Bali on missions often indistinguishable from tourism.

Tourism began in Bali in the 1920s. By 1930, as many as 100 visitors a month were experiencing the delights of the island. They came to Bali for a few days of romantic escapism; an assortment of artists and writers, aesthetes and expatriates, even came to stay.

One of the first and most famous was the German musician and painter, Walter Spies. He moved to Bali in 1926 after having already spent a few years as bandmaster in the court of the Sultan of Yogyakarta. In Bali, Spies built himself a simple house on the edge of a scenic ravine just outside the

The solid gold Garuda radiator cap that adorned the royal Fiat of the raja of Gianyar in the 1930s, left, a Balinese icon gone modern.

town of Ubud, Gianyar. He proceeded to produce two or three paintings annually that were of such radiant and revealing beauty that he established a new aesthetics which the Balinese have since made their own.

Spies was joined in the early 1930s by the German novelist, Vicki Baum, who wrote *A Tale of Bali*, a story sufficiently romantic, tragic and authentic to rate as one of the classics of Balinese studies. The Mexican artist-ethnologist, Miguel Covarrubias, and his American wife, Rose, moved in nearby to produce the great study, *The Island of Bali*, which remains unrivaled in English as an exposition of Balinese culture. Even Margaret Mead carried out important anthropological inquiries in Bali. The painters, however, usually outnumbered the writers.

In addition to Spies, they included the Dutch painter Rudolf Bonnet and the Belgian, Le Mayeur de Perpres. All of these early European painters and most of their successors accepted Balinese understudies who have created their own schools of painting which now flourish throughout the island.

The Japanese Occupation

Among the foreign residents at least, the only real cause for concern in Bali in the 1930s was the prospect of war in the Pacific, a threat which suddenly became a reality in December 1941. Japanese troops then began their march down the Malay Peninsula to capture Singapore, the key to the whole region, including the dangerously exposed, weakly defended Indonesian archipelago.

The Japanese invasion forces made Bali an early target of their campaign in the Indies, sending in a small expeditionary force several weeks after they seized the Moluccas and several weeks before they invaded Java. On the morning of Feb. 19, 1942, the Japanese landed about 500 troops on Sanur Beach, the traditional point of debarkation of military expeditions, and marched unopposed into Denpasar. In the next few days, they assumed control of the entire island and installed administrative offices in Denpasar and Singaraja.

The Japanese did not perpetrate atrocities in Bali comparable to those common in other areas, but they almost immediately acquired the reputation of being arrogant and obtuse. The one word which they immediately taught the general population was *bakkaro*. It meant, "You stupid beast!" and was usually accompanied by a kick or blow. The *Kempeitai* military police force of Japan was soon activated and began making arrests, especially among persons closely associated with the Dutch civil or military establishment. But even *Kempeitai* tactics in Bali were almost singularly gentle.

One positive development of the occupation was the emergence of military and paramilitary resistance movements opposed to the Dutch presence as well as the Japanese. One of the prominent leaders was a young military officer named Gusti Ngurai Rai, the son of a warrior caste family of Badung. He proved to be a charismatic hero and martyr for whom the occasion called — a military leader who relied not upon tactics and logistics but rather upon intuition and indeed at times upon mystical guidance. His slogan was *"merdeka atau mati"*, "freedom or death", and he put it to the ultimate test.

Ngurah Rai created the Tentara Keamanan Rakyat, or TKR, the People's Security Force. In time, he merged it with most of the other paramilitary movements and commanded what was regarded as a Balinese people's army.

Meanwhile, major events occurred in the outside world that would have great impact on Bali. Hiroshima and Nagasaki were bombed. The Japanese High Command capitulated. On Aug. 17, 1945, Sukarno and Mohammed Hatta declared Indonesia's

The Dutch artist Walter Spies in Bali in the 1930s, above. The Dutch *controleur* arrives at his residence in Denpasar in a 1930s photograph, at right.

national independence. The Balinese persuaded the Japanese to withdraw into self-imposed seclusion on Oct. 8, 1945, and the new Balinese officials occupied the provincial offices and residences.

The Dutch eventually drove out the Japanese once and for all. But they also arrested Balinese officials and attempted to reestablish a Dutch civil administration on the pattern of pre-war days. Ngurah Rai and his companions saw to it that they did not.

The Long March

Ngurah Rai devised the grand strategy of the "Long March to Gunung Agung." He rallied all available men in west and south Bali to concentrate them in east Bali with

heroes' cemetery.

With Ngurah's defeat, Balinese military resistance had been effectively broken. But in the ensuing years, continued attacks against the Dutch in neighboring Java finally led The Hague to concede Indonesian independence in 1949. Bali became part of the Republic of the United States of Indonesia on Dec. 29, 1949 and later a state in the Republic of Indonesia that was declared in 1956.

A Decade of Disaster

Under the leadership of its first president, Sukarno, the Indonesian archipelago underwent the inevitable growing pains that accompanied the transition from colony to

safe sanctuary on the slopes of the sacred mountain, hoping to lure Dutch forces into areas vunerable to guerrilla attacks. The strategy proved both heroic and tragic.

The Dutch forces surrounded the encampment of Ngurah Rai and his men. Initially, they escaped annihilation only by climbing up and over the volcanic peak and across formidable mountain terrain to Tabanan. But in Tabanan on Nov. 16, 1946, the Dutch again surrounded them. Called upon to surrender and negotiate, Ngurah Rai asked his men to join him in a suicide attack upon the heavily armed Dutch. It proved to be yet another *puputan*. Ngurah Rai and 95 of his men were killed. The site of the "Margarana Incident" as it is known, is now a national

nationhood. In Bali, the transition proved particularly difficult in part by reason of historic Balinese-Javanese antagonisms. Even though Sukarno was part Balinese, he ruled the vast new nation from Jakarta, the long-time capital city of Java under its Dutch name of Batavia.

Sukarno always claimed empathy with the Balinese soul. He elected for himself the age-old role of raja, as patron of island drama. But he did not at the same time discharge the raja's responsibilities for enhancing the spiritual and material welfare of his people. He left Bali a collection of monuments. Most, like the Tampaksiring palace and the Bali Beach Hotel, symbolize ill-chosen priorities if not ill-advised objectives.

But on a more beneficial note, Sukarno established Udayana University.

By the early 1960s, there prevailed throughout Bali the premonition that some awful disaster impended. It was feared that the supernatural powers were being provoked to some truly dreadful visitation and retribution. Human beings would somehow be compelled by acts of nature or the gods to revert to the standards and the values of the past and to impose order upon the present.

The first unmistakable signal that the divine powers were seriously displeased came in 1962 when a plague of rats infested the fields and the granaries. Rats by the millions, huge insatiable rats such as had never been seen before, feasted upon the grain ripening in the fields and then upon grain

Balinese 210-day years. The Eka Dasa Rudra is held in what is regarded as the most ancient and hallowed of the island's shrines, the magnificent Besakih temple complex on the slope of Mt. Agung. The mountain still evokes the prehistoric animistic worship of the spirits of the great volcano which dominates the island and signals the attitude of the gods toward the people by its serene or violent aspect.

As preparations were nearing completion on Feb. 18, 1963, Mt. Agung began to spit smoke and ash and occasional earth tremors could be felt. Despite the ill omens and inauspicious signs that the time was not right for the ceremony, the Eka Dasa Rudra began on March 8. Four days later, the volcano began to throw out mud and rock, and by

that had been harvested and stored. The government was unable to cope with the emergency. Eventually the farmers and their families engaged in an all-out war of extermination which put an end to the affliction. They then piled up token mounds of corpses and gave them symbolic cremations in order to atone for taking even rodent lives. But the conviction persisted that the gods were displeased. The conclusive evidence came in 1963 with the first great eruption in modern times of the sacred Mt. Agung.

To make the disaster even worse, the eruption occurred as the Balinese were making preparations for the Eka Dasa Rudra, the most sacred of all island religious rituals which normally occurs only once every 100

March 17 great rivers of molten lava were pouring down the mountainside. Flames leaped higher into the sky and smoke and volcanic ash blotted out the sun. The Besakih temple complex miraculously escaped major damage, but the Eka Dasa Rudra was prematurely ended. Entire villages were wiped out. Thousands died during the eruption and the ensuing famine and disease. Relief efforts continued well into the following year.

A Balinese artist's painting of the 1963 eruption of Gunung Agung, above. At right, President Suharto and his wife, Tien, at Pura Besakih for the 1979 Eka Dasa Rudra ceremonies.

In 1965, more sorrow engulfed the island. An attempted takeover of the Indonesian government in Jakarta by communist insurgents resulted in the murder of six top army leaders. Hundreds of thousands of Indonesians died in the reprisals and fighting that broke out following the unsuccessful coup attempt. Bali was the scene of some of the worst violence. As many as 100,000 people, not all belonging to communist political parties, may have been killed as members of the island's political parties turned upon each other.

Bali bounced back from the tragic decade of the '60s, as it had so many times before. Under the new Jakarta government led by President Suharto since 1968, Bali has en-

ture, production of livestock or industry.

The new Bali is one of the 27 provinces of the Republic of Indonesia — a unique province in that it has preserved and enhanced the ancient Hindu culture which, in adjacent Java, has been deeply overlaid by the Islamicc. Despite Javanese conquest and massive infusion of influences in early times, Bali has always been a discrete entity within the Indonesian archipelago. And despite widespread dissemination through the schools of the nationalist outlook, the islanders still feel themselves as much Balinese as Indonesian.

Today, the province of Bali is divided into eight *kabupaten,* or districts that correspond geographically to the traditional rajadoms. Each has its elected *bupati,* or district head;

joyed years of comparative peace and tranquility. Tourists began flocking to the island in great numbers in the 1970s, bringing a measure of prosperity to many of its artists and craftsmen whose work became prized souvenirs. The Balinese even managed to stage a successful Eka Dasa Rudra ceremony in 1979 with President and Madame Suharto in attendance during its climactic moments. Mt. Agung did not utter a single rumble.

There has been improvement and expansion of educational facilities and health services and per capita income has increased somewhat. But problems remain. The island has become overpopulated, and there appears little room for expansion of agricul-

its assembly and its branches of civil and military provincial offices. The stabilizing forces of ancient *adat* still regulate the life of the ordinary villager not only in his contacts with his immediate family and neighbors but also with village elders, the temple priests, and, the new agents of the centralized governments — the school teacher, medical personnel of the clinic, the agricultural agents and others.

The genuine Bali and the authentic Balinese are still to be found. It is therefore perhaps imprudent to assay Bali's prospects by referring to facts and figures that may be either inaccurate or inconsequential. The Balinese magic still works, which in itself is a reassuring miracle.

a world of sharing

In Balinese paintings, trees become the secret abodes of fantastic birds and monkeys, the nights an invitation for mischievous spirits, and the temple ceremony a panorama of offerings, sales stands, stylish dress, mystical figures of the theatre, fighting cocks, lovers' rendezvous and family worship. The Balinese world is one of sharing. The joys of everyday life merge with social duties and religious obligations, in the same way that one's personal fears are projected onto the mysteries of nature. The arts reflect an unconscious integration of environment, religion and community of which every individual is a part.

This feeling of continuity is the cornerstone of the local society. Every form of work or creativity is given group expression. The organization of villages, the cultivation of farmlands, and even the creative arts are a communal effort. Within his village, a man belongs to his family, his clan, his caste, his community, and to the total of the Balinese people who share in his heritage and surroundings. Religion is as essential as his livelihood. Every new occasion, whether it be the first birthday of a child or the completion of a house, receives the priest's blessing. Every personal calamity is treated as a shared problem among family, friends and divine guardians. Only in rare moments throughout his life would a Balinese feel oppressive solitude. Nor is death a separation, but a journey of the soul to a resting place in heaven where "life is just as in Bali, but devoid of all the trouble and illness," until it is reborn on earth, possibly in the person of a great-grandchild.

CHILDREN are privileged Balinese, for the smaller the child the closer his soul is to heaven, and the purer is his spirit. It all began in the tales of legendary times:

Held tenderly by watchful parents and an older brother, a child first touches the ground during the six-month-old ceremony here taking place in Kerambitan.
Preceding pages: Artist's view of life in Bali: contemporary painting by Ida Bagus Rai of Sanur.

After creating the world and mountains, trees, fruits and flowers, the deities made four human beings whom they provided with tools of work and houses to live in. The divine Siwa then made four women as wives for the four men. The god of love, Semara, made mating a pleasure so that the women could be fertilized, and eventually, the four couples had many children. (From the ancient Catur Yoga.)

A child born in Bali awakens to a wondrous world of expectation. His father has long centered his hopes on having children, preferably a male child who will care for him in his old age and, after his death, perform the necessary rites to liberate his soul for reincarnation. A newborn baby is believed to have just emerged into this life from a spiritual realm, and is respected as holy. As an infant, he is not permitted to touch the impure earth and is carried everywhere, often riding on the hip of an older sister. Ceremonies are held for him at prescribed intervals, culminating in his first Balinese birthday at 210 days. Offerings are made by the priest and he is allowed to touch the ground for the first time.

As soon as he can walk, the child is set free to wander all over the village with other children his age, sometimes going on excursions that last all day. In this society of his own, he grows to be self-reliant at a very early age. At home he is treated cordially, taken by his parents wherever they go, and coaxed into obedience as an equal. He is never beaten, for were one to strike a child, it may harm his tender spirit. This manner of raising children with independence and respect accounts for the exceptional maturity and sense of responsibility in Balinese children. In the most crowded village festivals, seldom do you hear a child cry or see him fight with other children.

During adolescence a child becomes formally initiated into the adult community. When a young girl of a high caste family reaches the age of puberty, a ceremony is held to announce her status as a mature woman. First she goes into strict seclusion and thoroughly cleanses her body. After three days she emerges in gold brocades and a crown of flowers to receive a

purification blessing from the priest. Frequently, a tooth-filing ceremony follows, also a custom of initiation for both boys and girls. By having a specialist, usually a priest, file a small portion of the upper teeth to form a straight line, one diminishes the six evil qualities of human nature: desire, greed, anger, intoxication, irresoluteness, and jealousy. With this ceremony completed, a Balinese looks forward to a life less prone to human frailty and error. Straight teeth make for prettier smiles, too. Ferocious snarls, with long canines swerving from the mouth, are reserved for the ghastly grimaces of witches and demons.

MARRIAGE is the final initiation into the community; only a settled married man can become a member of the village association. The Balinese marry at an early age. The average age for a girl is eighteen to twenty, and for a boy between twenty and twenty-five. A young Balinese feels it is his most important duty to marry and to raise a family to perpetuate his family line. To go unmarried is abnormal. It is said that if a male adult dies a bachelor, in the next life he will feed sows, a woman's chore; and if a woman does not bear any children, she will be suckled by a giant caterpillar.

As with everything in Bali, marriage customs vary from village to village and caste to caste. The two most popular forms of marriage are the *mapadik*—marriage by request, and *ngrorod*—marriage by elopement. *Mapadik* is the respectable form of courtship, in which the boy's family bearing offerings and presents visits the girl's family and openly proposes the marriage. *Ngrorod* is more exciting and clandestine, for here the honeymoon precedes the wedding, and the man is considered to be more heroic, like the romantic lover Prince *Arjuna*, hero of the *Mahabharata* epic.

The couple secretly decides to run away, usually to a friend's house a good distance from the girl's village. On the appointed day, the girl is suddenly carried off by her suitor.

With responsibilities of their own, children grow self-reliant at a very early age.

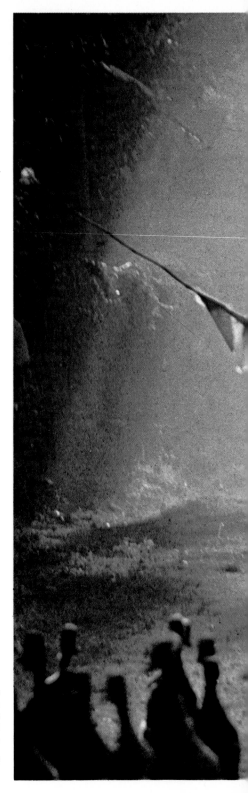

(Nowadays, it's fashionable to kidnap one's bride in a car.) The girl's family pretends to be very worried (and sometimes is). The enraged father is supposed to search the surroundings, asking everyone in the household who took his daughter. Of course, even a close friend who may have helped the daughter pack her clothes, innocently denies any knowledge of the affair. Sometimes even a search party is organized. Usually an envoy is sent to inform the girl's parents, who generally know the suitor and realize that if their daughter took some clothes, she willingly eloped.

Most Balinese agree—the advantage of *ngrorod* is that it is economical. In the formal courtship which precedes a *mapadik* marriage, the suitor must visit the girl's home several times—small gifts and bus fares do mount up. On the first night of elopement, a small religious ceremony is held to make the marriage official by customary law. Offerings are presented to Ibu Pertiwi, goddess of the earth, who bears witness to the union. Later the entire village is invited to a formal wedding ceremony when the couple is blessed by the priest, and their union is announced through offerings and prayer to their ancestors and deities of the house temple. It is then that the woman formally joins the man's family and becomes a member of his caste and clan.

Divorce is not difficult in Bali. A man merely reports to village authorities that his marriage is finished; or, if it is a woman, she simply returns to her home and the children are cared for by the man's family. However, divorce does not occur often. If the situation arises, it is more likely that a man takes a second wife, and the first remains as head of the household.

THE COMMUNITY revolves around family and religion. A man raises a family that worships common ancestors in the family shrine of each household. The various families composing a village all worship at the three village temples: Pura Puseh, the temple of origin dedicated to

Bathed in morning sunlight, a duck shepherd sets out for the fields.

Visnu, where the village founders are honored; Pura Desa honoring Brahma, the temple for official ceremonies involving the living village community; and Siwa's Pura Dalem, the temple of the dead, for revering the deities of death and the afterlife. Together these temples form the core of the community.

For thousands of people, the community is in the crowded neighborhoods of district capitals—towns alive with traffic of bicycles, horse-drawn carriages and motor vehicles, with market places and the busy enterprise of merchants who own the innumerable shops that line the avenues. But for the majority of Balinese, whose livelihood is agriculture, the community is near the rice fields in rural villages. It is these quiet hamlets with shaded pathways overhung by vegetation, thatched roofs scattered behind interminable mud walls, herds of farm animals and the children who are their caretakers, that one pictures when remembering Bali.

A village (*desa*) is made up of family compounds that line either side of several streets and lanes. Where the two main streets cross at right angles in the center of the village, there often is an open space (*alun alun*), around which are the temples, the town market, the cockfight arena, the home of the descendants of the local prince *(puri)*, a large tower containing the signal drum *(kulkul)* to call meetings, announce events or give warnings, and usually a giant banyan tree, the sacred tree of the Hindus. On the outskirts of the village are the public baths, often a riverine laundry, and the unadorned cemetery near the temple of the dead.

Although every male citizen with a family generally owns the land he lives upon and labors, theoretically the island is divine property and is leased to the people who cultivate it and live from it. The *desa* authority, a governing council of married villagers, oversees all that is built upon the land within the village. Formerly, *desa* control was very strict. If a man moved to another town, he asked to be re-

Though only men plant the rice, everyone joins in the harvest.

leased from the *desa* association and took the value of his share in village property, but his house and land remained with the *desa.* Nowadays the *desa* authority is more lenient. Decisions concerning land ultimately rest with the individual landowner. But in some conservative communities, like Tenganan of East Bali, the *desa* retains a stern control over all village property.

Within the village are smaller communities, the *banjars:* cooperative groups of neighbors bound to assist each other in marriages, festivals and especially during cremations. Every adult belongs both to his *desa* and to his *banjar*, where he carries out most of his responsibilities to the village. The *banjars* own the community's orchestras and dance properties, and have a kitchen for preparing banquets, a signal drum tower to call meetings, and a communal temple. The *banjar's* meeting hall, an open pavilion with a large porch, is a familiar sight to every traveler. Called the *bale banjar*, it serves as a local clubhouse where men can gather in their leisure hours practice with their *gamelan* troupe, watch a rehearsal of a play, hold council or just sit and chat.

WORKING THE RICE begins shortly after dawn when the men set out to the fields, accompanied by flocks of ducks that are brought to bathe and feed all day in the flooded paddies. The cascading terraces of rice fields are the most striking feature of the landscape. Each individual plot of rice, *sawah,* is irrigated and contained by dikes of black earth, one flowing into the next as in a rhythmic pattern on green silk. Every farmer owning one or more *sawahs* is compelled to join a *subak,* an agricultural society that controls the distribution of irrigation water to its members.

Like other Balinese associations, the spirit of the *subak* is communal. All members abide by the same rules with each allotted work in relation to the amount of water he receives. *Subaks* help the small agriculturalists by as-

Around the compound, rhythmic thumping of women pounding rice is a familiar sound.

79

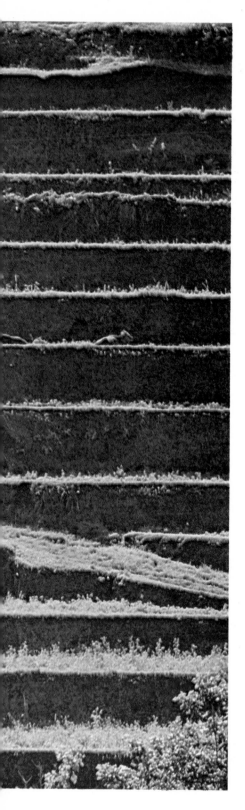

suring them of water, guard irrigation channels against strangers diverting the water for their own use, repair any damages in the dikes, and organize banquets at a propitious time, such as the completion of a harvest. At least once a month a general meeting is held in the small temple of the *subak,* a shrine in the middle of the rice fields dedicated to the agricultural deities. *Subak* associations are important to the prosperity of the Balinese people. The mountainous nature of the land makes irrigation extremely difficult. Only through this full cooperation among neighboring farmers have the Balinese become famed as the most efficient rice-growers in the archipelago.

Before the fields are planted, offerings are made to gain the goodwill of the deities who provide the crop with water and favorable conditions for a successful harvest. Characteristically, a little shrine resembling a Thai spirit house, constructed of bamboo, stands near every *sawah* as an altar for the offerings that are placed there at specific times during the growing season. Although only men plant the rice, everyone joins in the harvest, and often it is an opportunity to meet future sweethearts.

No set hours are reserved for working the rice. Farmers begin soon after daybreak and are also at work at dusk, since working is most comfortable during these cooler parts of the day. Noontime is spent at leisure at home or at the *bale banjar.* Some seasons demand more labor than others. During a harvest the village streets are almost deserted, the *banjars* empty —everyone is out in the fields. At other times, after the rice has just been planted, few hands are needed. Work and leisure run together in a smooth rhythm.

THE HOUSEHOLD is run by the women. Women are up at dawn with their husbands, preparing snacks for the men, fetching water from the village stream, and laying out morsels of rice

Carved from hillsides in huge steps, irrigated rice fields are the achievement of generations of farmers.

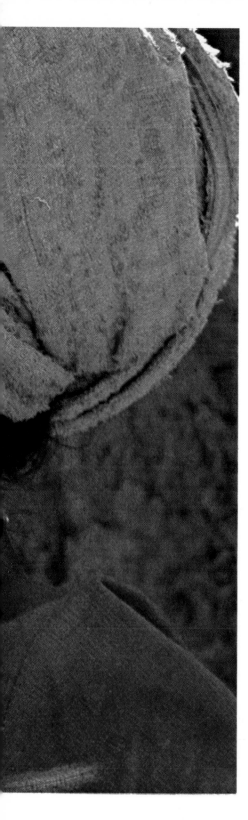

and flowers as small offerings to protect the homestead from evil spirits. The Balinese house can be viewed as a living organism. Like a human being, it has a head–the ancestral shrine; arms–the sleeping quarters and living room; legs and feet–the kitchen and rice granaries; and an anus–the garbage pit in the back yard. Each compartment is a separate pavilion *(bale)*. For affluent families, the sleeping and living rooms are combined in a modern, whitewashed building with a tiled roof; but usually all the *bales* are constructed of brick and wood with thick roofs of thatch. The *bales* are distributed within a well-kept courtyard surrounded by a high mud wall. Villagers feel uncomfortable without a wall around their homes for privacy during the day and security at night. Directly behind the entrance gate stands a small wall, *aling aling*, which not only screens the interior of the compound, but also guards against dangerous influences, for it is said that evil spirits have trouble turning corners in the darkness.

Outside the compound lies a fruit garden with a corner reserved for a pig sty. The Balinese pig, a tamed descendant of the wild hog, is the timid dweller of every household; raising pigs and chickens is one of the main sources of income for the women. On market days, it is not uncommon to see a woman carrying a food stand on her head and walking her pig to market at the end of a rope.

With the exception of cattle sales, the market is the woman's dominion. There she may spend the entire morning gossiping with a friend who has settled on an adjacent spot. The market has a mood about it—all the smells of the island's delicacies and domestic animals (chicks, ducks, piglets, and hungry dogs), seeds, beans, ferns, pastes of all hues and textures, instant one-pot kitchens offering soups and curries wrapped in palm leaf, local medicines to stop nose-bleeding and fainting, mysterious fruits and betel nuts—in short, a total experience in marketing. The grounds are so filled with determined saleswomen that you wonder who is doing all the buying. Yet, there

The sculptured proportions of a Balinese profile.

is always a constant coming and going of people and the hubbub of excited bargainers. Prices vary with the buyer. They are lowest to fellow villagers, higher to strangers, and considerably higher to foreigners—a customary procedure which is logical in a society so strongly oriented to the village community.

After a jaunt to the market, the women return to prepare the morning meal: steamed rice with spicy side dishes and hot, hot, hot sauce. During a harvest, they deliver the food to the men in the fields, but ordinarily the meal is set out for the family who may eat when they wish. Meals are eaten silently, leaving the relaxing time after dining for conversation. The day sets to the deep, rhythmic thumping of women pounding rice for tomorrow's meal.

In the evenings, after a refreshing bath, the men return home for dinner, usually the same food as lunch, served cold. Night is the time to put on clean clothes and stroll in the night markets in town, or meet under the lamplit food stands in the villages. The roads after dark always provide lively scenes of *gamelan* recitals, *banjar* activities, or an impromptu meeting of friends who lounge on the warm asphalt of the streetside. If a temple festival or a cremation is approaching, the entire village is mobilized making preparations. Women fashion high offerings and palmleaf decorations, *banjars* rehearse for the ceremony, and men construct ornamental gateways of bamboo at the village entrances and long slender poles, *penjors*, which gracefully bend above the road to announce the occasion.

DEATH AND CREMATION are a passage from this life to the next in the soul's journey to heaven. A death is the time for sharing one's feelings, when all the friends of the deceased gather in his home to visit. Night after night, while the corpse is still kept in the house, they stay up until late hours to keep the family company. Women help prepare refreshments for the men and assist in making the necessary

After a refreshing bath, farmers lead their cattle home from the fields.

offerings for the purification of the body. The men build high altars for the offerings and aid in cleansing the corpse. On the appropriate date set by the priest, the body is purified for burial in the village graveyard.

The body is buried only temporarily until it is cremated. Many villagers, who do not wish to hold a cremation on the first auspicious day indicated by the religious calendar, may wait several years until a mass cremation is held for which everyone shares the expenses. On the other hand, the body of a Brahmana priest cannot be buried under the ground and must be cremated as soon as the family is able. A man of wealth, aware that a cremation is the most important and most costly of ceremonies, sets aside a fund which will aid his family after his death.

As the date for a cremation approaches, everybody in the village is engaged in making the offerings, coffin, and huge tower—all beautifully deccrated to emphasize the importance of the grand send-off. The Balinese believe a person consists of three "bodies" (*sarira*)—the material body (*stulasarira*), the body of thought and feeling (*suksmasarira*), and the soul (*antakaranasarira*). When a person dreams, it is the body of thought and feeling that wanders. The cremation ceremony returns the material body to its five constituent elements, and weakens the attachment of the soul towards worldly desires, the world of thought and feeling which clings to the soul and causes it to be reborn. Only when the body is destroyed and the soul freed from all worldly attractions, can the soul be reunited with the Supreme Being. The soul cannot be released as long as the body remains. Thus, a cremation is a happy occasion, for it represents the accomplishment of the most sacred duty of every Balinese: the liberation of the soul of a parent or relation.

Most surprising to visitors first seeing a cremation is the lack of solemnity. On the awaited day, friends and relatives arrive from all over the island bringing small gifts for the family. (The traditional present is a piece of white cloth, signifying purity, which is used as part of the shroud.) The body has been brought from the graveyard to the home and placed upon a special pavilion encircled with offerings. Throughout the morning the guests are entertained with refreshments, and at noon are treated to a splendid banquet by their hosts. Then what seems a casual reception suddenly explodes in activity. Urged by the thunderous beat of the *gamelan*, dozens of village men rush into the household and carry the corpse from its resting place. All try to participate in carrying the body, for by doing so one shows his loyalty to the deceased. The carriers hoist the corpse above their shoulders and turn it about in all directions. This is in order to confuse the soul so that it will not be led astray and wander back to the house. The corpse is finally lifted to the awaiting tower, a high structure of wood or bamboo glittering with paper ornaments, mosaic mirrors and bright fabrics.

The tower represents the cosmos. Its wide base is in the shape of a turtle entwined by two *nagas* (crowned snakes) — symbol of the foundation of the world. Above is an open platform where the body is placed: the space between heaven and earth. The platform supports a multi-roofed tower symbolizing the receding heavens. The number of roofs varies according to the caste of the deceased. Brahmanas and the highest aristocracy may have towers of eleven roofs; the lower aristocracy seven or nine roofs; and the common people from three to seven. Nowadays, to save on cost, the tower often has but a single roof. The cremation tower of a high priest has no roofs at all.

Standing nearby is the large animal sarcophagus, which also varies with each caste. The Brahmanas burn their dead in a bull, or a cow if it is a woman. The Satrias use a winged lion, and the Sudras a fantastic half-elephant half-fish. But since customs are always changing, nowadays most of the nobility uses the bull, once the privilege of the priestly class.

The procession to the cremation ground provides an astonishing spectacle. Larger

The most lavish royal cremation in 1979 was that of Ubud's late Cokorda Gede Agung.

ceremonies need as many as a hundred men to carry the huge tower and bull in the tumultuous parade through town to the burning site near the temple of the dead. Led by a single line of women who carry the offerings and holy water, the bearers lift the towering constructions above a sea of followers. The tower is led by a long white cloth held by the relatives. In the magnificent cremations for Brahmana priests and high aristocracy, the cloth takes the form of a serpent which guides the soul.

As the procession crowds into the cremation ground, the body is passed from tower to bull, its path marked by the long white cloth stretched above the heads of women relations. Close relatives supervise the final details when the shroud is cut and the body exposed. The high priest mounts the bull's platform to recite the final prayers and pour holy water upon the corpse, letting the pots of water break upon the ground as is the custom. (Elements connected with the Hindu Trinity—water, fire and wind—relate to the ritual of cremation: water as the final blessing, fire for burning the body, and wind which carries the smoke to heaven.) The *adegan*, an effigy used in the ceremony as a symbolic container of the soul, is placed upon the corpse and thousands of old Chinese coins (*kepengs*) are spread all over it, traditionally as a ransom to Yama, the deity of death. When proper offerings and prayers have been made to ensure the soul a safe journey, the bull is set ablaze. Everyone stays to watch the fire until the bull is a singed skeleton, the body ashes and the soul lifted from this world.

After the body has burned, the procession marches to the sea to deposit the ashes, or to the river if the sea is too far away. This custom is the final purification, the washing away of all uncleanliness. Twelve or forty-two days after cremation, the Balinese hold a second funeral ceremony, *nyekah* or *mukur*, which releases the soul from the body of thought and feeling still clinging to it. Finally the deified soul is enshrined in the family temple, but a distinction remains between the soul and gods.

Cracking of a burning cremation tower.

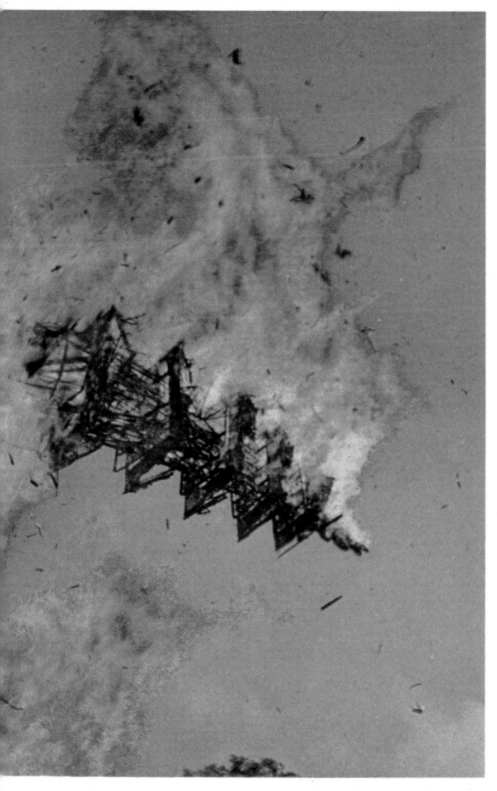

a faith of harmony

I praise the eternal victor over death, who causeth longevity, force and power ... who art the omnipresent and maintaineth the world, who causeth freedom for all those who perform devotions and have faith ... I praise thee who hath vanquished death.

(From a prayer recited by the high priest during a cremation.)

Religious rites and festivals guide a Balinese from birth to death and into the world thereafter. They provide the cohesive forces within the family unit and form the common basis of a village community. Religious observances regulate the plan of a town, the order of a home and the ethical code of the people. Holidays, entertainment and social gatherings are based upon the religious calendar and occur within the milieu of religious ceremonies. It takes only a short stay in Bali to become acquainted with the unique religion of the island. In the innumerable shrines that mark the landscapes, in the *Pendet* offering dance that greets you, even in the gracious personality of the people, religion is essential to the identity of the Balinese and to their pattern of life.

From earliest times, the people of Bali have conceived of an ordered universe stretching from the heavens above the mountains down to the plunging depths of the sea. Everything within nature has direction, rank and place. All that is holy is associated with height, the mountains and the direction upstream toward the majestic volcano Gunung Agung. All that is threatening or harmful belongs to the forces of the underworld, the fathomless ocean and the direction downstream toward the sea. The dwelling place of the people is in the intermediary sphere: the fertile plains between the mountains and the sea.

It is natural for the Balinese, who live so close to the earth—gaining nourishment from the soil and mountain streams, holding cele-

Preceding pages: marching rhythms of gongs and cymbals accompany deities carried in processions from the mountains to the sea. At left, high priests pray at the Besakih mother temple during the enormous Eka Desa Rudra ceremonies of 1979.

brations in courtyards under the evening sky, living in homes where the wind blows freely through open pavilions—to bestow nature with a magic and spiritual significance. On top of the lofty mountains dwell the divine spirits who bring prosperity and good fortune to the people. Beneath the unfamiliar sea lurk fanged giants and demons—forces inimical to man. So all nature is eternally divided into pairs—high and low, right and left, day and night, the east where the sun rises and the west where it sets, strong and weak, healthy and sick, clean and unclean; in general: good and evil, life and death. Each illuminates the other within the scope of creation, and the Balinese ritual strives always to maintain a middle ground—a harmony between the two poles.

AGAMA HINDU, the religion of Bali, upholds the peaceful life of a people who have settled below the blue mountain peaks and above the sea's horizon. The divine spirits (the deities and ancestors) are honored through worship and devotion. The evil spirits (demons, witches and ghosts) are placated through purification and exorcism. Both must be provided for since happiness and contentment come only to those who take both forces into consideration. Even during *Galungan,* the island-wide festival when all the temples ring with merriment, women do not forget to lay offerings of rice, sweet cakes and flowers as a token to pacify the evil spirits.

Yet beyond good and evil, life and death, nature and the universe, there exists a single unity—the source and totality of creation. This is Sanghyang Widi, God omnipotent to the Balinese. In this universal God, all the deities and ancestral spirits achieve a higher unity. It is Sanghyang Widi who lies behind the offerings, rituals and temple cult, so much a part of this festive island. But though Agama Hindu is a monotheistic religion, the supreme God is not often directly worshipped. None of the temples, altars and shrines is dedicated to him directly, but to God seen in his many manifestations.

When the Balinese first settle upon new land and wish to build a village, they erect a "shrine of origin" where they may pray to Sanghyang Widi. Later, when the village temples have been built and all the altars constructed, the people pay homage to the deities of the *desa,* through whom they honor God. Generations afterwards, when the souls of the village founders have been sufficiently purified to attain a divine state, the people also revere their ancestors in the Pura Puseh, or "temple of origin". Traditionally, it was forbidden to refer to an ancestor by his personal name. Instead the title *Batara* is used to address the deified spirit of a deceased person, particularly one who has been outstanding during his lifetime, like a holy man, a *raja,* a scholar or a courageous fighter.

The Balinese are a deeply religious people. The common folk—villagers and farmers—dutifully perform the devotions they have been taught since infancy. During a temple festival, you can't help but notice that nobody is excluded however young. Even the smallest child, his hands closed in prayer between those of his father, participates in a faith that grows with his consciousness and remains with him throughout his life. The educated and the priests, who have studied the complicated theology of Agama Hindu, guide the villagers in their reverences and introduce the island's religion to those first experiencing it. One Brahmana explained, "The Balinese know but one God, yet they honor many deities and ancestors. The multiplicity of divine spirits involves function. As we are one person but use our eyes to see, our hands to work and our feet to walk, so Sanghyang Widi is one God. Yet in his power as creator he is Brahma, in his power as preserver he is Vishnu and in his power to destroy he is Siwa."

The Brahmana was speaking of the Hindu Trinity—Brahma, Vishnu and Siwa (Shiva)—which in Bali is called the *Trisakti:* "three in one". In many of the large state temples there stands a three-seated pedestal enshrining the *Trisakti.* Before a ceremony the temple guardians decorate the pedestal with bright wraps of colored cloth: red for Brahma, white for Siwa and black for Vishnu. In the streaming processions that pass by, the symbolic colors red,

Symbolic male figure with "flames" emanating from his body represents Sanghyang Widi, the Supreme Being. This figure is carved on top of many temple shrines, and appears in an endless variety of magic amulets. Whenever a new-built house receives a blessing from the priest, a figure of Sanghyang Widi is hung above the doorway to signify "God be with us". Drawing by I Gusti Rundu of Sanur.

white and black predominate. Most of the Balinese worship according to the Siwaistic sect of Agama Hindu, since Siwa — God in his manifestation as destroyer — is most seen and felt by the people through suffering and sickness.

In the hierarchy of the divine, below Sanghyang Widi and the Trinity are many other deities — *Dewa* (male) and *Dewi* (female) — each closely linked to nature. Again the Brahmana has an example. "If one could imagine an indivisible whole seen from many different angles, so the *Dewa* and *Dewi* are different manifestations of Sanghyang Widi, each having its own associations." God in his power to create the wind is Dewa Bayu (deity of the wind), in his power to create the rice he is Dewi Sri (goddess of fertility), in his power to create the ocean he is Dewa Baruna (deity of the sea), and so on. Thus, the Balinese venerate many personifications of the same universal God. Whatever deity the people honor, their reverence is also paid to Sanghyang Widi, but indirectly through tangible things, like the sun, the sea, the rice, or a remembered forefather.

Were Bali to be under the care of only the deities and guardian ancestors, it would be truly heavenly. But there is a darker, mysterious side to the island, when a moonless night falls and the back roads turn pitch black, when the forests rustle in eerie shadows and the dogs begin to whine. Then the graveyards and crossroads become enchanted by nocturnal goblins and witches who assume forms of weird animals and monsters to waylay innocent passers-by. Reports range from monkeys with golden teeth to baldheaded giants sighted by eye-witnesses walking along the roads at midnight. Of course, everyone knows who is responsible for the ghostly visions: *leyaks* — witches or the spirits of living persons practicing the art of black magic.

Every Balinese has a tale to tell about *leyaks*. One is bound to make their acquaintance, whether it be by hearing a spooky story, watching a play about Rangda (queen of the *leyaks*), or possibly even a personal encounter. It's whispered that *leyaks*, like vampires, are fond of sucking the blood from sleeping people and

like to capture little children for a tasty meal. They also grow indignant if one neglects to bring them offerings and may vent their anger by plaguing the community with sickness or death. Yet, somehow *leyaks* are shy when it comes to foreigners and seldom reveal themselves to outsiders. Those who are curious may have to content themselves with hearsay, dramas of magic, stone statues at the Pura Dalem (temple of the dead), and of course, the gruesome, sabre-toothed masks with flaming tongues and long tendrils of goat's hair, which one sees everywhere.

While *leyaks* may seem more at home in fantasy than in fact (none have been captured before they have disappeared), the witches are most vivid characters in the spirit world of the Balinese. And they are not alone. The wicked *butas* and *kalas*—invisible spirits which haunt the desolate seashores and dark woods—also can pollute a village with uncleanliness and disease. Should these evil spirits predominate even in one household, the entire village is thrown into jeopardy, and elaborate rites of purification become necessary to cleanse it back to health again.

This assemblage of deities and demons is as much a part of Bali's population as the people themselves. Yet it would be misleading to think the Balinese believe in many gods. Their religion grew from a long succession of Hindu and Buddhist influences upon deeply rooted cults of animism and ancestor worship. From the teachings brought by mendicant priests traveling from India and Java, the people adopted practices to suit their needs. The strength of Agama Hindu has long been its flexibility in adapting to the changing times. In its pertinence to the customary law of the land *(adat)*, to civil and domestic ceremonies, to science and superstition, labor and leisure—in short, to the whole of Balinese society, Agama Hindu has guided a community in achieving a life of harmony and peace.

Pemangku, temple priest, presents an offering of spilt wine to the deities.

PRIESTHOOD AND WORSHIP gather people from all walks of life in common devotion. The serene figure of the priest, clad all in white and seated upon a high pavilion, is a familiar sight to all those who have attended temple festivals. Villagers make their devotions with the guidance of a priest so their prayers are properly directed and received. Ceremonies connected with civil law, such as marriages or the blessing of a newborn child, are conducted by a priest to bestow official authority, much like a state guarantee. Even for informal celebrations, for example, on completing a house, the priest is called upon to give God's blessing before the family moves into their new home. At times of rejoicing or times of sadness, the community first turns to its clergy which in Bali is divided into two levels: the *pedanda* or high priest, and the *pemangku,* the temple priest.

No momentous ceremony would be complete without the services of a *pedanda*. As spiritual leader of the community and carrier of the Agama Hindu theology, the high priest serves as a medium for the people during ceremonies. Through an intricate ritual of hymns and mantras, bell ringing and hand gestures, the priest temporarily achieves unity with God. By absorbing divine power into himself, he is able to prepare the purifying holy water essential to worship. This ritual may take several hours. Meanwhile the temple overflows with devotees–arriving in processions, parading among the shrines with offerings, crowding around the courtyard which has been transformed into a stage. Only in the tingling sensation that filters from the constant soft ringing of a bell, does one become aware of the priest's presence as he silently recites the powerful mantras.

The divine spirit of God is embodied in the water prepared by the high priest. When the ritual has been completed, the priest passes the holy water to the *pemangku* (the temple priest), who sprinkles it upon the people as a blessing and purification. The hard-working *pemangkus,* as curators of the temple, are the

Offerings on Nyepi, day of silence.

supervisors of temple feasts. Whether they be distributing holy water to their congregation, receiving offerings or directing a large procession, it is they who officiate at the temple and take an active part in the ceremonies. The high priest does not participate in worldly things. He is respected as a holy man set above the people. He dedicates his life to meditation, the study of theology and the performance of the ritual. The devoted assistants of the priests are their wives, who through marriage become priestesses and take on the same responsibilities as their husbands.

TEMPLES, large or small, plain or elaborate, are found everywhere on the island. Besides the house temple in every compound, each village must have at least three temples—the Pura Desa, Pura Puseh and Pura Dalem—if it is to be considered a complete village community. There are countless others: the *subak* temples, the clan temples, the *banjar* temples, and those shrines near the public bathing places dedicated to the spirits of the lakes and springs. As sites for renewing contact with the spiritual world through offerings and prayer, temples are essential to the land. If not, the harmony between nature and the people would be disrupted, leaving these places susceptible to accidents and danger.

Most of the time the temples are left unoccupied. It is only during holy days, when the deities and ancestral spirits descend from heaven to visit their devotees, that temples flourish with festivity. For this event, everyone arrives beautifully dressed, presenting the deities with food, music, prayer, devotions and the best entertainment to amuse them during their sojourn on earth. Usually after one or three days, the deities return to heaven and the temple empties until the next holiday. Temples then, as places for renewing contact with the divine, are the true centers of the arts and the nexus of Balinese culture.

Besakih, mother temple of all Bali, flourishes with festivities high on the slope of Gunung Agung volcano.

101

The plan of a temple reflects the spirit of Bali's religion. Rather than a sombre, massive structure, the temple is "a gay, open-air affair" —a spacious enclosure surrounded by walls and partitioned into courtyards. To enter, you pass through the monumental *candi bentar*, split gate. Resembling a tower cut in two halves, this passageway probably takes its form from the old *candi* monuments of ancient Java. Once inside it seems you're far away from the hurried traffic and commerce of the street-side. In the absence of all the ceremonial decorations, the crowds, dances and food stands, everything about a temple is quiet and withdrawn. Stone carvings of demonic faces, overgrown with weeds and moss, peer out from the walls onto the wide courtyard. All around the courtyard stand a number of simple, thatched pavilions—an assembly hall where the *desa* authority holds meetings *(bale agung)*, a shed for the temple orchestra *(bale gong)*, a shelter for preparing offerings, and sometimes a cockfight arena.

Shaded by frangipani trees and a tall *kulkul* (alarm drum) tower, the outer courtyard functions as an antechamber for social affairs and preparations. A second closed gateway, *paduraksa*, guarded by statues of two fierce giants, leads to the inner courtyard: the temple proper. Here, lined in rows on the sides closest to the mountains, are the shrines that serve as "sitting places" for the visiting deities. Perhaps the old *pemangku* is there placing some small offerings before the shrines and brushing the fallen leaves aside to keep the place tidy. The multi-roofed towers of the *meru* shrines taper upwards to the sky. The receding roofs are always in odd numbers, the highest *meru* having eleven roofs in dedication to the spirits of Gunung Agung or Mt. Batur.

In the inner courtyard there are often shrines which house the temple's heirlooms. Medieval stone statues of Hindu deities, jewels, ancient manuscripts and shapeless stones are preserved in temples as sacred relics. Either

Streams of offerings float above a line of women draped in gold brocades.

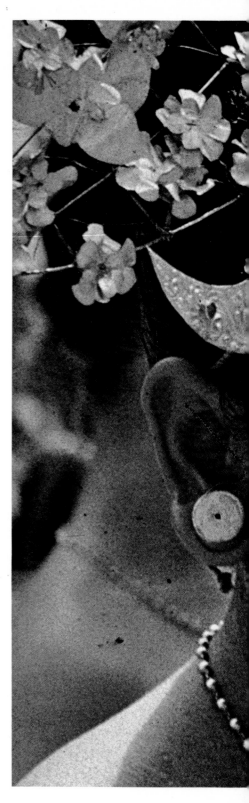

because of their antiquity or because they were found under extraordinary circumstances, these objects are considered divine gifts to the people. Yet a statue is never venerated for its own sake. There are no idols in Bali. Both a thing and a person may be respected as holy because of a spiritual presence which dwells within.

TEMPLE FESTIVALS and holidays are held throughout the year. To pass a week without hearing of at least several celebrations in different villages is highly unlikely. Certain days are designated for special prayers, others for purification rites and others for offerings to the lower spirits. If a village is threatened by disease or an unexpected mishap, a ritual exorcism becomes necessary. A ceremony may also be prompted by divine inspiration through a trance medium, or by the fear of black magic. Then there are holiday seasons with festivals in all Bali's temples (see calendar), and the first nights of full moon and new moon are a time magically favorable for religious observances.

Among the most frequent ceremonies and one especially well known to visitors is the *odalan*. Held once each Balinese or lunar year on the anniversary of the temple's initial consecration, an *odalan* festival is long anticipated by the entire village as a day of prayer, feasting and entertainment lasting late into the night.

In the morning of an *odalan* all the men gather around the *wantilan*—an open pavilion for staging cockfights. Originally, cockfighting served as an essential preliminary to temple feasts. The spilt blood of the cocks was a sacrifice to evil spirits so they would not interfere with the religious proceedings to follow. Later, ritual became secularized into a favorite sport. A recent edict of April 1981 forbade cockfighting outside of temple festivals. Although cockfighting still retains its traditional place at the beginning of a festival, the ban, aimed primarily at limiting the gambling which was so great a

Traditional grace and beauty.

104

part of the local excitement, has taken a lot of punch out of the proceedings; it remains to be seen whether cockfighting will disappear forever from the Balinese way of life.

For years, the cocks have been groomed, tested and coaxed for the special event. Before the fight, two men exchange their cocks to see if in strength and size the birds are evenly matched, and if they have a mean eye for each other. When the contest is agreed upon, the cocks' feet are armed with vicious blades of polished steel. The thread bindings must be tight and bound properly. A jury member stands by to see they are fixed by regulation.

Amid all this excitement, the cocks are put down in a small square which marks the starting point. The arena falls silent as the cocks are provoked and released. In attacks too swift for the eye to follow, the cocks entwine in aerial combat, each striving to gain leverage for the lethal descent of its spurs. A round may last a few seconds, and for all the commotion that precedes them, the actual fights are quick and to the point—a blood-stained cock unable to rise marks a defeat. The birds are swiftly retrieved and, if they are not too badly injured, nursed back to health to fight another day; the less fortunate reappear that night as a delicacy on the family dinner table.

Cockfighting is definitely a man's sport. Women rarely watch, but usually they are preoccupied either selling snacks at the surrounding food stands *(warungs)* or arranging the high offerings. All during the day of an *odalan*, lofty pyramids of fruit, cakes and flowers arrive at the temple, sometimes in the most startling fashion. At one festival, one-meter-high offerings came gliding in on the heads of girls riding bicycles, who dismounted with unbroken balance and entered the temple without once touching their heads!

Offerings should not be taken literally as

In a brilliant display of color, mosaics of flowers, fruits and rice cookies arrive at the temple to honor the gods.

actual food for the deities and evil spirits. Rather, they are given in the same spirit as one presents a gift—a sort of modest token to strengthen the people's request: that the divine bring more prosperity to the community and that the evil spirits bring the least possible trouble. Thus, offerings are always sharply divided into two kinds: those to the evil spirits which are disdainfully left upon the ground, and those to the deities, exquisitely made and appropriately placed upon high altars. Near the high offerings burn fragrant wood and incense to carry their essence *(sari)* upward toward the divine. Ordinary people take what is left; the material part is later brought home and eaten by the family. So both the divine recipients and the donors enjoy the banquet.

While the offerings continue to arrive, the *pemangku* recites prayers of invitation requesting the deities to descend to the temple, their earthly residence. Often, the presence of the deities is represented by little figurines of gold, bronze or gilded wood *(pratimas)*. The deities are asked to occupy the *pratimas* as a more tangible form to which the ceremony may be directed. These figures in themselves have no power. Like the temple shrines which support them, they are merely receptacles for a divine presence.

In the afternoon, everyone congregates among the long tapering flags that elegantly adorn the courtyard. All the shrines are smothered with splendid offerings and hung with traditional paintings and glittering brocades. The *pratimas* rest enclosed with flowers upon the shrines and high altars. Nearby, the *pemangku* sits before a brazier of incense and a water vessel, and blesses the people who have come with offerings. Everyone performs his duties seriously, yet there is no solemnity about a temple festival. All is gay and casual, since an *odalan* is as much a social occasion as a religious one. The *pemangku's* family is there

Enshrined with offerings and burning incense, sacred Barong and Rangda masks overlook the ceremonies from pavilion in temple of the dead.

to assist him, and it couldn't be merrier when his little daughter sprinkles holy water on the bowed heads of her playmates.

At times, the temple's *gamelan* sounds a rhythmic march and a procession is formed to take the deities to the ocean (or nearest large river) for a ceremonial bath. When the procession reaches the sea, the deities are entertained with music, dancing, hymns of praise, and receive many offerings before they are carried back to the temple.

At night, the temple courtyards are transformed into a county fair. Outside the towering gate is a carnival of sideshows—rows of food and candy stands, toys, balloons, and *batik* sales, animated card games, spinning wheel lotteries, prize contests, lively displays of sales-talk by vendors selling wonder medicines, and invariably a drama performance which begins around midnight and lasts late into the morning hours. Everybody looks his best, especially the shy young girls who sell food at the *warungs*. (It's a custom in Bali for a girl who reaches the age of marriage to set up a food stand. Being much in the public eye, she attracts many suitors. The young man who wins her fancy, it is told, pays less.) Needless to say, girl watching wins out over the prize games as the number one attraction for the bachelors present.

Once inside the temple, the proceedings take on a more formal, mystic tone. *Pemangkus* and priestesses continue to chant songs of praise before shrines clouded with smoking incense. They are joined in their devotions by a group of women who rise to dance a slow round of *Pendet*, honoring the deities of each shrine with incense and offerings and prayers. As attendants to the festival the women may go unnoticed among other villagers, but as dancers each comes alive with exuberant individuality and grace. None of the dancers is a professional; nor do they use costume or make-up. The dance in itself is an offering to the deities, and true to the Balinese spirit it is

Young trance dancers enchanted by witch queen Rangda, who observes from behind.

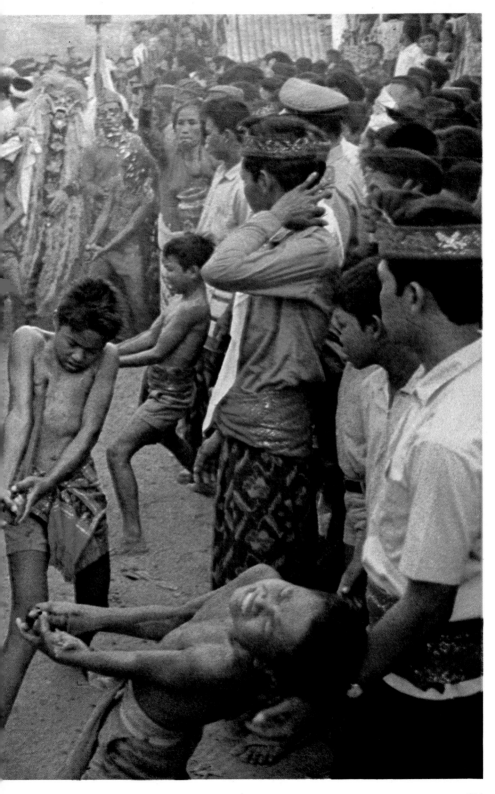

to pay homage to God through the beauty of motion, song and music.

During the course of these rituals, a *pemangku* may become possessed by a divine spirit and fall into trance, crying and shaking violently. He is calmed by a fellow priest and presented with offerings for it is believed he has been entered by a deity. When all is quiet the priest asks him questions—if the ceremony pleases him, if all the offerings have been properly prepared. Trance is taken as a religious experience, a form of communication with the spiritual world. Certain men and women in every village serve the deities as established trance mediums in the temple ceremonies. Each temple has its own trance mediums who attend all the ceremonies there, and every medium has his own deity with whom he communicates during trance. Most mediums belong to a special family of trancers, as do the trance dancers in the Barong and Rangda plays. But they may also be chosen by a deity who "enters" them during a trance ritual. Usually the head *pemangku* of a temple is a trance medium and may attend ceremonies at other temples as the spokesman for a deity.

Through a trance medium, a divine request may be made or advice given. If a person goes into trance and speaks during a ceremony, it is taken as a good sign—a divine gesture to the people that their prayers have been heard and their offerings accepted. When the message is passed on to the priest, he revives the *tapakan* with prayers and libations of holy water. The medium awakes fatigued and dazed, rarely remembering what he had spoken during trance.

An *odalan* ends with the dawn. The long tragic tale of the drama reaches its climax, the *gamelan* closes its stately song, and elderly women dance a final round of *Pendet* in farewell to the deities. Before returning home, the *pemangkus* recite prayers politely requesting the deities to depart in hopes that they have been well provided for during their visit and will return to heaven pleased.

At the end of a temple festival, courtyards are covered with a carpet of offerings.

island travel

Yells, giggles and wild laughter: six children scamper out of their houses to shout the favorite playwords: *"Turis! Turis!"* A somnolent dog lazily raises its haunches and shies away. Stately ladies in festival dress, bearing towers of fruit offerings upon their heads, turn to watch the passer-by. The road is a meeting place for everyone. Temples, shrines, ruins, dances, palaces await you everywhere as destinations.

Not all the roads in the island are streamlined. Those in the best condition and with the most traffic connect Denpasar with the main towns and centers of tourism. If you relish smooth traveling, it's best to limit yourself to these chief towns and villages. But if bumps mean little, nearly every place of interest is accessible by car or jeep. To be safe, before going exploring, inquire for current information about road conditions. The map on the following pages also indicates the types of roads.

Swiftest transportation is by hired car or microbus. An adequate number of taxis, operated by travel agents and hotels, serve the island. Independently run taxis are stationed at the **Suci** bus terminal in Denpasar. To head off the beaten track, a jeep or motorbyke is best; both are easily available, you have only to ask around. Though recommended only for the hardy, seasoned traveler, the Balinese bus is an incomparable conveyance. Hundreds of buses traverse every district of the island at generally reasonable fares. There are two main bus stations in Denpasar: **Kreneng** serving the east (toward Ubud and Klungkung), and **Ubung** serving the west (Tabanan and Bedugul). Quick microbuses, called "Colts", also leave from these stations. *Bemos*, small trucks carrying up to twelve people, offer economical transit in Denpasar and surrounding areas. The sound of bells and hoofbeats are the accompaniment for a jog through Denpasar in a *dokar*,

Preceding pages: tourists snap away in a Balinese painting. Left, a temple relief in Kubutambahan. Following pages: maps of Bali; even automobiles are blessed with offerings; and, a youngster cools off.

a horse-drawn cart carrying up to three passengers. It is advisable to settle the price with the driver before starting on a journey.

An exciting thing to do in Bali is to get lost. In the innumerable village compounds off the main streets everyone is about his business as usual. The atmosphere of ease and affability is unmistakably Balinese. It is most fun to go by motorscooter or bicycle, choosing one's pace and stopping frequently. Vespas, Lambrettas, Yamahas, Hondas and bicycles are rented in most large villages. Where the road ends, take to the sea. *Jukungs*, outrigger *prahus* used for fishing, sail with two or three passengers to **Serangan**, "The Turtle Island", a short distance from Sanur. Larger Sanur-based transport diving parties to the incomparable coral reefs around the island. From Kusumba, beyond Klungkung in the east, *jukungs* sail to Nusa Penida island. From Padangbai boats ferry to Lombok island.

Much of islands travel is left up to the special interests and ingenuity of the individual. You may enjoy anything from hiking down the crater of a volcano to seeking out a secluded beach to pass the afternoon sunbathing. The following trips are guidelines, to spotlight interesting places and to give an overall view of the possibilities of exploring the island. They are designed to be flexible so that you may pick up and depart from them as you please. Many parts of Bali remain unknown, yet to be discovered.

The nicest times to travel are in the morning hours and late afternoons, leaving midday free for a leisurely meal. Local food stands offer hot drinks, fruits and cakes for snacks. Modern toilet facilities and running water are scarce outside the main tourist centers. A guide knows the best places to make stopovers if you plan to be out all day. For those whose stay is short, the Ubud-Kintamani Tour is a good introduction to Bali and its opportunity for shopping. Trips to the east and to the west cover the more remote parts of the island. The trip south concentrates on the shoreline and beachlife, and the Northern Round Trip bridges the mountain range to the coast of North Bali.

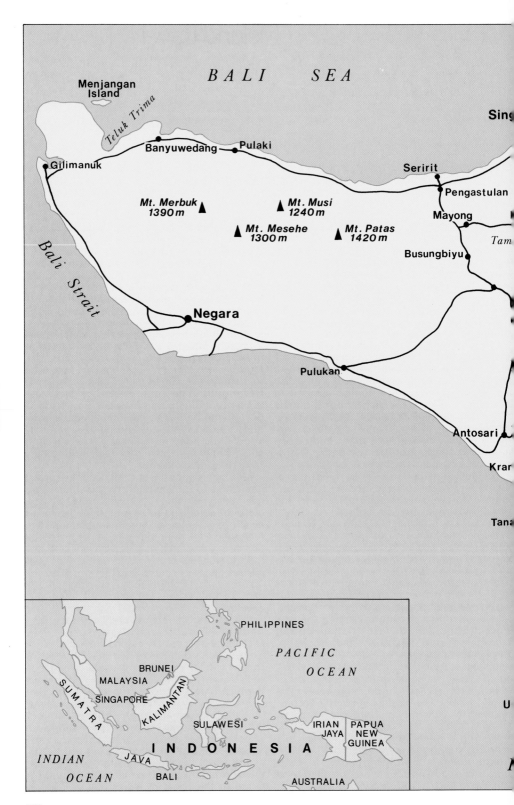

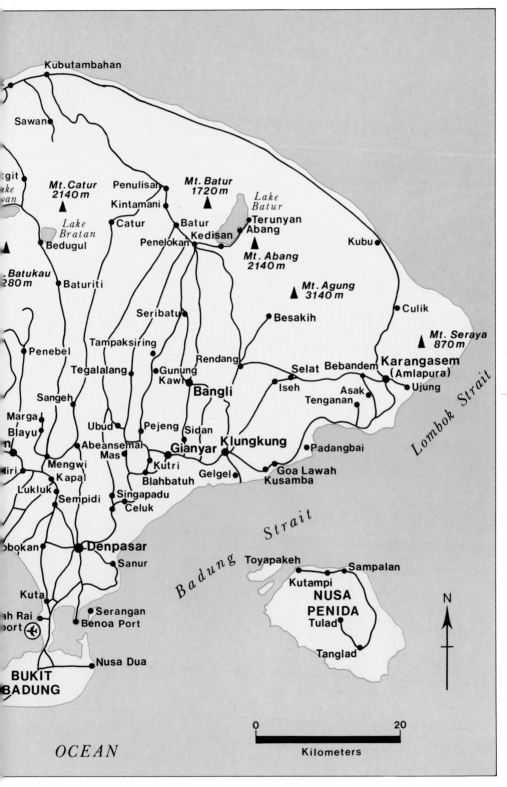

Kubutambahan

Sawan

git
ke
wan

Mt. Catur
2140 m

Penulisan

Mt. Batur
1720 m

*Lake
Batur*

Kintamani

*Lake
Bratan*

Catur

Batur
Kedisan

Terunyan
Abang

Bedugul

Penelokan

Kubu

. Batukau
280 m

Baturiti

Mt. Abang
2140 m

Mt. Agung
3140 m

Culik

Seribatu

Besakih

Mt. Seraya
870 m

Penebel

Tampaksiring

Sangeh

Tegalalang

Gunung
Kawi

Rendang

Selat

Bebandem

Karangasem
(Amlapura)

Iseh

Asak

Ujung

Marga
Blayu
n

Ubud

Pejeng

Bangli

Tenganan

Sidan

Abeansemal
Mas

Gianyar

Klungkung

Padangbai

Miri

Mengwi
Kapal

Kutri

Gelgel

Goa Lawah

Lukluk

Blahbatuh

Kusamba

Sempidi

Singapadu
Celuk

bokan

Denpasar

Badung Strait

Sanur

Toyapakeh

Sampalan

Kuta

Kutampi

NUSA
PENIDA

Lombok Strait

ah Rai
ort

Serangan
Benoa Port

Tulad

N

Nusa Dua

Tanglad

BUKIT
BADUNG

0   20

OCEAN

Kilometers

119

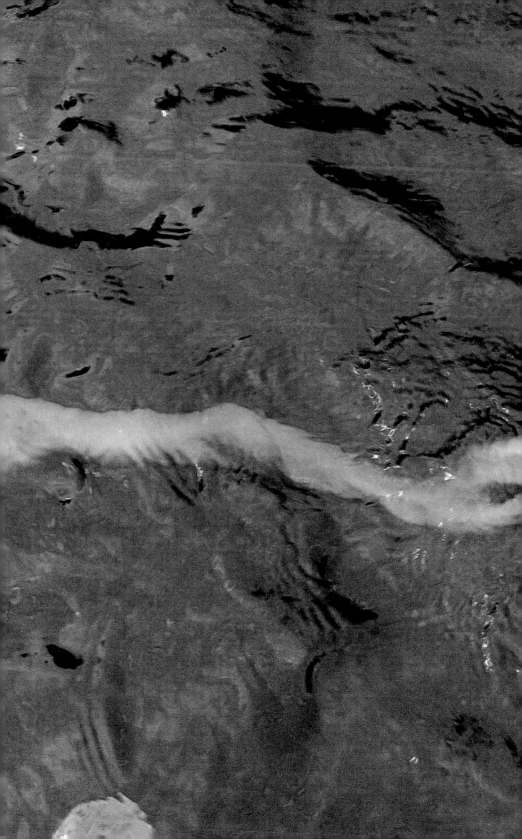

denpasar

With a population over 100,000, Bali's capital is the largest city in the island. It is also the capital of the Badung regency. Since the late 1960s and the tourist boom, Denpasar has grown quickly into a bustling little city in which narrow streets, many of them one-way, can barely handle the crush of traffic. In the center of town is a large open square, called **Puputan Square** after the suicidal battle between the *rajas* of Badung and the Dutch militia in 1906. On one side stands the Museum Bali and the Pura Jagatnatha, a state temple. Across the square is the national military complex. On the third side are the Governor's offices.

The great statue with four faces and eight arms at Denpasar's main intersection (at the northwest corner of Puputan Square) represents the god Guru manifesting himself as the lords of the four directions. It was erected in 1972 as a secular monument to commemorate the *puputan*, though its imagery symbolizes Hindu concepts. It replaced an old street clock.

Denpasar's two main shopping streets come together at the Guru statue. **Jalan Gajah Mada** is block-full with general stores, art shops, restaurants, banks, and a couple of ice juice stalls. The colorful local market is also nearby. **Jalan Veteran** and the little street behind the *Bali Hotel* are good places to buy handicrafts. Many shops close between 1 p.m. and 5 p.m., but thereafter stay open until 8 p.m. The *Hotel Bali*, dating from Dutch times, is on Jalan Veteran. The *Hotel Denpasar*, the other large hotel in the capital proper, is on Jalan Diponegoro. More than 80 smaller hotels are scattered throughout the city.

Denpasar means "north of the market". True to its name, every morning industrious saleswomen open up their stalls in the marketplace, **Pasar Badung**, with assortments of spices, yarns, weaving, hardware, baskets and

125

mats, and fruit and vegetables and meat—every food and commodity imaginable. Each merchant presents a small offering to Ratu Mas Melanting, goddess of prosperity, whose shrine is on the premises. In the evening, Jalan Kartini, just off Jalan Gajah Mada, changes into a string of gaslights, illuminating food and fruit stands, shoe and batik displays of the night market (*pasar malam*).

The capital has enough places of interest to make a trip in itself, especially if you are staying nearby. Right on the Kuta turn-off stands **Puri Pemecutan**, a rebuilding in 1907 of what remained of a much larger palace which was destroyed during the *puputan* conflict. The buildings and ground plan follow the design of royal residences of the old Badung kingdom. Shaded pavilions house *lontar* leaf manuscripts containing works of classical literature; a full *gamelan* orchestra called *gong mas*, or "the golden orchestra", that survives from the original *puri*; traditional

weapons; and a fine collection of contemporary Balinese painting.

Kokar is the everyday name for the Konservatori Kerawitan, the Conservatory of the Performing Arts. There one can watch dancers practicing many different dances with a variety of *gamelan* orchestras. The school was built in 1960 and teaches Balinese and Javanese dance and music besides more general subjects. Although the students are in their teens, a dance instructor will assure you that there is no definite age for a good dancer; dancing years are between the ages of six and eighty. The Academy of Indonesian Dance **(Asti),** a higher level institution, is on the same premises.

Every full moon, citizens of Denpasar may pay homage at **Pura Jagatnatha**, a newly built temple next to the Museum, dedicated to Sanghyang Widi, the Supreme God. The tall *padmasana*, constructed solely of white coral, symbolizes universal order. The turtle

An island-wide
center for the
performing and
fine arts

At Museum Bali, an
historical survey of
Balinese art

Bedawangnala and two *naga* serpents represent the foundation of the world; the towering throne signifies the receding heavens. This design, so prevalent in the island, also relates to the Hindu myth of the churning of the sea of milk, when the gods and the demons stirred the cosmic ocean to create the nectar of immortality.

The **Museum Bali**, built by the Dutch government in 1932, presents an excellent survey of Balinese art from prehistoric times to the early 20th century. Items range from Neolithic stone implements, Metal Age sarcophagi, and Buddhist and Hindu bronzes through a fine variety of modern woodcarvings and paintings, to ceremonial masks and *ukurs*—human effigies made from silver and Chinese coins used in death rituals. The architecture of the museum combines the two principal edifices in Bali: the temple and the palace. The split gate, the outer and inner courtyards and *kulkul* ("alarm drum")

tower are characteristic of the temple. Opposite the *kulkul* stands an elevated pavilion once used in palaces as a lookout for a prince viewing his lands. The main building with its wide, pillared veranda resembles the Karangasem palaces of East Bali, where the porch once served ministers and authorities who had an audience with the *raja*. The windowless building on the right reflects the Tabanan palace style of West Bali, while the brick building on the left belongs to the northern palace style of Singaraja, making the museum a true monument to Bali.

A permanent exhibition of modern Balinese painting and wood carving may be seen at the Art Center at **Abiankapas** on the edge of the city. This grandiose complex includes a large dance arena and a sales room. Exhibitions, dances, and recitations of classical literature are organized by the center. A calendar of events is available. Visiting hours are 8 a.m. to 5 p.m., Tuesday to Sunday.

sanur, kuta, and the south

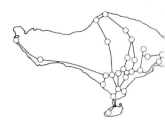

It is curious that the two famous tourist centers of Bali are at Kuta and Sanur, villages on opposite sides of the narrow isthmus to Bukit. No longer typical Balinese villages, they have changed much as tourism developed and are now satellite suburbs of Denpasar, connected by a steady stream of *bemos*. Bali is becoming an increasingly popular S.E. Asian conference center and international surfing and yachting events swell the number of tourists to the island annually. A government decision has restricted hotel centers to the far south at Denpasar, Sanur and Kuta and to the development of a new tourist center at Nusa Dua on the Bukit peninsula.

Throughout the island's history this same area (together with the northern villages around Singaraja) have been the first to welcome or defend against outsiders. In popular belief, the demon Jero Gede Macaling annually haunts the coasts of South Bali from his home in Nusa Penida. At Belanjong, beyond the Hotel Sanur, an inscription engraved on a low pillar commemorates the victories of Sri Kesari Warmadewa over his enemies in A.D. 913.

In later times, famous priests from Java trod these shores. The three best-known temples of the area—Pura Sakenan, Pura Luhur Ulu Watu, and Pura Petitenget at Krobokan—are associated with the itinerant 16th-century priest Nirartha.

The first European to settle in South Bali was a Danish trader, Mads Lange, who built a copra factory in Kuta around 1830. By befriending kings of these regions, he persuaded squabbling *rajas* to give up their quarreling to some degree and unite against Dutch pressures from North Bali. Partially successful at this quest for continuing Bali's independence, Mads Lange was beloved by some rulers and detested by others. He was believed poisoned by enemies in the late 19th Century; his grave may be seen at Kuta.

In 1906 the Dutch invaded the south at Sanur, the opening clash taking place on the beach as the Dutch militia landed. Battles were waged all along the road from Sanur to Denpasar. The three ruling princes of the kingdom of Badung climaxed their defence and defiance in battles unto death, *puputan*.

'Surfing at Kuta Beach', painted by Batuan artist I. Made Budi (previous pages).

The Dutch were left in control. After t upheavals of the Japanese occupation a Independence, the Dutch in 1946 again land troops at Sanur.

Sanur has been long famous for its paint and orchestras. You need only walk a sh distance inland to hear village music clu engaged in their nightly practice sessio Often, in the evening, streets are packed w spectators awaiting local theatre performanc Sanur has always been a great center of t *Arja*, a traditional opera of courtly romanc and to this day is an avid patron of the *Waya Kulit* puppet day.

A great sport of the children of Serang "The Turtle Island", is to fly huge kites, so 8 meters long, by hoisting them into the from outrigger canoes. In fact, kite flying such a popular pastime here that officials Bali International Airport feared the kites mig be distracting to landing aircraft and suggest everyone shorten their strings. Sanur, Serar

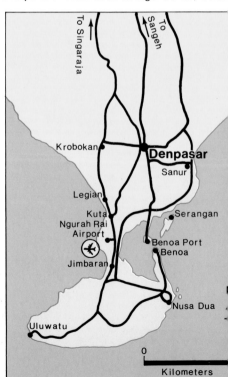

130

an, and Kuta are close by. The journey to the sea temple of Ulu Watu is an enjoyable trip.

SANUR. Save for a few scattered villas owned by lords and heiresses, during the thirties Sanur beach was left in seclusion. Pandy's Art Gallery was then an aquarium and coffee shop. Tandjung Sari was a solitary temple on the cape, and *Hotel Bali Beach* had not neared its conception. The only surviving home of those times is that of the Belgian painter Le Mayeur, who moved to Bali in 1932 and lived there for 26 years. The house, with its statued gardens, luxuriant gold and crimson carvings, and Le Mayeur's own paintings is now cared for by his widow, Ni Polok, once a renowned *Legong* dancer and famed beauty—the ideal Balinese of his paintings. On his death Le Mayeur willed the house to the Indonesian Government. A guidebook is available. The house is situated close by the Hotel Bali Beach.

By the fifties, the first cluster of bungalows was built as a small hotel. The villagers were amazed that someone would want to settle by the ocean, as beaches were traditionally shunned by the Balinese because of spirits. Yet Sanur continued to attract an international elite and today is a prominent luxury resort area in the Far East. The Hotel Bali Beach, a Soekarno-era project, was opened in 1966. While the Hotel Bali Beach expanded into a new wing and bungalows (called the Bali Seaside Cottage), more than 30 hotels opened their doors up and down the beach.

When the Hotel Bali Beach first opened, and even to this day, it was a source of wonder to the Balinese. They came from all over the island to set eyes upon what, to the modern world, were everyday matters—sky-high rooms, running water, electricity and elevators. The *Bali Hyatt* and *Sanur Beach* are the next largest hotels. The building boom reached its peak for a PATA Conference in 1974 when hotels at Sanur alone provided

Facing east, the beach
is ideal in the early
morning

about 1,600 rooms. A new, open highway now links Sanur to Denpasar and Nusa Dua. The volume of traffic to the Bukit Peninsula has increased since more luxury hotels opened at Nusa Dua resort in 1982.

A wise government regulation that forbids buildings taller than a coconut palm has allowed Sanur to retain much of its village character. The luxuriant vegetation soon covers building scars, and moss transforms a new stone wall. The regulation encouraged the growth of bungalow-style hotels based on the Balinese norm of many small buildings within the one-house compound. The hotels of Sanur are all comfortable and elegant.

Built along the beach, the hotels of Sanur are ideal in the early morning, for the coast there faces the sun rising over Nusa Penida. On the clearest days, Lombok's Rinjani volcano floats distantly above its collar of clouds, with Bali's own Gunung Agung closer by. Elegant triangular sails of fishing *prahus* glide on the calm sea. These boats are called *jukungs* and there are many for hire for trips along the shore. At low tide, the waters recede leaving great swathes of sand and coral that stretch for hundreds of meters to the reef. It is then that villagers wander among tide-pools to collect coral, which they burn nearby to make building lime. At night, fishermen wade by torchlight to catch shrimp and bait.

It is easy to spend a day around Sanur: lazing by the pool-side, walking on the beach, or following paths through the surrounding hamlets, rice fields and coconut groves. You can take a look at the coral pyramid in the sea temple or the old pillar inscription at Belanjong.

In the evening the choices are several. Relax on the beach (especially around the full moon) or on the porch of a bungalow. Wander down to the beach market and try the local food stalls. Watch a dance or drama (your hotel can tell you when they are on).

KUTA. Sunsets make memories at Kuta beach, one of the island's loveliest seacoasts. Skylight descends in warm waves of color, leaving shy stars behind. Village fishermen often set off at dusk, the sails of their *prahus* shrinking to frail silhouettes that drift across a wide, red sun. They vanish into the night, lulled by the rhythm of waves breaking on a beach longer than vision can discern. They return when the young warmth of early morning lights up the slopes of Mt. Batukau and, on clear days, the mountains on the eastern tip of Java.

Save for the fishermen, the villagers usually busy themselves at sundown and rarely wander down to the beach to sit quietly watching the sun set into the sea. Mads Lange, South Bali's first European resident, must have enjoyed it though. An Englishwoman, Ketut Tantri, who lived through the early years of the revolution in Bali and Java, built a house at Kuta beach. The *Kuta Beach Hotel*, built on the same site, was opened in 1959, but guests were few.

Only in the late sixties did young travelers, at home riding the waves of Hawaii and California and elsewhere, begin to frequent the beach. At that time, almost everyone stayed in Denpasar, coming to Kuta for a swim, the sunset, a kris dance and sometimes a night on the beach.

The villagers of Kuta were farmers and fishermen and metal smiths, and they were rather surprised at the great interest their beach received. But like many Balinese, they saw there was a profit to be made. For a small charge they invited the travelers into their homes. Home-stays were set up everywhere. These are clean, simple and cheap accommodation. A number of larger hotels, such as the *Kartika Plaza Bali* and the *Oberoi*, have also sprung up. There are many restaurants serving all kinds of westernized dishes and "soul" food, and mini-boutiques selling Bali beach fashions

abound everywhere. Tourist activity has spread north up the coast to Legian and beyond on the road to Krobokan.

As the size and fame of Kuta spread, the beach became popular with the residents of Denpasar. Indonesians from the large cities of Java came by the tour load. Dozens of art shops opened along the main streets. On the beach, girls and women carry bundles of sarongs and batiks on their heads, looking for customers. Young boys sell dance tickets, and young girls sell cold drinks. At sunset, the beach is a lively place, and the roads are full of cars and motorbikes.

It is said the goddess of the sea claims at least one victim each year at Kuta beach, so be careful—at times there is a strong undertow. Mostly, however, it is fine swimming and the body surfing is great. Kuta and Ulu Watu have waves as fine as anywhere in the world for board surfing. Boards are for hire. The Surfing Club of Bali was set up by an Hawaiian-in-residence and a Lifesaving Club patrols one section of the beach. In 1981, Kuta hosted international surfing and lifesaving events on its golden beaches.

At Kuta, the water stays warm late until after dusk, like its saffron reflections; and the smooth descent of the shore suits anything from building sandcastles to taking long walks. Local beachcombers are on hand gathering fans of white coral and stringing cowries into long necklaces to sell. The Balinese sometimes come from near and far to perform rituals by the ocean.

Although all the ritzy nightclubs are at Sanur, Kuta after dark is a popular place for young visitors to eat, drink and be merry. There is a night market, one or two informal discotheques and numerous bars and restaurants serving good food at moderate prices. Almost every evening there is a performance of Balinese dance somewhere in Kuta. To know what is on, just ask around.

A sacred temple
festival in the
island of turtles

Perched between the
spirit and the
deep blue sea

SERANGAN. A pleasant sail by *prahu* from Sanur or Benoa, carries you to Serangan, an island just off the coast south of Sanur, nicknamed "The Turtle Island" for the large sea turtles caught there and fattened on sea grass until they are sold as the speciality of village feasts. At low tide it is possible to walk there. The island's sea temple, Pura Sakenan, is held sacred by all the people of South Bali, especially those of the Denpasar and Mengwi areas. It is associated with the 16th-century priest Nirartha. Within both this temple and the nearby Pura Susunan Wadon are slender pyramidal shrines called *prasada* or *candi*, which are rare in Bali. Over a three-day period, once every six months, thousands of devotees cross over the sandbanks. Towering giant puppets – *Barong Landung* – are carried by canoe in a water procession from the mainland. *Gamelans* ring throughout the day, amidst the steady flow of women bearing offerings to be blessed.

ULU WATU. Connected to the mainland by a low, narrow isthmus, the limestone tableland of Bukit peninsula, at 200 meters above sea level, is in striking contrast to the lush Bali mainland. Cacti grow upon this arid land. Some parts are used for grazing cattle. A good surfaced road meanders across Bukit to its western tip, where rocky precipices drop almost one hundred meters to the ocean. The small sea temple of Pura Luhur Ulu Watu balances picturesquely on the cliff's edge. Perhaps dating from the 10th century, it is one of the six prominent temples revered by all Balinese. Honoring the protective spirits of the sea, the temple has an unusual arched gateway capped by a Kala head and flanked by fine statues of Ganesa. At the end of his life, the priest Nirartha chose this spot to achieve *moksa*, deliverance from this life. Vantage spots on the Bukit road afford vistas of the heartland of Bali rising to the peaks of distant volcanoes.

135

ubud–kintamani tour

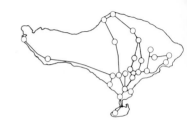

Taking the round trip to Kintamani, including a visit to the Ubud area, provides a good opportunity for getting acquainted with Bali.

Your first introduction to the island is the capital city of Denpasar with large town markets, an old palace, and a dancing school. The Museum of Denpasar houses an art collection of admirable scope beginning with prehistoric finds and continuing to traditional arts in practice today. Out of Denpasar, through villages specializing in stone carving and metalwork, the route leads to districts rich in the ruins of a fascinating civilization: the early Hindu-Balinese kingdoms that vanished in the 15th century. Bronze Age antiquities, awesome stone monuments and ancient statues recall legendary kings. Contemporary styles of painting and woodcarving flourish in the upland villages of Ubud and Mas, thus completing an historical view of Balinese art from past to present.

Green seas of rice, so abundant in the fertile soils of the southern plains, are scenes of quiet beauty. Fanciful palmleaf scarecrows and thatched huts to give shade are scattered throughout the countryside. A field is never without a shrine or small temple, honoring the deities of agriculture who give their blessings for a successful harvest. In village communities, women are threshing rice for tomorrow's meal, fetching water, washing along the river banks, or caring for bands of playful children who cannot resist energetically welcoming every passing visitor. The highlight of the trip is the ascent to the holy volcano Mt. Batur, and the sanctuary on the crater dedicated to the fertility goddess who dwells there. At about 1,700 meters, the slopes of Batur determine the lie of the land for central Bali. Waters enriched with volcanic minerals flow from the Batur highlands, led from one rice terrace to another, in descending steps to the sea.

Take your time; one day is not enough for the island's many surprises. No sooner than you begin to sightsee, you may find yourself in the middle of a festive religious procession: your best and most exciting guide to a Balinese temple ceremony. Many of the places mentioned here make beautiful side trips. Morning walks through family compounds lead to out-of-the-way retreats. The highlands of Kintamani invite explorations down the crater to a cloistered mountain village, where people adhere to customs surviving for over a thousand years. Batur's peaks break through the mists around noon, so it is advisable to leave Denpasar early in the morning and plan for a full day excursion.

Within the Kintamani Tour to the volcano, there is a shorter round-trip taking a half day. This trip passes through Celuk, a center of gold and silver work, to Kutri, (see page 141) and from there crosses over to Bedulu (see page 151) to concentrate on Ubud and Mas, the centers of painting and woodcarving. A worthwhile visit to view examples of some of the best in Balinese painting and sculpture over the years can be made at Ubud's Museum Puri Lukisan. Opened in 1954, the museum now has extra buildings for individual and group exhibitions as well. If you are pressed for time and are especially interested in the arts and in shopping, you'll find this shorter round trip most convenient.

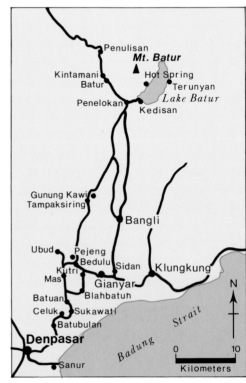

Batur temple in the mists (previous pages).

Gifted young sculptors
merrily carving demons
in soft *paras* stone

Formerly each
kingdom had its
smithing center

BATUBULAN. Driving northeast of Denpasar, one is soon among the fields and streams of Badung and Gianyar. Badung's district border is marked by a spinning factory named Patal Tohpati. Tohpati means "where people risk their lives" and alludes to a former battle between two rival kingdoms. Entering Batubulan, stone statues of divinities and demons, humans and animals line the roadside. They are sold to tourists and to the Balinese as protective figures or for family shrines. You can watch boys carving at the workshops, for the boys form the bulk of the dozen or so groups. Batubulan also boasts many dance clubs that regularly perform. Antiques and handicrafts are on sale, besides the stone carvings. Because its stone sculptors are exceptionally gifted, Batubulan is an area of beautiful temples. Particularly interesting is the Pura Puseh, lying 200 meters inland. Here, on the temple gate, deities from the Hindu pantheon are juxtaposed to a meditating Buddha.

CELUK. A silver-spun dragon twice encircles the wrist to form a bracelet sold in the village of Celuk, a center of gold and silver work. Original designs in delicate filigree make Balinese jewelry one of the most unusual styles in Asia. Although individual pieces are elaborate, they have simple origins in their making. Artisans use a tree stump with a protruding iron spike as a pounding base, a bamboo stem to catch the filings, and a manually operated gas pump for heat. As with most Balinese crafts, gold and silver work is largely an hereditary trade. Apprentices begin young. By the time the boys are twelve, they are already producing fine ornaments from the precious metals. However, the increased demand by tourists has resulted in the craft extending beyond the traditional clan. Almost every family in Celuk now makes or sells gold and silver work. Kuta and Kamasan (near Klungkung) are other such smithing centers, the latter famous for large silver bowls.

Batuan—a village
with a distinctive
style of painting

Darkly flow the
waters of the
cursed Petanu

SUKAWATI AND BATUAN. After crossing the River Oos by the large new bridge, the road turns sharply north into Sukawati and then Batuan. In 1022 king Marakata issued an edict creating these two villages out of the old Sukawati. The important Sukawati market even attracted Chinese merchants and the *puri* became a center for the arts. It is today still the *wayang* center of Bali, besides owning famous dance groups.

Batuan specializes in dance, painting and weaving. Its painters took part in the development of modern Balinese painting in the thirties and possess their own distinctive style. There are many art shops in both villages.

Beyond Sakah, the road bridges a deep ravine of the Petanu River. This river is an important historical landmark. The strip of land between its borders and the eastern river Pakrisan contains numerous antiquities surviving from the early Balinese-Hindu period beginning at the end of the 10th century.

Broken bas-reliefs, rock monasteries and Hindu statues are found scattered among the temples and rice fields.

The Petanu River has a fabled origin. A popular legend tells of the King Mayadanawa, whose pride in his great magical powers brought the gods to wage war against him. Defeated in battle by Indra's forces, he created a spring of poisoned water. Many of the gods died from drinking or bathing in its waters. But Indra and his priests produced a spring of holy water—the famous Tirta Empul—which revived Indra's fallen allies. To escape his fate, Mayadanawa changed himself into a cock, then into rice, finally into a stone. Indra shot an arrow into the stone. Mayadanawa's blood poured forth into the Petanu River. For many generations, this river was believed to be cursed. Until this century, it was forbidden to use its waters for irrigation, because it was thought that should the rice ever be cut, blood would spurt from the severed stems.

The massive stone
head of a legendary
strong man

An unusual Indonesian
antiquity of Durga, the
goddess of death

BLAHBATUH. The Pura Gaduh of this market village is associated with Kebo Iwa, a legendary personality famous for his size, strength and magical power. Many landmarks and buildings are attributed to him, including the original gate of this temple. Enshrined in a small pavilion is a massive stone head over a meter high, said to be a portrait of Kebo Iwa. The head cannot be dated precisely and does not resemble usual Hindu-Javanese iconography; it is probably solely Balinese in creation. Kebo Iwa was a high official of the last king of Bedulu before the Majapahit conquest in 1343. Gajah Mada, the great prime minister of Majapahit, realizing he could never conquer Bali while Kebo Iwa lived, enticed him to Java with the promise of a beautiful princess, and had him killed. The present temple is a reconstruction following the earthquake of 1917. Many of the statues are unfinished; some gay carvings are on the main stairs.

KUTRI. For those with a special interest in the antiquities of Bali, a path leaves the lower temple of Pura Bukit Dharma and climbs a steep hill covered with banyan trees to a single shrine on top. Here is the famous statue of Durga killing the bull-demon under her feet. Durga is the goddess of death, the angry aspect of Siwa's wife Uma. Although the statue is defaced, the fluid motion of the body defies the conventional pose of Balinese and Javanese sculpture, especially of female figures, and is closer to Indian prototypes. Standing over two meters high, this statue of Durga is one of the finest works of art remaining from the early 11th century. Kutri was probably then part of the village Buruan where inscriptions say there was a burial temple honoring Mahendradatta. So the Durga statue is thought to commemorate this East Javanese princess who came to Bali to rule with her husband Udayana—and earned the reputation of being a Calon Arang.

GIANYAR Before Gianyar, traveling from Kutri, there is a road junction. For a shorter round trip (skipping the Gianyar-Kintamani circuit) which allows more time for shopping in Ubud and Mas, take the road left to Bedulu and follow the tour from there (pages 151-157). Or, if there is time, take the road right to Gianyar and Kintamani. Just outside Gianyar there are several textile and weaving works with rows of bright, freshly dyed cloths hanging outside. Visitors are welcome inside to watch the nimble-fingered weavers at work.

Looking on to the square in the center of town is the *puri*, surviving intact from the former kingdom. A policy of war enabled its early rulers to carve out a powerful realm early in the 19th century, until its expansion was checked by the Dutch. The *puri*, inside and out, presents fine examples of traditional architecture, stone and wood carving. The eating stalls near the cockfight arena are good, especially for roast pig. A side-road from Gianyar links with Lebih on the coast, where once a year people from all over the Gianyar regency hold a large celebration to placate the demonic forces that bring disease to man and rice. On the road from Gianyar to Blahbatuh is the village Bona, a center of basket weaving and the home of the modern *kecak* dance. About three kilometers beyond Gianyar, the road onward to Kintamani branches left.

On a curve in the road near the village Sidan stands a small, elegantly carved temple—a particularly fine example of its kind which is the Pura Dalem—the temple of the dead. The *kulkul* drum tower is decked with reliefs showing tormented wrongdoers being punished by devilish giants. The gates are flanked by deities of death who symbolize the Pura Dalem, particularly Durga, manifested as the witch queen Rangda. To the left is a separate shrine which always accompanies the Pura Dalem. It is dedicated to Merajapati, caretaker of the dead.

In a cooler setting,
temple reliefs and
statues

Demulih hill,
conducive to
relaxation

BANGLI. Further inland the weather is cooler. Plots abound with sweet potato, peanut, corn and spices. A high *kulkul* drum tower marks the entrance to Bangli, capital of a kingdom descended from the early Gelgel dynasty. The largest and most sacred temple of the district is Pura Kehen, the terraced mountain sanctuary and state temple of Bangli. An ancient document tells of the slaughter of a black bull during a feast held at this temple in the year 1204. Down below at the foot of the stairway, there is an old temple which contains a collection of historical records inscribed on bronze plates. Statues, in *wayang kulit* shadow play style, line the first terrace from which steps lead to a magnificent closed gate the people of Bangli call "the great exit". Above the gate looms the hideous face and splayed hands of Kala Makara, the demonic one who catches harmful spirits to prevent them from entering. On either side are statues of villagers gesturing a welcome. An enormous banyan tree shades the first courtyard, where the walls are inlaid with Chinese porcelain. An eleven-tiered *meru* dominates the inner sanctuary. Here, on the right, you see the three-throned shrine of the Hindu trinity: Brahma, Siwa, and Vishnu. A hierarchy of deities is carved on the back of the shrine. By turning left at Bangli, you may bypass the volcano and take a short cut to Tampaksiring (see page 148). Just 3 kilometers out of Bangli on this road is Demulih hill. It is well worth the climb up, for the view of central Bali is superb, and the hilly setting (worthy of being declared a sanctuary) is conducive to peace and relaxation. Bangli itself, a little town that is usually passed through, is rewarding and worth a walk through to view some of the stone statues and temple reliefs. To reach the volcanoes of Batur and Abang, continue straight. Many villages in this mountain region have retained an older form of culture that was not deeply influenced by the courts of the lower slopes.

143

The "place to look"
upon the mountain
craters

PENELOKAN. From the bamboo forests north of Bangli, the road emerges to a lookout above a huge volcanic basin. Ribbons of black lava ripple down the valley from the misty peak of Mt. Batur. This is Penelokan, "the place to look", where the world changes colors. Sometimes, the still lake there resembles blue glass, and at others, a sheet of platinum. In chartreuse and vermilion blouses, the mountain girls stride along the rim of an ancient crater surrounding Mt. Batur. Legend tells of Pasupati (Siwa) dividing the sacred Hindu mountain Mahameru and placing the halves in Bali, as the volcanoes Gunung Agung and Batur. Next to Agung, Batur is the most revered of Bali's mountains. Temples throughout the island honor the deity who dwells at its summit. Penelokan is a good place to make a lunch stop at one of its high standard restaurants.

A short steep corkscrew road leads down to Kedisan on the lakeside where boats can be hired. On the flank of the volcano opposite Trunyan at Tirta Bungka, are hot springs set beside the cold waters of the lake, nature's sauna for tired travelers who have climbed Mt. Batur. Nearby, the hotel Tirta Yatra, is a convenient place to stay before or after climbing the volcano.

Formerly, the people of this area lived relatively unperturbed at the base of the holy volcano. In 1917, Batur violently erupted destroying 65,000 homes, 2,500 temples and more than a thousand lives. Lava engulfed the village of Batur but miraculously stopped at the foot of the temple. The people took this as a good omen and continued to live there. In 1926, a new eruption buried the entire temple except the highest shrine, dedicated to God in his manifestation as Dewi Danu, goddess of the lakes and waters. The villagers were then forced to resettle on the high cliffs overlooking Batur. They brought the surviving shrine with them and rebuilt the temple, now known as Pura Ulun Danu of Batur village.

A remote and secluded
dwelling place of the
"original Balinese"

A severe temple
style honoring the
capricious volcano

TRUNYAN. From Kedisan, on the shores of Lake Batu, a *prahu* takes you across the lake to Trunyan, hemmed in by the towering crater wall. A path down the rim of the crater also leads there. Cut off and relatively inaccessible, Trunyan is ethnically and culturally outside the Balinese mainstream. The inhabitants–who call themselves the *Bali Aga*, or the "original Balinese"–to this day retain a social order aligned with prehistoric traditions. Cremation is not practiced here. On the lakeside, not far from the village, lies a simple fenced-off area where the dead are placed and allowed to disintegrate by natural process. Secretive and protective about the customs exclusive to their community, the people keep hidden Bali's largest statue 4 meters high, that of Ratu Gede Pancering Jagat, the patron guardian of the village. From the village of Songan, past Kedisan, there is a long but interesting walk back to Kintamani.

BATUR. In 1927, the people of Batur began rebuilding Pura Ulun Danu, the temple which once lay at the foot of the volcano. It was an ambitious project. The majority of the 285 planned shrines are yet to be completed. At present, the temple is finely and simply designed. Two august gateways, severe in contrast to the elaborate split gates of South Bali, open onto spacious courtyards laid with black gravel. Rows of *meru* towers silhouette against the sky in full view of the smoking volcano. The *bale gedong*, a storehouse of precious relics, contains a bell of solid gold. As the story goes, the bell was presented to the treasury of the temple by a king of Singaraja in atonement for his having insulted the deities. The ritual in this temple is closely linked with the veneration of Lake Batur and supplication for the blessing of irrigation water. The mountain lakes help regulate the flow of water to the fields and villages through the many natural springs lower down the slopes.

Your base for an
exciting trek to
Batur's crater

Bali's highest temple
shrouded in mist

KINTAMANI. Inscriptions from the 10th century indicate that this high mountain district—which takes its name from the ancient, wind-blown town at 1,500 meters—was the earliest known kingdom in Bali. Its small houses are constructed of wood and bamboo tiles to give warmth in the cold evenings of the highlands. Plentiful vegetables and fruits prosper in the damp climate. Like many of the old villages in Bali, the center of community affairs is the *bale agung,* the village assembly hall, where the elders of the *desa* authority meet once a month. The dances of Kintamani are varieties of the *Sanghyang* trance dance, rarely performed in other parts of the island. Every third morning, the main street becomes a gay bazaar for all the surrounding villages. There are several small hotels for an overnight stay while exploring the area. Not far north of town, a dirt road branches left down towards Lake Bratan, and to the village of Selulung with its interesting little, stepped pyramids.

PENULISAN. The main road continues its ascent to a hillside in the clouds where, symbol of modern civilization, Bali's television aerial, claims its high-tech place beside the long flight of steps rising to the mountain sanctuary of Pura Tegeh Koripan. The highest temple in Bali, at 1,745 meters, Pura Tegeh Koripan is actually a complex of temples at which a circle of surrounding villages worship. The sparsely adorned *bales* shelter lines of fine statues; portraits of Balinese kings, queens and divinities; and *linggas.* Several statues bear dates of the 11th century, another that of the 15th century. It is thought that this temple was the mountain sanctuary of the old Pejeng kingdom, just as Pura Besakih was the state mountain sanctuary for the later Gelgel dynasty. The clouds often wrap themselves around the high peak, but on a clear day, the view from Penulisan encompasses half the island: from the crest of Mt Bratan in West Bali to the Java Sea. This temple is the farthest point north on this tour

but one can continue north to Singaraja.

On the return trip south of Penelokan bearing right, you pass three villages striking in their uniformity. The identical rooftops and continuous high walls are seldom seen in the more relaxed organization of typical villages. Although such conformity could only come from old communities where individualism is still minimal, the true explanation for their construction is the eruptions of Gunung Agung and Mt. Batur in 1963. Because the soil was poisoned by the volcanic ash, all occupants of this region had to be evacuated to emergency camps, set up all over the island. When the people resettled upon their land, they rebuilt their entire village at the same time. Thus all the buildings look alike.

You are now entering territories that were settled by the Bronze—Iron Age, which began about 300 B.C. and continued well into the first millenium A.D. The great bronze drum of Pejeng, and various axes, jewellery and figurines are still preserved in temples as sacred heirlooms, or have been found in the rice fields and entered private collections. From the 10th century till the Majapahit conquest in 1343, this area was the heartland of the kingdom of Pejeng-Bedulu. Its kings issued decrees written on plates of bronze, from which scholars have been able to reconstruct the history of the kingdom. These inscriptions, found all over Bali, tell of village and state affairs. Both Hinduism and Buddhism were practiced, and priests served as advisers to the kings and as members of the royal court of justice. Many inscriptions describe the founding of monasteries within a village territory and the freeing of that village from certain state taxes to pay for the monasteries' upkeep. The ruins of these monasteries survive to this day, many bearing reliefs cut into rock. Statues of gods and kings dating from these centuries are also preserved in dozens of temples.

A sanctifying spring
for Bali's *Agama
Tirta*, or "Religion
of Water"

TAMPAKSIRING. The hallowed spring of Tirta Empul in Tampaksiring dates from legendary times. In popular folklore, it was made by Indra when he pierced the earth to create a spring of *amerta,* the elixir of immortality, with which he revived his forces who were poisoned by Mayadanawa (page 216). The waters are believed to have magic curative powers. Every year people journey from all over Bali to purify themselves in the clear pools. After leaving a small offering to the deity of the spring, men and women go either side to bathe. On the full moon of the fourth month each year, the villagers from nearby Manukaya take a sacred stone to be cleansed at Tirta Empul. When the weathered inscription found on the stone was deciphered, it gave the date of Tirta Empul's foundation as A.D. 962 and described the cleansing ceremony. For a thousand years these villagers had been abiding by this tradition without having been aware of the meaning incised on the stone! In 1969 the temple at Tampaksiring was completely renovated. Many of the shrines were built anew and painted in bright colors. Outside the temple are rows of sales stands where you may buy souvenirs—the bargain being carved bone jewelry.

On the hill above the sacred spring is the Government Palace built in 1954. Once a resting place for Dutch officials, the site was chosen by former President Soekarno as his residence during his frequent trips to the island.

South of Tirta Empul, on a line joining it with Gunung Kawi, is Pura Mengening. There is a definite connection between these three places. At the latter temple there is a free-standing *candi* similar to those *candis* the facades of which are hewn from the rock at Gunung Kawi. Like Tirta Empul, the temple has a spring of pure water, which is also a source of the River Pakrisan. Pura Mengening might be the commemorative temple of King Udayana.

Ancient rock-hewn
candis and
monks' cells

GUNUNG KAWI. From the lookout above a long stairway, ghostly habitations appear on the far side of the valley. The young River Pakrisan bubbles down over boulders, as it winds through the rice terraces. This is the striking setting of Gunung Kawi, a complex of rock-hewn *candis* and monks' cells.

Legend has it that the gigantic strongman Kebo Iwa carved out all the monuments one night with his fingernails. Remarkably preserved in their deep niches over 7 meters high, they are only facades without interior chambers. There are ten in all—the main group of five east of the river, a group of four west of the river, and one by itself at the southern end of the valley.

Each has a complex of monks' calls nearby. The *candis* however were not places of burial, but served as memorials to deified royalty. Short inscriptions on some of the *candis* have enabled archaeologists to attribute them to the end of the 11th century, soon after the

death of Anak Wungsu in about 1077. But the identity of the kings and royal spouses honored there has not been determined with certainty. One theory says the main group of five *candis* honored Udayana, his queen, his concubine, and his two sons, Marakata and Anak Wungsu. Another theory suggests they honored Anak Wungsu and his royal wives. The group of four *candis* is thought to enshrine Anak Wungsu's concubines. The tenth *candi* honors a high state official. Perhaps Anak Wungsu ordered the Gunung Kawi monuments sculpted at a place where he himself used to meditate.

Similar though smaller rock-hewn *candis* and monks' cells have been discovered in other parts of this central heartland of the Pejeng kingdom, several of them also on the River Pakrisan. By the suspension bridge at Campuan, Ubud, are a couple of cells. In those times the monastic tradition must have been strong.

The art of painting
flourishing with the
tourist boom

PEJENG. There are no great ruins here or ancient palaces. The remains of the old kingdom are mostly statues kept in many temples. One of the most impressive antiquities in Indonesia, however, is the monumental bronze drum called the "Moon of Pejeng", loftily enshrined upon a high pavilion in the Pura Penataran Sasih. It is a thousand years older than the Pejeng kingdom, for it survives from the Bronze Age in Indonesia which began about 300 B.C. First made known to the West in a book published as long ago as 1705, it is the largest drum in the world to be cast as a single piece. Shaped like an hour glass and over 3 meters long, the drum is of a rare type, decorated with eight stylized heads. A stone mold for a similar drum found in Bali proves that a highly sophisticated technique of bronze casting was used in ancient Indonesia.

The old Balinese, however, tell a different tale: once there were thirteen moons in the sky each year instead of twelve. One night, one of the moons fell to the earth and was caught in a tree. It shone so brilliantly that it prevented the local thieves from their nocturnal depredations. The boldest among them determined to extinguish the light. He climbed up the tree and urinated on it. The "moon" burst, killing the thief, and fell to the ground in the form of a drum, explaining why it is now broken at the base. The large stones lined in back of the pavilion are said to be fallen black stars.

Besides in the Pura Penataran Sasih, which was the state temple of Pejeng, important antiquities are found in three other temples. Pura Kebo Edan (Crazy Buffalo) houses a giant statue 3.6 meters tall. In Pura Puser ing Jagat (Navel of the World) a remarkable stone vessel tells in carving the story of the Churning of the Ocean by the gods and demons to obtain the elixir of life. Two kilometers east of Pejeng is the old monastery of Goa Garba.

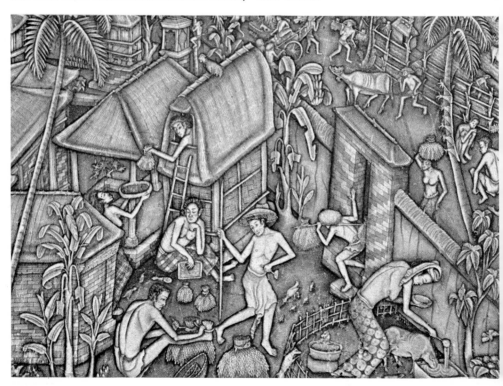

BEDULU. The village at the crossroads beyond Pejeng was once the center of early Balinese dynasties. In the 14th century, the armies of the Majapahit dynasty in Java threatened many parts of the archipelago. One ruler refused to submit: Dalem Bedaulu or Raja Tapolung (Fall from Meditation), the last king of the Pejeng dynasty, a man reputed to be endowed with supernatural powers. Boastful of his awesome powers, he was punished by the gods. According to one version of the legend, Bedaulu at his own command would have his head cut off by a servant and then replaced, without causing him harm. One day, however, the king's head accidentally fell into a river and was carried away by the torrent. The desperate servant hastily decapitated a pig and thrust its head onto the shoulders of the king. Ever after, the king dwelt on a high throne and forbade his subjects to raise their eyes in his presence. Alas for all secrets in Bali, the sharp eyes of a passing child espied him. The word was spread throughout the land of "Bedaulu", "He-Who-Changed-Heads".

In other versions of the story it is the Majapahit prime minister Gajah Mada who discovered that the king had a pig's head. Granted an audience, he asked to eat boiled ferns and drink from a spouted water pot. But to eat and drink he had to raise his head, thus discovering Bedaulu's bestial appearance. Scholars have a more prosaic theory for the origin of the name: formerly the name may have been *Badahulu*, or "(the village) upstream".

Dalem Bedaulu was the last monarch of the Pejeng dynasty which fell in 1343 to Gajah Mada's forces from Java. Shortly thereafter a new ruling dynasty which owed allegiance to Majapahit was established at Samprangan, just east of Gianyar. A century later the capital was moved to Gelgel near Klungkung.

GOA GAJAH. A short distance from Bedulu stands the mysterious Goa Gajah or Elephant Cave. A fantastically carved entrance depicts entangling leaves, rocks, animals, ocean waves and demonic human shapes running from the gaping mouth which forms the entrance to the cave. The monstrous Kala head that looms above the entrance seems to part the rock with her hands. Similarly decorated hermit cells are also found in Java. The large earrings indicate that the figure is that of a woman. The T-shaped interior of the rock-hewn cave contained niches which probably served as compartments for ascetics.

Recent excavations carried out in 1954 unearthed bathing places in front of the cave with six female figures, representing nymphs or goddesses holding water spouts.

An energetic clamber down rocks and rice terraces fifty meters behind the cave leads to the fragments of a fallen cliff face with the broken bas-reliefs of stupas and a tiny cavern enshrining two ancient Buddha statues.

An old Javanese chronicle written in 1365, some twenty years after the Majapahit conquest of Bali, says that one of the two Buddhist bishops in Bali at that time had his hermitage at Lwa Gajah, the "elephant river", which probably alludes to the Petanu River which flows nearby in its deep gorge. However, Goa Gajah dates back certainly to the 11th century. Whether it was originally a Buddhist or Hindu hermitage cannot be answered with certainty, for there are both Hindu and Buddhist sculptures inside or outside the cave. Perhaps monks of both religions had hermitages close to one another. In pre-Majapahit Java and Bali, the two religions, both influenced by Tantric beliefs and practices, had begun to amalgamate into what is called the Siwa-Buddha cult. Buddhist practices and doctrines survive to this day amongst a small segment of the Brahmana priests who are mostly found in East Bali.

An enigmatic story
carved in gigantic
proportions

The carvings are
angular and stylized,
yet forceful

YEH PULU. A strenuous walk inland along borders of rice fields leads to the unfrequented ruins of Yeh Pulu. It's best to take a guide there, though you will always be accompanied by dozens of curious children who scamper along with you. Yeh Pulu is a small temple walled by a carved cliff face—an enigmatic frieze 2 meters high and 25 meters long. Of the figures carved in high relief, none appear to be deities except the seated Ganesa, the elephant-headed son of Siwa. In the first scene of the frieze, a man carrying two vessels of palm beer walks behind a woman of high caste wearing an elaborate headdress. They approach a house where an old woman appears from behind the doorway. Next, a man with an axe converses with a woman. Sitting near him is a hermit wearing a turban, which surprisingly is almost identical to the crown the high priest wears today. There follows a violent scene involving a bear (?), in which a man thrusts a special double-ended knife into the beast's open muzzle. Beside it, in a comic representation, a frog imitates the hero's attitude and action by thrusting a knife into the mouth of an attacking snake. Next, two men carry two animals on a pole between them, and the final scene shows a rider on horseback with a woman being pulled along behind. Making fun of this last scene is a little relief depicting a female monkey clinging to her mate's tail.

Although the reliefs were excavated in 1925, their exact meaning remains conjectural, like many mysterious carvings in this district. The reliefs may represent a story of Krishna, the last scene depicting the hero returning home triumphantly with Jambavati, the daughter of the slain bear, tied to the horse's tail. Krishna later marries Jambavati.

At the far end of the frieze is a hermit's niche near a small underground spring. It is presumed Yeh Pulu was a hermitage dating from the 14th century.

UBUD. The trip to Ubud is a time change: from stone dwellings of antiquity to a current center of fine arts noted for its painters. On the threshold of Ubud is the village of Peliatan with an especially active dance troupe and *gamelan* orchestra. These famous musicians have represented Indonesia abroad in Europe and the United States. The village *puri* continues the tradition of fine performing with private dance lessons for aspirants from the age of five. It's delightful to watch a *Legong* instructor glide through the motions of the dance trailed by four little girls, their feet weaving patterns over the courtyard and their faces set in concentration to the essential rhythm of the drum.

A quieter rhythm guides the daily life of Ubud. Each morning farmers set their fighting cocks along the roadside to bask in the sun. Covarrubias says they do this so the cocks will be amused watching the passers-by: sturdy women suspending hemispheres of pots to be sold at market, farmers bearing sheaves of

rice, and nowadays passing automobiles. It's nice to join them and stroll through the plentiful shops that line the avenue opposite the old *puri* in the town's center. Ubud is excellent for shopping. Galleries display contemporary styles by old masters of thirty years experience and young boys who have developed a manner of their own—the "Young Artists" style. Many shops have studios at the back where you may watch painters at work.

For decades the serene beauty of this village has lured celebrities and artists from all over the world, some of whom stayed to build their homes here. Down the road at Campuan, the junction of two rivers that flow through Ubud, are the former residences of Walter Spies and Rudolf Bonnet, artists who lived here during the thirties. With the support of Cokorda Gede Agung of Ubud, these two painters founded the Pitha Maha, a society which encouraged the young artists of the area, criticized them, provided

Like carpeted steps,
rice terraces mold
the landscape

them with materials and encouragement, and patronized their work. Spies' own paintings inspired the Balinese artists to abandon the rigid forms of the traditional style and adopt such European techniques as perspective. (Spies died during World War II.)

Since the turn of the century the art of North Bali had come under European influence. The modern styles of Ubud and Batuan drew their inspiration from the scenes of everyday life about them, besides from the classic stories of Old Javanese literature. Many Balinese painters associated with Pitha Maha are internationally renowned, like the late I Gusti Nyoman Lempad, and others remain to this day among the island's most outstanding artists: A.A. Gede Sobrat, Ida Bagus Made Poleng, I Gusti Ketut Kobot and several others, each working in his own style. An outstanding woodcarver was I Tjokot from the village of Jati, 15 kilometers north of Ubud. Mas and Nyuhkuning are other early woodcarving cen-

ters still active.

At the present time, Dutch-born Han Snel and the American Antonio Blanco are the long-resident foreign painters. They have galleries in their homes where their works may be seen. Dutch-born Arie Smit encouraged young artists to create bold, simplistic paintings from which arose the "Young Artists" style with its bright colors. The patronage of the arts continues, with friends and collectors intermittently sponsoring exhibitions abroad.

The Museum Puri Lukisan (Palace of Fine Arts), also called the Museum Ratna Wartha, was begun in 1954 and opened two years later as a permanent collection of modern Balinese art. Beautifully situated above a garden, the museum displays sculpture and paintings in chronological order, giving a clear view of the modern movements in Bali's art centers. In the early seventies two new buildings were added, one being used for exhibitions. Bonnet returned to Bali in 1973 to help expand the per-

manent collection.

Ubud is the only important tourist center in Bali outside the Denpasar-Sanur-Kuta area. There are several hotels, and recently in 1975 electricity came. Many tourists like to make Ubud their home while in Bali and travel out from there. Besides the main trips, there are many roads and places near at hand that are enjoyable to visit. The terraced fields and waterfalls in nearby gorges invite one to leave transport behind and set off on foot. Any direction is fine. The best-known walk is to the monkey forest, just south of Ubud, where a troop with a fine-looking king inhabits the surviving patch of jungle. A great banyan tree straddles the nearby gorge on the path down to a delightful bathing place. The Pura Dalem on the edge of the forest has exceptionally fine statues of Rangda gorging herself on young children. The road south through Padangtegal leads on to Pengosekan, a village of painters since the

thirties. It is well known for the varied and individual style of its artists and was visited by Queen Elizabeth II in 1974.

Cross over the suspension bridge at Campuan, and turn left several hundred meters beyond, for the path to Penestanan, main village of the "Young Artists". On trips further afield on the back roads, a motorbike is best. From Ubud, two roads, besides the usual one via Tampaksiring, lead to Kintamani. One road goes through Payangan, famous for its lychees which grow nowhere else in Bali. The second road is surfaced as far as Tegalalang. Jati, where I Tjokot lived, is just off the latter road beyond Tegalalang. There are several art shops along the road. Up nearer the crater, be prepared to encounter thick volcanic sands left behind where Gunung Agung erupted in 1963. Ubud serves well both the traveler who wants to get about and those who prefer a quiet relaxing stay

*"Young boys have
no worries; they
just carve."*

MAS. According to the Balinese chronicles, Danghyang Nirartha (Padanda Sakti Bahu Rauh) came to Bali from Java at the end of the 15th century and made his home in this village. This priest, from whom almost all of Bali's Brahmanas claim descent, gave Balinese Hinduism the form it now presents, including its highly complex offerings and spectacular cremation rituals. He became court priest of the Gelgel ruler. Dozens of temples in Bali are associated with his name, for he made long trips on foot through the island. Most of the villagers of Mas (which means "gold") are Brahmanas who honor their ancestor in the Pura Taman Pule built upon the site of Nirartha's residence.

In the olden days, the fine arts of wood-carving and painting were reserved almost exclusively for royal and religious purposes. Nowadays they are also produced for enjoyment and commerce. Men of every caste are artisans, and in Mas live some of the most talented. The best known is Ida Bagus Nyana, who in 1974 received a high national reward in recognition of his art. For many years he has not sold his beautiful and original carvings, which may be seen at his home. His son, Ida Bagus Tilem, is one of several accomplished sculptors working at Mas. Some carvers specialize in masks for the Topeng and other dances.

Do not be surprised when you visit an art shop to find a corps of woodcarvers making statues—the Balinese do everything in groups, and many of the young carvers work under the direction of a master. A carver selects his seasoned block of timber—often, an ebony from Sulawesi—then shapes the rough form with an axe. With a mallet and dozens of small chisels, the carving is worked into its finished form and finally smoothened. The polish is nothing more than shoe shine. Again, the sculptors begin young. The most expensive carving is often done by boys of twelve years.

to the east

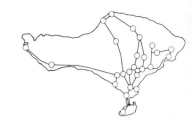

According to mythology, when the deities made mountains for their thrones, they set the highest peak in the east, a place of honor to the Balinese. During centuries of isolation, the islanders knew this sacred volcano, Gunung Agung, as "Navel of the World". In every temple in Bali a shrine is dedicated to the spirit of Mt. Agung. The tapering form of cremation towers, *merus,* and even high temple offerings bear the shape of a mountain, mirroring the people's reverence for their holy volcano. Here, on the slopes of Gunung Agung, lies the mother temple of all Bali, Pura Besakih. A cluster of temples, Pura Besakih represents religious unity within Hindu-Balinese beliefs.

In February 1963, devotees of this temple were busily engaged with last preparations for the Eka Dasa Rudra, the greatest of Balinese sacrifices, which occurs once every 100 years. Suddenly, a glow of fire shone from the crater and Gunung Agung began to rumble. A priest-ess interpreted the ashes of the volcano as a sacred portent sent to purify Besakih, and the people continued with their festal arrangements. By the time the great sacrifice was held on March 8th, thick columns of dark smoke were surging from the summit. Shortly after, Mt. Agung exploded, destroying hundreds of homes and killing over a thousand people. It was a remarkable coincidence, for the volcano had been dormant for centuries. To most Balinese, of course, the eruption did not occur by chance, but was chastisement for having offended the gods. The volcanic ash destroyed most of the crops in the island. Although Eka Desa Rudra is generally held once every 100 years there is a sacred proviso that, should the world be in a state of upset due to natural or human disharmony, it may be held earlier. Eka Desa Rudra was held once again in March 1979, this time without undue incident.

East Bali offers a different impression from the southern plains. The east is a quiet country of high bare hills ribbed with ancient terracing. The coastal strip along the eastern shore consists primarily of coconut and banana groves. Coral is gathered for making into building lime, but gradually the coral reefs are being destroyed. Partly hidden by the eastern coastal ranges is the colossal cone of Gunung Agung, the peak of which on clear days soars high above the countryside.

Resplendent Pura Besakih (previous pages).

To reach Klungkung, follow the Ubud-Kintamani Tour to Gianyar (pages 138-142), and then drive directly east. In the area between Gianyar and Klungkung are lush river gorges, valleys sheltering farm villages, and country tracks down to the sea. East of Klungkung, landscapes are still blackened by the lava streams of the '63 eruption, which isolated this area from tourist travel for several years. Along the eastern shores palms dip their branches above the waves of the strait which separates Bali from the island of Nusa Penida. Many interesting places are side trips from the main route. To see the east, it's better to plan two separate day trips: the first—to Klungkung and Besakih, and the second—a full day's outing that embraces parts east of Klungkung and the territories of Karangasem. Seasonal changes affect the condition of side-roads; so, especially for traveling in the Karangasem district, inquire for information on present road conditions.

Before heaven and
hell in the
Hall of Justice

KLUNGKUNG. As the seat of the Dewa Agung, nominally the highest of the old Balinese *rajas*, Klungkung holds a special place in the island's history and culture. As artistic centers, the palaces of Klungkung's *rajas* and noblemen patronized and developed the styles of music, drama and the fine arts that flourish today. The capital was shifted to Klungkung from nearby Gelgel in 1710, and a new palace built. Probably towards the end of that century the original Kerta Gosa, Hall of Justice, was erected. An exquisite example of the Klungkung style of painting and architecture, the present Kerta at the town's main intersection is beautifully laid out within its moat. Three Brahmana priests acting as judges presided over this royal court which continued in existence through Dutch times. Cases were brought here only if they could not be settled among families or individual villages, as the Kerta was the island's highest court of justice and by far the strictest. Imagine a terrified defendant kneeling before the tribunal, his gaze chancing to wander to the ceiling on which were painted scenes of the horrors he would meet after death, were he guilty. If he dared to look higher, he found each punishment complemented by a reward in heaven. At that time, perjury could bring a curse upon three generations.

The Bale Kambang, the Floating Pavilion, likewise decorated, was used by the attending royal family. Pan Semaris and Mangku Mura directed the present paintings in 1945.

Two kilometers south, between Klungkung and Gelgel, lies the village of Kamasan, the present-day center of the Klungkung-style painters. Indeed that style is often called the Kamasan or *wayang* style, as it draws its main themes from Old Javanese literary classics. Kamasan is also a famous center of gold and silver smithing. In the shops of Klungkung one can buy modern and antique Klunkung-style paintings, carvings, silverwork and silks.

161

BESAKIH. A climb north, through the astonishing landscapes of Bukit Jambul, ascends over 900 meters up the slopes of Gunung Agung to Pura Besakih, the holiest of all temples in Bali. It originated most probably as a prehistoric terraced sanctuary where worship and offerings were made to the god of Gunung Agung, the dominant landscape element in the Balinese world. Over a thousand years and more, it was enlarged and added to until it grew into the present complex of about 30 temples. In the 10th century it was apparently a state temple. According to inscriptions kept here, an important event took place in the year 1007. If can only be guessed that this was associated with death rituals for Queen Mahendradatta, Udayana's co-ruler who died the previous year. Since the 15th century it was the state temple of the Gelgel-Klungkung dynasty which built a series of small temples in honor of its deified rulers. Now it is the state temple for the provincial and national govern-

ments which meet all expenses. Today, Pura Besakih is revered by all Balinese as the "mother temple" of Bali.

Within the Besakih complex, the paramount sanctuary is the Pura Panataran Agung which rears its lofty *merus* on a high bank of terraces Steps ascend in a long perspective to the austere split gate. Inside the main courtyard stands the three-seated shrine enthroning the Trisakti, the trinity of Brahma, Visnu and Siwa During festivals the shrines are wrapped in colored cloth symbolic of the deities. The Pura Panataran Agung and two other important temples higher up the slope likewise together symbolize the Trisakti. In the centre Pura Panataran Agung is hung with white banners for Siwa; to the right, Pura Kiduling Kreteg with red banners for Brahma; and Pura Batu Madeg, to the left, with black banners for Visnu. These latter two temples are taken care of by the Karangasem and Bangli regencies respectively, certain other shrine

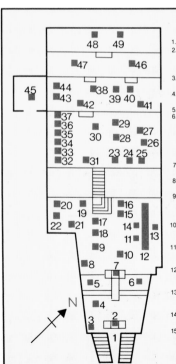

PURA PANATARAN AGUNG (BESAKIH)

1. Candi Bentar — Split gate.
2. Bale Pegat — Special pavilion where the gods, seated in their palanquins, are honoured.
3. Bale Kulkul — Tower for the wooden slit-gong.
4. Bale Pagambuhan — Pavilion for gambuh musicians.
5. Bale Mundar-Mandir (Bale
6. Ongkara) — Pavilions where worshipper utters prayer on entering the main courtyard. Ongkara is the holy syllable A-U-M, a symbol of the Trinity, Brahma, Wisnu and Iswara (Siwa).
7. Gelung Agung — Gateway to main courtyard.
8. Bale Pagongan — Pavilion for the gamelan orchestra.
9. Bale Kembang Sirang — Pavilion where the raja used to sit during major ceremonies.
10. Bale Pawedan — Pavilion where brahmana priests perform their ritual.
11. Panggungan — A little pavilion where offerings are place.
12. Bale Agung — Long pavilion of 24 posts for important meetings.
13. Gedong Kawas — Pavilion associated with flesh offerings.
14. Bale Pepelik — Pavilion for offerings.
15. Sanggar Agung — Tripartite padmasana "seat" for Brahma (to the right or east), Wisnu (to the left or west) and Iswara or Siwa (center).

16. Pasamuhan Agung — Pavilion where the gods gather at times of ceremony.
17. Bale pelik — dedicated to Ratu Sanghyang Siyem.
18. Bale pelik — dedicated to Mpu Bharada (Airlangga's court priest):
19. Meru with 11 roofs — dedicated to Ratu Manik Makentel.
20. Meru with 9 roofs — dedicated to Ratu bagus Kubakal.
21. Bebaturan (open altar) — dedicated to Ratu Sula Majemuh.
22. Bale Paruman (Pyasan) — Pavilion for decorating statues of the gods.
23. Bale pepelik.
24. Kawitan — shrines dedicated
25. to deified ancestors of three
26. descent groups.
27. Kehen — Building for storing temple possessions including old charters written on wood.
28. Meru with 7 roofs — dedicated to Ratu Geng.
29. Meru with 11 roofs — dedicated to Ratu Maspahit.
30. Bale pepelik.
31. Bale pawedan — pavilion for high priest ritual.
32. Gedong — Shrines dedicated
33. to Ida Gusti.
34. Meru with 3 roofs — dedicated to Ida Tohjiwa.
35. Meru with 5 roofs — dedicated to Ida Panataran.

36. Meru with 7 roofs — dedicated to Ida Tulus Sadawa.
37. Meru with 5 roofs — dedicated to I Gusti Ngurah Dauh.
38. Meru with 11 roofs — dedicated to Ratu Sunaring Jagat.
39. Shrine dedicated to widyadara (male heavenly beings).
40. Shrine dedicated to widyadari (female heavenly beings).
41. Bale pelelik.
42. Shrine dedicated to Bhatara Surya-Candra (sun and moon).
43. Shrine dedicated to Ratu Ulang Alu.
44. Shrine dedicated to Ratu Subandar (Ratu Waruna, god of the sea).
45. Sub-temple belonging to the Pande or genealogical group of the goldsmiths and blacksmiths.
46. Meru with 11 roofs — dedicated to Sanghyang Wisesa.
47. Meru with 3 roofs — dedicated to Ratu Ayu Magelung.
48. Gedong — Shrine dedicated to Ratu Bukit Kiwa (or Ratu Pucak).
49. Gedong — Shrine dedicated to Ratu Bukit Tengen (or Ratu Pameneh).

N

being the responsibility of the other regencies. All of Bali comes together at Pura Besakih. Religiously, oneness is symbolized in the *padmasana* in Pura Panataran Agung, dedicated to Sang Hyang Widdhi, the Supreme God.

Pura Besakih is most fascinating at festival times, but it is grand and impressive whenever you go there.

The drive up the mountain to Besakih, with a stopover in Klungkung for sight-seeing and shopping, takes a full day. To resume the tour of East Bali, if you are staying in Denpasar, it is best to leave early in the morning the following day. By passing through Klungkung before noon, you may choose a site to lunch on the beach or in the shaded countryside and visit the Bat Cave, fishing villages and Tenganan before reaching Karangasem in mid-afternoon. Now that the new road linking Rendang and Karangasem has been finished, it is possible to make a Besakih-Karangasem

round trip comfortably in a day. You may be lucky to arrive in Bali during a time when eastern villages are holding ceremonies. Festivals, unique to these villages, should not be missed, so check the calendar of events at your hotel to find a good time to visit.

Enroute to Kusamba, one passes the first of numerous solidified lava streams which swept through Karangasem. Where there were once rivers, rice fields and villages, now lie wide strips of lava rock reaching down to the sea. The eruption of Mt. Agung in 1963 destroyed the roads, isolating one fifth of the island and leaving many homeless. Recently, roads and bridges have been restored, but the island remains desolate in many places. A line of fruit trees, rising from the ash, once bordered a village street. On holy days, women walk kilometers with their offerings over the barren rock, faithful to places of crumpled brick which they remember as grand temples containing many shrines and *bales*.

Sprightly outrigger
canoes plying to
and fro Nusa Penida

KUSAMBA. Colorful outrigger *prahus* line the black sand shores of this fishing village, directly across from Nusa Penida, an island of 40,000 people. The strait between the two islands is filled with fish, and when the weather is calm the seas are bespeckled with white sails. Twice a day fishermen set out for Nusa with cargoes of peanuts, fruit and rice, for that dry, hostile island is only sparsely cultivated. The sailors of Kusamba boast that their large *prahus* with crews of five, can carry up to one and a half tons of cargo. They also carry passengers across who wish to visit the coral gardens and white sand shores of Nusa. Another trade of east coast villagers is salt panning. Where the road nears the sea, rows of brown, thatched roofs emerge from the sands. These huts are small factories for making salt. Wet sand is gathered from the sea and spread in sand banks along the beach. After drying, it is dumped in a large bin inside the hut. Slowly, a pure water of high salt content drains through the sands, which is then poured into bamboo troughs to evaporate in the sun, leaving the salt crystals. The entire process takes one day, and on a good day the salt panner makes five kilograms of salt which he sells in the market of Klungkung. Although Kusamba is a fishing village, the people live a bit inland because of the old Balinese fear that the ocean is magically dangerous.

A trip to Nusa Penida is for the traveler who can appreciate out-of-the-way places without comforts. The Kusamba *prahus* come in at Sampalan, the fishing center for Nusa particularly beautiful in the morning with Bali looming across the strait. All the terraces in this rocky island are faced with stone. Several villages weave a reddish *ikat* cloth that can also be bought at Klungkung. With its own peculiarities of language and art, the island has interesting temples—Pura Ped on the north coast, and one at Batukandik where the sun seat takes the form of a woman.

An eerie cave
temple honoring
the serpent Basuki

The entrepôt for
trade with Lombok

GOA LAWAH. The road continuing east parallels lovely seascapes with a full view of Nusa Penida, inviting sunbathing, picnics and refreshing swims. One passes close to the sinister Goa Lawah, the Bat Cave, whose walls literally vibrate with thousands of bats—their bodies packed so close together that the upper surface of the cave resembles undulating mud. The sight would be more eerie if it weren't that whenever the creatures venture out of the cave into daylight, their radar sense directs them back into their murky dwelling place. Being an extraordinary phenomenon, Goa Lawah is considered holy. A temple with shrines protects the entrance. The cave is said to extend all the way back to Besakih, and may contain an underground river, which comes up, it is said, at Pura Goa (Cave Temple) within the Besakih complex—a temple associated with the mythological *naga* or serpent Basuki which is also honored at Pura Goa Lawah, where a snake is said to live, feeding on bats.

PADANGBAI. A perfectly shaped bay cradled in the hills, the harbor of Padangbai is the main port of all transit to the neighboring island of Lombok, with passenger and cargo vessels departing each morning. International shipping lines making stopovers in Bali anchor to the left of the bay; visitors and cargo are ferried to the pier. An area enclosed by white sand coves and turquoise sea, the small harbor town makes a good visit for yachtsmen sailing to Bali. The history of this coastal village is connected with those eventful years that saw the deaths of Mahendradatta and Udayana at the beginning of the 11th century. There lived at Padangbai at that time a priest of great stature, Kuturan by name, who was capable of rejecting the wishes of a king and is remembered for his reforms of village organization. Pura Silayukti at Padangbai is said to mark his residence. Continuing east, the road passes through the beautiful area around Manggis, mountains on one side, the sea on the other.

165

TENGANAN. On a side-road, leading inland to the hills near *Karangasem,* is Tenganan, one of the most conservative villages of the *Bali Aga*—"original" Balinese. This is a walled village. Within the bastions, all living compounds are identical in plan and are arranged in rows on either side of the wide, stone-paved lanes which run the length of the village. The people of Tenganan claim to have come originally from Bedulu. The legend of how they aquired their land dates from the 14th century: the mighty king Dalem Bedaulu lost his favorite horse and sent the villagers of his kingdom in all directions in search of it. The men of Tenganan traveled east and found the corpse of the horse. When the king thereafter offered to reward them, they requested the land where the horse was found, i.e. all the area in which the carcass of the dead horse could be smelt. The king sent an official with a keen sense of smell to partition the land. For days, the chief of Tenganan led the official through the hills, yet still the air was polluted with odor of dead horse. At last, the tired official decided this was enough land and departed. After he had left, the *Bali Aga* chief pulled from his clothing a very smelly remnant of the horse's flesh.

Tenganan still owns, communally, these large tracts of well cultivated land. Traditionally, the men were not accustomed to work in the fields with their own hands and hired out their land to men of neighboring villages. The aristocratic Tenganese went to the fields chiefly to collect *tuak*, a popular palm beer. The women of this village weave the famous "flaming" cloth, *kamben gringsing,* which supposedly has the power to immunize the wearer against evil vibrations. Through an intricate process of weaving and dyeing, known only here, a single cloth takes five years to complete. Only the finest pieces are worn by Tenganan people for ceremonial dress. The imperfect ones are sold, since they are much in demand throughout Bali.

Sounds of a rare
gamelan and the
dreamlike *Rejang*
dance

During ceremonies here, girls, from the age of two, wrap their bodices in silk, don a multi-colored scarf and flowered crowns of beaten gold. Men begin to play the mysterious melodies of the *gamelan selunding,* an archaic orchestra of iron sound-bars, seldom heard outside a few cloistered villages in the east. Very slowly the girls file out of the darkness, their eyes cast to the ground. Silently, they lift their scarfs and let them fall again, always moving in slow, dreamlike elegance. This is *Rejang,* a ritual offering dance.

The Fight of the Pandanus Leaves at Tenganan takes place only once a year during a festival called *Usaba sambah.* To the accompaniment of the sacred *gamelan selunding,* two men each with a round, plaited shield attack each other with wads of pandanus leaves, the variety with thorns down either side of the leaf. The two favorite tactics are to rush and clench the opponent. The clench has one disadvantage: while one man rubs this thorny wad across his opponent's back, he is rather open to the same treatment. Occasionally, the earnestness of an expression makes one wonder if an insult is not being repaid. During this festival, ferris wheels, such as you pass on the road past Klungkung, are set up on the rising terraces of the village. Some have one wheel of seats, others two, and the whole wooden contraption is turned by the foot-power of two men at the tops of the poles on either side.

Within a few kilometers of Tenganan are other conservative and secluded villages that enact, unchanged, rituals peculiar to them. At Asak, dancers sweep their hair in a great coil to one side, as seen in old stone statues of noblewomen. Men play the ancient *gamelan gambang* of wooden keys. Beyong Tenganan, the main road crosses a pass overlooking a huge valley. At the highest point, where drivers often place offerings, a path climbs steeply up to Pura Gumang and a great view.

Eclectic building
styles created by
the late *rajas*

AMLAPURA (KARANGASEM). Crossing a wide, solidified lava flow which year by year is slowly being brought back to cultivation, you enter Amlapura, the main town of Karangasem regency. The former kingdom was founded during the weakening of the Gelgel dynasty late in the 17th century, and became in the late 18th and early 19th centuries the most powerful state in Bali. Puri Agung Karangasem long served as the residence of these kings, who extended their domain across the eastern straits to the island of Lombok. The *puri's* austere, three-tiered gate, penetrating the thick walls of red brick, is a notable introduction to Karangasem architecture.

During the Dutch conflict at the turn of the century, the *raja* of Karangasem co-operated with the European army and was allowed to retain his title and autocratic powers. Puri Kanginan, the palace where the last *raja* was born, is a 20th century eclectic creation of designs from Europe, China and Bali. The main building with a large veranda is called "Bale London" because the furniture bears the central motif of the Royal Crest of England. The wooden paneling appears to be Chinese work, while Ramayana reliefs, on the adjacent tooth-filing pavilion, retain a Balinese flavor. The photograph over the entrance to Bale London portrays the late king, Anak Agung Anglurah Ketut, as a young man studying with his religious teacher. It was his pleasure to make fantastic moats and pools. Five kilometers south, on the beach at Ujung, he helped design a moated water palace, opened in 1921. In about 1947, he built Tirta Gangga (6 kilometers north on the road to Culik) as a rest place, where he laid out a series of pools decorated with unusual statuary. It suffered damage during the 1963 eruption and at the hands of political agitators during that period as well as from an earthquake in 1979. The coast road continues through spectacular scenery to the northern capital of Singaraja.

SIBETAN, SELAT and ISEH. From Subagan, the village in the solidified lava flow outside Amlapura slowly putting itself back together, a road heads west along the foothills of Gunung Agung. It meets the Klungkung-Besakih road at Rendang, and thus makes possible a round trip in Karangasem. The inland route provides a chance to explore seldom-visited villages of the beautiful east. Women carrying loads of sweet potatoes, spices and bound piglets, men leading cows for sale, make their way to the village markets which teem with activity until around noon. Large markets come round every three days, that at Bebandem being especially interesting. A few kilometers farther west is Sibetan, rich in rice and fruit, famous for *salak*, a brown fruit with the texture of an apple and clothed in a skin resembling that of a cobra. Plantations of the low thorny *salak* palms cover the range between Sibetan and Selat. From Selat a back-road leads through Iseh and Sideman to just east of Klungkung.

Iseh, a mountain village where people grow rice and white onion, was chosen in 1932 by the German artist Walter Spies as a site for a country house. For many years after, Theo Meier, a Swiss painter, lived in the same house that gazes out on an uninterrupted view of the great volcano. The massive slope is cut by deep ravines, forming serpentine shadows descending to a wide valley of rice fields. In the landscape, hues vary from luminous yellow, to opulent light green of mature rice, to red-stemmed buff of stalks just before harvest.

Wherever you travel in the east. you take away impressions of serene landscapes, rustic villages and undulating rice fields often dotted with fruit trees, papaya, durian and bananas. The larger festivals are amazing: temple buildings and tall bamboo structures hung with colored cloths and decorated with rice cookies; the swell and bustle of the crowd; women running around with offerings; and the *gamelan* playing-all in worship and honor of the gods who have made it so.

to the west

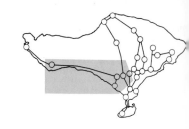

The western districts of Tabanan and Mengwi were once powerful warring princedoms. In 1891, Mengwi was engulfed by its belligerent neighbors—Tabanan and Badung. The days of absolute rule by *rajas* ended entirely with the Dutch conquest of South Bali in 1908. Unlike the *Raja* of Karangasem, the *Raja* of Tabanan did not have an agreement with the Dutch and, therefore, lost the rights to his lands. They were redistributed among councils of individual villages. With their own land, the communities prospered, and now Tabanan is a rich, prolific area.

Although the *rajas* were deprived of political powers, they remained leaders among their people. Palaces continued to serve as centers of the arts, and royal families retained their essential role of presiding over devotions at the state temples. Residents throughout Mengwi participate in the cult of Pura Taman Ayun, the old kingdom's state temple. In jungles near the peak of the western volcano Batukau, lies the mountain sanctuary of Pura Luhur, also a royal temple. The gigantic forests that surround the sanctuary are uninhabitable wilderness, yet processions of thousands have journeyed there to pay homage.

The western uplands of Batukau are famed for magnificent landscapes. The view from the mountain village, Jatiluwih, takes in the whole of South Bali. Perched on a high terraced slope, Jatiluwih earned its name, which means "Truly Marvellous". The mountain range extends to the western tip of Bali through the darkest, most mysterious regions of the island. Here dwell the ghosts of Pulaki, a legendary city destined to sink into the earth. Deer, crocodile and wild hogs roam these dense bushlands. Some even say the last tiger of Bali stalks here, though no one has seen it for some years.

As little known as the mystifying tiger are the enchanting beaches of the west that stretch for kilometers against a booming surf. Volcanic coves facing the Bukit Peninsula sometimes contain, etched upon their lava cliffs, the ruined foundations of ancient sea temples. And many of these secluded bays are a haven for sunbathers.

More than any of the tours, the trip to the west is a series of excursions to places of special interest, rather than a continuous round

Harvesting near Tabanan (previous pages).

trip. Each destination is a reason in itself to travel there: the Monkey Forest of Sangeh, the moated temple Pura Taman Ayun, the coral gardens of Tanah Lot, the beaches of Krambitan, or the far western capital of Negara with its bull races. If you are interested in making a short trip, many of these places are easily reached from Denpasar. For journeying to the more remote beaches and sanctuaries, check for current road conditions.

Many Javanese have moved to West Bali. The *subak* irrigation organizations there—the backbone of agricultural life and livelihood—operate well with their Hindu and Muslim members. The movement of Indonesians from densely populated areas (Java, in particular) to relatively open regions or wilderness is encouraged by the government's *Transmigrasi* scheme. Indonesians are becoming aware of the vastness of their own country. Balinese transmigration has worked well in the Palu area of Central Sulawesi.

SANGEH. Rawana, the villainous giant of the Ramayana epic, could die neither on earth nor in air. To kill him, the monkey general Hanuman devised a plan to suffocate the giant by pressing him between two halves of the holy mountain Mahameru — a destruction between the earth and air. When Hanuman took Mahameru, part of the mountain fell to the earth in Sangeh, along with a group of his monkey armies. And so they stayed to this very day.

Such is the legendary origin of Bukit Sari, or The Monkey Forest, a cluster of towering trees and home of hundreds of sprite monkeys. The forest is sacred and for many years no one has been permitted to chop wood there. A moss-covered temple lies in the heart of the woods and is a familiar hideout for the nimble inhabitants. You make many friends by buying a bag of peanuts, and for such a feast the monkeys often bring their families along. Rumor tells of a king of the monkeys who invariably has the first choice in selecting peanut handouts. He oversees one camp, while a rival king and his followers control another area of the forest. A beautiful restive place, Sangeh has long been an inspiration for painters and monkey-watchers.

The temple, Pura Bukit Sari, was originally built around the 17th century as an agricultural temple and has been restored several times, most recently in 1973. In the central courtyard, a large statue of Garuda, an old carving of uncertain date, symbolizes freedom from suffering and the attainment of *amerta*, the elixir of life. The forest of nutmeg trees in which it lies was presumably planted deliberately a long time ago, for it is unique in Bali.

There is a separate route linking Sangeh directly with Denpasar that begins at Jalan Kartini, making it a short trip. A side-road joins Blahkiuh, just south of Sangeh, with Mengwi which can also be reached by returning to Denpasar and taking the trip to the west. A sub-standard road links Sangeh with Ubud.

Quiet, inviting lanes
off the busy road
to Tabanan

A sense of beauty,
a sense of grace

SEMPIDI, LUKLUK and KAPAL. These villages west of Denpasar, are noted for decorative temple sculpture. Carvings of domestic scenes and mythological episodes are mischievously exaggerated and painted in bright colors, reminiscent of the exuberant North Balinese style of sculpture. The aphorism—the more you look, the more you see—certainly rings true here, especially at the Pura Dalem of Lukluk and the three *desa* temples of Sempidi. The most important temple in this area is Pura Sada in Kapal, an ancestral sanctuary honoring the deified spirit of Ratu Sakti Jayengrat whose identification remains uncertain. (According to one story he was a noble from Majapahit who came to Bali by sea—*kapal* means "ship"—his vessel being wrecked on a reef where the village now stands.) The temple, the original foundation of which may be as old as the 12th century, was rebuilt during Majapahit times by one of the early kings of Mengwi, perhaps in the 16th century. The oldest of the

Mengwi state shrines, predating Pura Taman Ayun, Pura Sada was destroyed in the great earthquake of 1917 and restored by the Archaeology Service in 1950. A large brick *candi* or *prasada*, ornamented with modern statues, dominates the complex. Seven Saints adorn the body of the *candi*, and at the top are the Nine Gods—the lords of the eight directions and of the center. The temple's 64 stone seats are believed to commemorate faithful followers who died in battle and are reminiscent of megalithic ancestral seats. Just outside Kapal village, on the opposite bank of the river, grows a unique coconut tree with a split trunk, bearing fruit on both branches. Nearby stands a huge banyan tree with a complete temple built in its branches.

(Left) Fine sculpture at Pura Sada in Kapal, possibly honoring a Majapahit noble. (Below) The many-tiered merus of Pura Taman Ayun's inner courtyard, Mengwi.

MENGWI A turnoff toward the mountain leads to the principality of Mengwi which, until 1891, was the center of a powerful kingdom originating from the Gelgel dynasty. These kings continue to be venerated in the state temples of Mengwi, in particular Pura Taman Ayun.

In Bali, each social unit—of increasing size beginning with the family—possesses a temple wherein they worship deified ancestors. The family ancestors are worshipped in the house temple, the clan ancestors in the clan temple, the founders of a village in the Pura Puseh, and previously the ancestors of a royal dynasty were collectively worshipped by a kingdom in the state temples. State temples include mountain temples, sea temples, and those at the heart of the kingdom, such as Mengwi's Pura Taman Ayun. Among the rows of *palinggihs,* (shrines that serve as "sitting places" to receive visiting deities during temple feasts) is a brick building facing east: the *paibon*, a royal ancestral altar. In the sur-rounding pavilions, priests recite prayers, village elders hold council, offerings are prepared, furniture and the temple's musical instruments are stored. For those interested in traditional woodcarving, the small doors of the shrines here are beautifully carved. The moat gives the impression of a sanctuary in the middle of a pond, explaining the name *taman*, "garden with a pond". The waters are a symbolic place of contact with the divine through *widadaris*, celestrial nymphs who bathe there.

Beyond the moat, the temple lies on slightly rising ground. The grassy expanse of the outermost courtyard, the fine array of *merus* and pavilions in the inner courtyard, and its well-kept appearance make it one of the most beautiful temples in Bali. Originally dating from 1634, Taman Ayun was restored and enlarged in 1937. On its festival day (*odalan*) hundreds of women file into the temple bearing colorful offerings, which they place together before the *merus*.

PURA TAMAN AYUN

1. Gedong dedicated to Bhatara Puncak Padangdawa (for the arts).
2. Méru Tumpang XI (11-roofed) — dedicated to Hyang Gunung Batukau (mountains and forests).
3. Gedong — dedicated to Dewan Gusti.
4. Candi Kuning dedicated to Dewi Ciligading
5. Candi-Padmasana dedicated to Bhatara Wawurauh (Siva and Buddha).
6. Candi dedicated to Hyang Purasada (for heroes).
7. Tugu — dedicated to Bhatara Dugul, for the gods of the rice fields.
8. Méru Tumpang XI (11-roofed) — dedicated to Ulunsuwi (Bhatara Sri).
9. Méru Tumpang XI (11-roofed) — dedicated to Bhatara Sakenon (for the sea god).
10. Gedong Palinggih Ibu or paibon, serves as ancestral altar where offerings to ancestors of the rulers of Mengwi are put.
11. Méru Tumpang IX (9-roofed) — dedicated to Hyang Gunung Batur.
12. Méru Tumpang XI (11-roofed) — dedicated to Gunung Agung (for the security of the state).
13. Dedicated to Hyang Siwa Raditya (for the Sun-god Surya).
14. Méru Tumpang IX (9-roofed) — dedicated to Hyang Puncak Pengalengan Gunung Mangu Bratan (for the irrigation god).
15. Méru Tumpang VII (7-roofed), dedicated to the ancestral gods of the Majapahit settlers.
16. Méru Timpang V (5-roofed) dedicated to Batungaus.
17. Méru Tumpang III (3-roofed) — dedicated to Syang Pasurungan.
18. Méru Tumpang II (2-roofed) — dedicated to Batu pasek Badak.
19. Balé — simple shed for offering to Ratu Pasek.
20. Balé Murdha — Assembly Hall of the village elders.
21. Gedong — For keeping temple clothes.
22. Balé Saka IX — For the Orchestra.
23. Balé Saka VIII — for relaxing and for preparing offerings.
24. Balé Pawedan — where the priests recite their weda.
25. Bale Papelik — the Communal seat of the Gods.
26. Balé Panggung — For offerings.
27. Balé Saka IX — For Keeping furniture.
28. Kolam, pond or moat.
29. Kuri Agung — Main covered gate. It is opened only when there is a ceremony in progress.

The ancient craft
of weaving golden
ceremonial cloths

Dedicated to the
indomitable spirit
of Bali

BLAYU. From Mengwi you may cross the range to the coast of North Bali (see page 184). A left turn off the main road leads to Blayu where the women are weavers. The clicking of bamboo looms resound, as locally dyed threads are interwoven in webs of gold embroidery to fashion ceremonial cloths worn during festivals. A *sarong* two meters long takes three weeks to a month to weave, depending upon the intricacy of the design. The Balinese clean such cloth by dusting it and letting it dry in the sun, since it is not washable. In the past, girls were weaving with their mothers by the time they were ten years old. Nowadays, they are away at school and the ancient Balinese craft is left to their elders. The sarongs the Balinese wear everyday are batiks from Java and cloths woven in Balinese factories. But the demand for *songkets* (the cloths with interwoven gold thread) for festival and ceremonial use is still sufficient to keep busy the women of Blayu and several other villages.

MARGA. On 20 November 1946, Lt. Col. I Gusti Ngurah Rai, a commander of nationalist troops in Bali, and his company of guerrilla fighters were killed in the Battle of Marga. Surrounded by a numerically superior Dutch force, and under bombardment from the air, the small band, only 94 men in all, refused to surrender; they attacked the enemy positions and died to the last man—a *puputan* reminiscent of the royal *puputans* carried out forty years earlier also against the Dutch. At Marga there stands a monument honoring these soldiers, inscribed with a famous letter written by Ngurah Rai refusing surrender until the cause was won. Stone medallions symbolize *Panca Sila*, the five principles of the Indonesian state: the star for belief in God, a linked chain for democracy, a bull for nationalism, a banyan tree for humanity, and rice and cotton grains for social justice. A Hero's Day is held on the anniversary of Ngurah Rai's death and the Bali International Airport is named in his honor.

TANAH LOT. From the village of Marga, the trip west returns to the main route leading to Tabanan. At the crossroads of Kediri, a side-road branches to the sea, ending on a green hill which slopes down to the beach and to the remarkable temple of Tanah Lot, suspended on a huge rock offshore. Set apart from the land by coming tides. Tanah Lot, with its solitary black towers and tufts of foliage spilling over the cliffs, recalls the delicacy of a Chinese painting. If hearsay is to be believed, there dwells inside one of the shrines at Tanah Lot a huge snake, discreetly left undisturbed by the Balinese.

Although a small sanctuary, Tanah Lot is linked to a series of sea temples on the south coast of Bali: Pura Sakenan, Pura Ulu Watu, Pura Rambut Siwi, and Pura Petitenget. All these temples are related to the principal mountain sanctuaries: Besakih at Gunung Agung, Pura Batur at Batur and Pura Luhur at Mt. Batukau. The upland temples venerate deities associated with mountains and mountain lakes, while the sea temples include homage to the guardian spirits of the sea within their ritual. These main temples are often listed with the *sad-kahyangan* the six holy "national" temples, which exact tribute from all Balinese.

The chronicles attribute the temple at Tanah Lot to the 16-century priest Nirartha. During his travels along the south coast he saw the rock-island's beautiful setting and rested there. Some fishermen saw him, and bringing gifts, invited him to stay at their hut. Nirartha refused, saying he preferred to spend the night on the little island. That evening he spoke to the fishing folk and advised them to build a shrine on the rock, for he felt it to be a holy and fitting place to worship God. The villagers kept their promise.

The beaches of Tanah Lot are ideal for relaxing, especially in the late afternoons, when the temple on the rock dissolves into a striking silhouette against the evening sky.

TABANAN. Pasar Hewan, in Kediri, a village en-route to Tabanan, is Bali's cattle market. Every three days, by the religious calendar, merchants from South Bali come to buy cattle for export to Singapore and Hong Kong. Other livestock on sale include geese, ducks, pigs, chickens, and fighting cocks. With such animated merchandise, there's never a dull moment at Pasar Hewan.

With Badung and Gianyar, the district of Tabanan forms the island's most prosperous region—the rice belt of the southern plains. Kept in impeccable order by the *subak* associations, the fertile fields stretch from the foothills of Batukau volcano to the south coast. Farmers adhere to no special seasons for planting and harvesting. The cycles of growth vary with individual plots, and planting continues throughout the year. There is, of course, a legend to explain this. It tells how after many unsuccessful harvests, these villagers went to the main temple to beseech the divine spirits for a good yield. They vowed in exchange to sacrifice a *guling buntut*, a roasted, tailless pig. When the fields prospered the people remembered their vow. Dismayed by the dearth of tailless animals, they decided to offer a human being. Everyone wondered whose child would be the unfortunate one. At last, one man found a solution: since they had promised the offering after the harvest, why end the harvest at all? They quickly replanted before the crops were reaped.

Tabanan became a separate and powerful kingdom during the shake-up of political domains during the 17th century. It has long been the home of famous *gamelan* orchestras and dancers, among them the great male dancer Mario. An anecdote is told of Mario. When he was shown his photograph in Covarrubias' book, he exclaimed, "That man is a good dancer. How is it I have never seen him?" and laughed with amazed delight to discover it was himself. Born around the turn

of the century, he was already dancing at age six. He developed and perfected the spectacular solo dance, *Kebyar*, which began in North Bali during the period of World War I. Mario's grace and movement enraptured European audiences who saw him dance in the thirties.

Tabanan, like the capitals of the other regencies, has been left behind by Denpasar. However, it is a spirited, growing town, with the shops as elsewhere in Bali being in the hands of Chinese merchants. The Chinese-Balinese artist, Kay It, who lives at Tabanan has had successful exhibitions in Australia. He is a painter, a batik artist, and a designer who has introduced new forms into the earthenware industry in nearby Pejaten. His tiles designed with animated little scenes are delightful in their variety. Many of his designs are based on two old Balinese human figures, the *Cili* and the *Barong Landung*.

Little known are the fabulous beaches of Tabanan. At the end of every side-road to the coast lies a long deserted shore with surf that sometimes breaks over 3 meters high. Remote villages along the way present a simpler view of Balinese life than those which line the primary routes. In many temples of this region, the carvings are brightly colored with silver paint. At first glance, they appear plated by the precious metal. The village of **Krambitan**, southwest of Tabanan, houses beautiful, traditionally designed buildings, such as the *bale gong*, the pavilion which contains the village's musical instruments. Krambitan was once a minor court under the *raja* of Tabanan. Carrying on this tradition, it is today the center of a lively group of Balinese literati who study and sing classics of the Old Javanese and Balinese literature. A dirt road continues past the village down to the west coast. There lies a beautiful black sand beach, so wide that the children use it as a football field.

The "Coconut-shell Stone",
venerated throughout
West Bali

BATUKAU. Mt. Batukau, the "Coconut-shell Stone", the most westerly of Bali's three towering peaks, at an elevation of 2,278 meters dominates the Tabanan landscape. All the temples in West Bali have a shrine venerating the spirit of Batukau. Along the road from Tabanan to Penebel, a turnoff leads to Wongaya Gede, the closest village to Pura Luhur, the main sanctuary located high on Batukau's slopes. (The road suits only a jeep or a motorbike.) The uninhabited jungle above Wongaya Gede encloses the temple, aloof within its solitary clearing far above the populated farmlands. The forest and the phosphorescent green moss growing everywhere are Pura Luhur's modest decorations. A Zen master would appreciate the masterly blending of temple with landscape.

A singular, seven-tiered *meru* exalts Mahadewa, the deity associated with Batukau. The adjacent stone shrines *(prasada)* are similar to those at Kapal and Serangan. Not far from Pura Luhur, a square lake recalls the moat of Pura Taman Ayun at Mengwi. Both temples are classed as *pura taman:* a temple which has a pond and is always maintained by a king. Lakes are also related to mountain sanctuaries, the rituals of which include veneration of lakes and a blessing for irrigation water. At Pura Luhur stand shrines for the three mountain lakes within its catchment: Lakes Bratan, Buyan and Tambelingan. When Tabanan was a kingdom, Pura Luhur was its state mountain and ancestral temple. Among old sanctuaries on Batukau's slopes around Jatiluwih are several megalithic ones.

Nearby Pura Luhur is the holy spring of Air Panas, where hot water surges from the river bank. All strange, natural phenomena are believed to be frequented by a spirit. Thus, Air Panas is enshrined by a small temple where people make their prayers with offerings. The cool western uplands, overlooking half the island, offer magnificent views.

NEGARA. A good distance from Tabanan stands Negara, the capital of Jembrana regency—a rugged strip of land partitioning the southwest coast of Bali. From Gilimanuk, the harbor at the westernmost tip of the island, ferries ply the narrow strait to East Java, the route by which most of Bali's import needs, and such exports as copra and coffee, are transported.

The most exciting event in Negara is the bull races, a secular entertainment that began less than a century ago. Possibly it developed from the custom of carrying home the harvested rice by bullock cart, or it may have been introduced from Java or Madura where the sport is strong. Bulls are carefully selected for strength and color, looked after and pampered, and never used for ploughing the fields. Dressed up in silk banners with painted horns and enormous wooden bells (now usually replaced with metal bells), they parade before the crowd of spectators. The course is a 2-kilometer stretch of road, and the teams are judged for speed and style. It is remarkable to see such ordinarily docile creatures thunder down to the finishing line at speeds up to 50 kilometers an hour. The agile charioteers often drive standing up and twist the bulls' tails to give them spunk. For the fans, this regional sport of Jembrana is a great opportunity for gambling. A family that owns a winning bull gains much prestige, and, besides, the price will double. A little magic is believed to help. If you are fortunate enough to be in Bali during the bull racing season, usually between July and October, do not miss seeing them.

Negara is the farthest point west cited in this trip. The road, however, continues around the island to Singaraja, through lonely regions of the northwest. The journey takes a full day, on the seldom-used roads.

From this point, your tours may take you through Gilimanuk and by ferry to East Java, where breathtaking scenery awaits you.

northern round trip

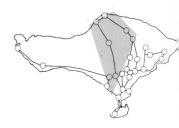

Every island has its round trip. In Bali this means leaving the south coast to pass over the volcanic mountain range that runs across the island and descending to the coastal region of Buleleng in North Bali. The geographical separation between north and south has developed cultural differences between the two areas making the Northern Round Trip a study of contrasts.

The feudal rule of local *rajas* in North Bali ended in 1848, with Dutch control here sixty years prior to colonial rule in the south. Many of the descendants of the *rajas* became officials for the Dutch at this time. As a result of the European influence, the way of life in North Bali is more Western than in the majority of rustic communities in the south. It was the women of Buleleng who first began wearing the Malay blouse, *kebaya,* by official decree "to protect the morals of Dutch soldiers". In Singaraja, the former Dutch capital, the *banjar* system of communal responsibility is not so institutionalized; the social order centers more around the individual family unit. Nor is the class system so stringent as it is in the south where the aristocracy continued to rule until 1908.

The art of North Bali is also distinctive. The intricate carving in grey sandstone on southern temples is more restrained than northern temples, where tall gates have a dynamic, flaming ascendency and are covered entirely with luxurious designs. The pink sandstone quarried near Singaraja is extremely soft, enabling northern carvers to give full vent to their imaginations, an advantage often leading to humorous Rabelaisian scenes. Burlesque caricatures of well-fed European officials are portrayed in cartoon strips along the walls of some northern temples. To add to the jubilance, many carvings are painted bright blue, white, red and yellow making them even more conspicuous. (Unfortunately, galvanized tin and zinc roofs are frequently used on temple pavilions, contrasting with the brilliance of the sculpture.) In Balinese art it was this area that first showed the influence of various European techniques.

◄ *Lake Bratan in Bedugul (over) The fertile Bratan basin is patched with vegetable gardens which supply the island with fresh produce.*

The round trip is a full day's excursion. The road west through Bedugul is shorter and much faster than the return route through Kintamani, so it is advisable to reach Singaraja in the late morning and begin back in mid-afternoon. It's wise to bring a sweater along since the temperature drops ten degrees in the highlands. Those who have time and don't mind roughing it a bit, can investigate the entire coast of the island by jeep, stopping over in village hostels. Before the advent of air travel, ships anchored off Singaraja and passengers drove from there to Denpasar. Nowadays, few travelers journey to the north—an intriguing area relatively undiscovered by the majority of island visitors.

In 1975, a golf course of international standards was opened on the shores of Lake Bratan near Bedugul. Set in the misty hills of Bratan, the course has hosted international tournaments. Bali, ever irresistible, is becoming a true tourist mecca.

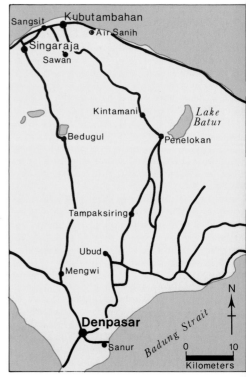

BEDUGUL. To reach the mountain range, you drive west from Denpasar through Mengwi (see pages 172-175). As you leave the southern plains, the landscape changes from flowing tiers of rice to motley patches of onion, cabbage and papaya grown in the cool climate of the highlands. The clusters of farmhouses along the way are no longer the familiar thatched huts of the south, but sturdy cottages made of wood and tile to withstand the steady downpour of heavy rains. This is rich alpine country. The earth, saturated by mountain streams, is smothered with thick moss and creepers. The road climbs and winds its way around steep cliffs hung with ferns, wild flowers and elephant grass.

In jungle terrain lies the serene lake of Bratan, veiled with mist. It fills the ancient crater of Mt. Bratan. Because the lake is an essential water source for surrounding farmlands, the people of Bedugul honor Dewi Danu, goddess of the waters, in the temple Ulu Danu on a small promontory on the lake. One can stay overnight nearby at a rest house on the shore. It is peaceful and cool. Children fish for minnows and canoes cross the still waters, carrying firewood to villages on the further bank. Just near Bedugul is the market of Bukit Mungsu selling wild orchids and both temperate and tropical vegetables grown in the fertile soil here. Near the market are the botanical gardens.

Lake Bratan is so lovely that it is easy to forget the surrounding forest-clad mountains. From the market a path leads through pine plantations up towards the primary jungle on the peaks. An old Dutch forestry house and the remains of a once extensive garden lie mysteriously within the forest. There is a small temple high up, its walls carved with superb reliefs. On the road north of Bedugul, past the new international-standard golf course, the road rises along the lip of Lake Buyan, affording a clear view of the Bratan basin.

A horse-drawn
dokar for a pleasant
jaunt through town

SINGARAJA. From the highest point on the mountain pass, 1,220 meters above sea level, a spectacular descent brings you to the northern coast at Singaraja, capital of Buleleng regency. Buleleng is a strip of land that stretches along the whole northern coast of Bali—open to the sheltered waters of the Java Sea, and bordering on most of the other regencies. Archaic types of social organization and antiquities are found in many villages that are mentioned in inscriptions dating from the 10th century onward. The inscriptions also tell of pirate raids. Throughout its history Buleleng has been more open than the rest of Bali to the influence of the maritime world of the Indonesian Archipelago and beyond. A province before and after Majapahit conquest, it rose to prominence at the end of the 16th century under Raja Panji Sakti, who added the conquest of the eastern tip of Java to his other successes. In 1604 he built a new palace called Singaraja on fields where men grew the grain known as

buleleng. Buleleng, gradually came to refer to the whole northern coast. The official day of Singaraja's foundation is 30 March 1604, and each year a festival is held to commemorate it.

In 1814 a British military expedition stayed several months in Singaraja when Raffles was governor-general. The British went, but the Dutch came, at first with demands and later bearing arms, accusing the *rajas* of raiding wrecked ships. The first attempts of the Dutch ended in defeat or stalemate. In 1849 a reinforced expedition captured the Buleleng stronghold of Jagaraga, after a fierce week-long battle. In 1882 the Dutch imposed direct colonial rule upon Buleleng and Jembrana. Singaraja became their capital and chief port and remained the seat of the colonial Indonesian government for the old Nusa Tenggara province (the Lesser Sunda Islands) until 1953. Longer exposed to European influence than other parts of Bali, Singaraja has often been in the forefront of changes in the arts,

Once the island's
capital and main
port of call

fashion (wearing the *kebaya* began here), and political and social movements.

As an important shipping center, Singaraja has a cosmopolitan flavor about it. The population of 15,000 comprises many ethnic and religious groups. It is not unusual to see an Islamic procession pass before a Chinese temple flanked by office buildings of European design. Residential sections of the town are named after such immigrant groups as the Bugis of Sulawesi, the Javanese and the Chinese. After the bustle of Denpasar, Singaraja seems subdued, no longer a leader amongst Balinese towns. A legacy from Dutch times, however, is its continuing importance as an educational center. The city also houses a historical library, the Gedong Kirtya, which is the storehouse of Balinese manuscripts, totalling some 3,000. *Lontar* books—leaves of the *lontar* palm cut in strips and preserved between two pieces of precious wood—contain literature, mythology, historical chronicles and religious treatises, some works relatively new, others almost a millenium old. Miniature pictures, incised on the leaves with an iron stylus, are masterpieces in the art of illustration. *Prasastis*, metal plates inscribed with royal edicts of the early Pejeng-Bedulu dynasty, are among the earliest written documents found in Bali.

Buleleng is the island's chief coffee growing area. Freighters anchored off the harbor load this cargo for export to Europe and the Orient. The climate here is drier than in the south. Rather than rice, the fields yield Indian corn, oranges and crops of dry agriculture. The following temples of North Bali are located near Singaraja. If there is time, a pleasant drive further east between stately colonnades of trees leads to Yeh Sanih, a shimmering pool of blue-green, flowing from underground springs. The clear waters have been enclosed to make a most refreshing place to swim. All along the northern shore are sea temples.

SANGSIT. The temples of North Bali differ from those in the south. Instead of the small shrines and *meru* towers of southern temples, a single pedestal, built on a terraced stone base, furnishes the inner courtyard. Often, the pedestal supports a *padmasana,* throne of the sun god, and sacred "houses" to store relics and serve as a resting place for deities during temple festivals. Next to the classical lines of southern decoration, North Balinese carving is forcefully baroque. Every crevice of the temple proper is gaily carved in curves, flames, arabesques and spirals, cascading a light ebullience everywhere.

A fine example of the northern style is Pura Beji in Sangsit, a *subak* temple dedicated to Dewi Sri, goddess of agriculture. *Naga* snakes form the balustrade of the fine gateway. Fantastic physiognomies of imaginary beasts and devilish guardians peer from the entangled flora, deliberately cocked at an angle to throw the facade slightly off balance. This dynamic asymmetry continues in the inner sanctuary. Jawless birds, fierce tigers and sunflowers project from every part of the pedestal. Rows of stone towers jut up from the terraces, forming a labyrinth of pink sandstone. To counterbalance the overpowering decor, the courtyard is spacious and decorated with only a few frangipani trees.

The North Balinese sculptural style with its caricatural tendency is found on other temples in the area—besides on the temples mentioned at Sangsit, Jagaraga and Kubutambahan—for example, on temples at Bungkulan and Bebetin.

As you drive along the north coast road, also keep your eyes open for wooden split-drums or *kulkuls* which are carved with a human head on top. For some reason they are rarely found in South Bali. Examples may be seen at Bungkulan (the village past Sangsit), at Kubutambahan, and the finest of all at Tejakula.

SAWAN. A side-trip southeast of Singaraja passes the small temple of Jagaraga whose reliefs portray: two smug Europeans in a model-T Ford suddenly taken unawares by an armed bandit (a robbery probably inspired by cowboy films); flying aces in one-propped aircraft plunging into the sea; and a Dutch steamer signaling an SOS upon being attacked by a crocodilian sea monster. Even the wicked Rangdas and fertility statues—a dazed mother buried under a pile of children—are skillfully hewn with a delightful sense of humor. This trip ends at Sawan, a village with a gong casting industry, a talented group of the bamboo *gamelan anglung* orchestra and a unique local market that takes place at night.

Sculpture that draws on modern motifs is not entirely lacking in the south. On the Pura Dalem of Blahkiuh near Sangeh a relief depicts a Japanese shooting at an airplane, and a temple relief at Panarungan (Mengwi) interprets the Japanese rape of Balinese girls.

KUBUTAMBAHAN. Here, Pura Maduwe Karang, "Temple of the Owner of the Land", honors Mother Earth and the sun which give prosperity to the crops of dry agriculture. As *subak* temples venerate the creative urge in nature that insures harvests on irrigated rice fields, this temple holds ceremonies to guarantee a "blessing" for plants grown on unirrigated land: fruits, coconut, maize and coffee. On its festival day farmers from surrounding villages come to ask for remnants of the offerings which are buried in the fields, a symbolic ritual to transmit the divine benevolence to the soil. Formerly, Kubutambahan was the center of a federation of villages, which helps explain the widespread importance of Pura Maduwe Karang. The temple carvings are startling—ghouls, domestics, lovers and noblemen, even an official riding a flowery bicycle (page 116).

From Kubutambahan, one turns south, crosses the mountains to Penulisan (see page 146) and descends to Denpasar.

lively visions

At the turn of this century, the native arts of Bali mirrored a well-ordered society governed by feudal lords and sustained by the guiding rituals of its religion. The palaces and temples, as political and religious centers of the island, were also centers of the arts. A prince would adorn his pavilions with the most exquisitely carved wood panels and the finest of paintings. His court would be entertained by the shimmering melodies of the *gamelan*, the soft sways of the classical *Legong* dance, or a parade of comics enacting a mask play. He would dress in the most lustrous silks and bear a splendid kris with a hilt of gold and precious jewels. Furthermore, as a ruling prince, he was expected to be well versed in the arts himself. He should be able to paint a picture, carve a block of wood, play a musical instrument, dance, and sing in the poetical *Kawi* language.

Of course, a prince who possessed all these artistic attributes belonged to the ideal world of superhuman heroes. In reality, if a ruler lacked talent he would support actors, artists and musicians as part of his retinue. Ordinary people, who looked upon their lords as models of conduct, would emulate them by learning the arts of dancing, poetry, music and painting. Thus, art was not exclusive to the aristocracy. Any farmer, merchant, even a coolie could become as fine an artist as his master.

The opulence of the court—the highest secular institution in the Balinese community—had its religious parallel in the lavish decoration and dances within the temples. Silken materials, gilded umbrellas, statuettes and sacred masks graced the temple shrines during festivals, while throughout the night the temple's orchestra would beat the rhythms of ceremonial offering dances, shadow plays and dramas of magic.

This convergence of beauty and ritual explains why the arts have endured to such a great extent in Bali. Ritual demanded a continuous renewal of communion with the divine through temple celebrations. The people poured all their artistic talents into preparations for these occasions. New offerings had to be made, new shrines constructed, dances rehearsed, music practiced and dramas created. Because of the island's climate and the materials used, frequent renovations were necessary. The only readily available stone was, and still is, soft volcanic stone that crumbles easily and is quickly eroded by rain. This kept carvers and masons constantly occupied creating new sculptures or retouching the older ones. Artists were called upon to replace cloth paintings that had rotted in the humidity, or woodcarvings which had been eaten away by white ants. Periodically, the island was struck by earthquakes that destroyed hundreds of temples in a matter of hours, causing scores of villages to engage in massive reconstruction. Because artifacts were assured only limited life, the Balinese were continually building and rebuilding, and this necessity has kept the arts alive and dynamic.

As artistry was inseparable from courtly life and religious practices, so it was from the everyday experience of the people. The Balinese language has no words for "art" and "artist". In former times there had been no need for such definitions. Art was never considered a conscious production for its own sake. Rather, it was regarded as a collective obligation to make things beautiful: food exquisitely presented as an offering; a cloth wrap of gold brocade; motion in the pattern of a dance; sound in a musical rhythm. And this was always done with a definite purpose: to create beauty in service to society and religion. A woodcarver carved the pillar of a royal pavilion as his duty to his prince. A sculptor sculpted a stone temple gate as an act of devotion to his faith. Just as an aristocrat demanded the highest standard of work for his palace, so did the people for work in the temples of the revered deities.

While the artist was a respected member of his community, he was not set apart as belonging to an elite. As a "figure-maker" or "picture-maker" as well as a farmer or merchant, he was

Preceding pages: clinging vegetation colors a temple statue; and, an elaborate temple offering fashioned from rice.

194

called upon when his skills were needed. These he gave gratuitously. He neither signed his name to his work, nor received money for his labor. His prime aim was to serve his community.

In the first decades of this century, Bali entered a new era as a colony of the Netherlands. Western education, modern technology, films, magazines, and a steady tourist trade opened up a new world for many Balinese, and this broadening of outlook was reflected in the arts. For the first time, craftsmen began to treat their work as art for art's sake, experimenting in new styles, themes and media. Some accomplished artists received recognition from abroad, and it was during this time of invention and renewal in the 1930s that many of Bali's finest works were produced.

What distinguishes Balinese art today is a fusion of the lively, ornamental folk art—beauty in service—and the recently added element of self-conscious "art". Anyone passing by a temple gate can see that the love of decorative splendor which highlighted the past is still very much alive. As was true in the olden days, the majority of Bali's artists are highly skilled craftsmen who learned their trade by mastering the traditional forms inherited from their forefathers. The qualities they admire—attention to detail, technical precision and sureness of hand—are the mark of a fine craftsman. Like so many things in Bali, art is an expression of collective thought. Many paintings, carvings and sculptures are made communally in workshops, where a master craftsman supervises a group of apprentices. A small number of outstanding artists who have developed unique styles do create individually, their best work often setting the trend for many imitators.

The Balinese artist is intensely aware of his surroundings. He feels his environment as one who is a participant rather than an observer. Local painters rarely draw from nature; they *know* nature, and in their art they distill from it an essence which is uniquely Balinese. They scan their experience, select details from it, and give each detail a fresh significance. The Balinese style is an art of particularism. Certain formulas of reality must be adhered to, whether from nature or myth. Dutch-born painter Arie Smit, who often sketches scenes of Bali in a rapid, impressionistic style, showed one of his paintings of a temple to a local artist, who criticized it because the bricks of the temple gate did not look properly laid.

One would never find here, as one does in Chinese painting, a quick brush stroke representing a tree. In Bali, a tree is a trunk with twenty gigantic leaves, each leaf drawn with precision and care. And a tree is not only a tree, but also a boarding house for mysterious birds, snakes, lizards, butterflies and devilkins. Such a vision is true to an island community charged with cosmic and magical influences; it is "realistic" without being photographic.

A virtue of Balinese art is that it retains its own distinctive character. The people are extremely proud of their creative traditions, yet they are also progressive and if a new idea catches their fancy, they accept it wholeheartedly. Their art has assimilated Javanese, Indian, and Chinese styles into an Indonesian folk art rooted in ancient magic. The relatively new influence of the West will inevitably increase, and with it so will the possibilities and challenges for contemporary art in Bali.

The present art community has two criteria: (*a*) a work of art is praiseworthy in the eyes of fellow Balinese, or (*b*) it appeals to the foreign market and is sold. Among Bali's prominent artists who have gained international renown, the two standards of success merge conveniently. But when there is a conflict between them, problems arise which may have a greater impact in the future. A fine artist by Balinese standards may not win the understanding of foreign buyers, and in order to earn a living might sacrifice the quality of his work for commercial reasons. The foreign market sometimes distorts the judgment of the Balinese. Many of the mass-produced half-sized copies of dramatic masks, the conventionally posed nude figures, and "home-made" antiques now on sale seem out of character for a people who take pride in superior craftsmanship and attention to detail. Every country has its souvenir items and it would be wrong to look at this as representative of contemporary art, yet much of the superb execution in the antique carvings and early modern paintings is absent today.

One of the reasons for this lies in the structure of Balinese society. Modern art, created for its own sake, does not have a traditional place and function within the community. The important patronage of Balinese nobles has virtually ceased in the last four decades, and with it, the most influential aesthetic guidance among the Balinese themselves. Unfortunately, the island's two main museums in Denpasar and Ubud no longer have the funds to continue to buy contemporary works. Except for established painters and woodcarvers who have their own studios, the working artist has little choice but to display his work in commercially oriented art shops. Because a new place for modern art has not yet been found within the native community, many of the most beautiful examples go overseas and are lost to Bali.

With encouragement from discriminating foreign collectors, perhaps local artists will recapture the refined standards of elegance which prevailed in the past. Also if high quality works are priced according to merit, artists would gain the appropriate time they need to do fine work. If galleries recognize an audience that expects superior work, they may become veritable showcases for the best art currently created in Bali.

Though styles and traditions are now in flux, the all-pervading artistry of the people is more lively than ever, and the heritage of beauty in service to religion remains vital to Balinese life. A society today is rare, where the arts are continually enlivened in every temple, village and community. With the stimulus of a growing foreign market, a wider introduction to new media and materials, and the restoration of peace and affluence to Indonesia, the prospects for Balinese art have never been higher.

Traditional Balinese literature inscribed in Lontar books made from leaves of the lontar palm are cut in strips and preserved between pieces of precious wood, right.

ARCHITECTURE AND STONE SCULPTURE. In few other places in the world does a traveler encounter such a profusion of decorative carvings, splendid gateways and monumental sculptures as in Bali. After an hour's drive, you are already acquainted with a panorama of flourishing styles that seem to spring into view everywhere along the roadside.

Judging from the multitude of carved temple and palace walls, drum-towers, gates, public baths, shrines and art galleries, it would appear there was an army of carvers scouring the island in search of barren stone. In truth, such lavish adornment is reserved for the public buildings in the villages. Domestic architecture is of little concern to sculptors. The majority of Balinese homes are made simply from bamboo and thatch, or whitewashed brick and tile. Their construction is left to carpenters, contractors and thatch-workers, with only sparse decoration carved above the gate or upon the family shrine. Formerly, *rajas* and lords built glorious palaces *(puris)* embellished with elaborate carvings and gilded woodwork. Now, as the residences of prominent families, *puris* remain among the finest examples of Balinese architecture, but they are monuments to an era that has passed. A sculptor today devotes his talents to beautifying private and public buildings of a secular nature (including communal places) and, by far the most important edifice in the community, the place of worship.

Surprisingly, the origin of the Balinese temple does not stem from Hindu Java, but can be traced to prehistoric megalithic sanctuaries — crude monuments built of large uncut stones which were laid in an open space surrounded by a wall. During the ritual ceremonies of ancient Bali the great nature gods — deities of the sun, of the mountains, and of the sea — would descend upon these megaliths when summoned by a priest. Megaliths are the direct forerunners of the shrines found in the inner courtyard of Bali Hindu temples. In some mountain villages that retain ancient customs indigenous to Bali, megaliths are still preserved in the form of stepped pyramids made of rough stones.

Unlike India and Hindu Java, where the temple is a house or a hall, in Bali the temple is a rectangular plot of ground set apart from the profane world by a high stone or mud-brick wall. The enclosed area — a sacred tract of land upon which the deities descend — is just as significant religiously as the buildings and shrines within; this priority is reflected in the architecture of the Balinese temple, in which space is emphasized over mass.

Although its austere, tapering gateway stands apart from streetside life, the Balinese temple is not a self-contained unit. It encompasses in its design a universal order essential to the religious rites carried out within its enclosures. A temple is always oriented to the four cardinal points: the direction toward the sacred mountains, the direction toward the sea, east and west. The "seats" of the deities are found at the farthest end of the temple nearest the mountains, while the entrance faces the opposite direction toward the ocean, which is why the temple walls never enclose a circular space.

No special class of architects design the temples. Master sculptors in charge of the construction often take part in the manual labor of building, with the assistance of a number of stone and brick workers. A master sculptor usually has inherited the trade from his father and forefathers. He knows the traditional regulations of building a temple which are derived from a written system of proportions and rules passed down through the ages. All units of measurement are based upon the human body (that of the master sculptor). The temple gate must be so many times as high as the length of his outstretched arms, and so many times as wide as the length of his foot. The front walls must be so many times as long as the gate is high, and so on. Needless to say, no two temples are exactly the same size, but this makes no difference to the Balinese. The beauty of a temple is judged by its proportions and how it harmonizes with the surroundings.

Widow-witch Rangda confronts viewers entering a Pura Dalem near Tampaksiring.

A master sculptor, well practiced in the art of stone-carving, knows by heart the many varia-tions of decorative motifs that are the finishing touches to the walls and gate. Above the en-trance should be placed the figure of Kala, a leering monster with outspread hands who catches any brazen evil spirits who seek entry. Or the ancient swastika symbol, a magic sign of good fortune and prosperity. Odd in-ventive motifs such as the upper part of a bird's beak or a grotesque face with a single eye are designated to finish each corner. They enclose row upon row of intricate volutes, spirals, ara-besques, leaves, flowers, vines and tendrils that overshadow a temple facade in a riot of entwined vegetation. The Balinese penchant for gilt and bright colors frequently leaves these carvings boldly accented by strong lines of white paint, and blotches of pinks, blues and yellows. They go so far in some parts of West Bali to coat an entire shrine with brilliant silver chromotone!

Together with its overwhelming decoration, a temple has its own personalities: the visionary fantastics—giants, devils, sorceresses, serpents and magic birds—that are energetically sculpt-ed in bold postures, as if they were caught in a momentary dance movement while flashing their eyes, stamping and snorting. Their robust bodies and sumptuous costumes reveal the characteristically baroque traits of Balinese art (see page 190). A temple is never without these awesome portrayals of deities, heroes and ma-gical guardians which stand dignified on either side of the gate. They derive from an imagina-tion unique to this island which conceives the supernatural and divine not as ethereal spirits, but as vigorous super-Balinese.

The gateway and front walls of a Pura Dalem (temple of the dead) usually present a ta-bleau of ceremonial figures such as the witch-queen Rangda, posed in her conventional stance or enshrined in an elaborate niche. Yet there also exists a more playful, naturalistic art that enlivens the formality of temple sculpture.

Topsy-turvy demon dancing on the back of the Tampaksiring Rangda shrine.

One can find in the same temple as Rangda, on the back of the same shrine, a topsy-turvy de-mon dancing on his hands, a lively figure carved in refreshingly simplified contours, with more movement than the frozen upright posture of the Rangda.

Formerly, in the absence of art galleries and museums, it was the public buildings, mainly the walls of temples and palaces, that served as display cases for informal, amusing carvings; although they were always given secondary importance to the official statues. One can imagine an old Balinese sculptor, after dutifully carving all the principal statues and motifs, taking delight in finding an inconspicuous corner along the wall where he could freely chisel a miniscule scene of his own fancy. Tucked away at the foot of a stairway, on a pedestal supporting a monumental witch, or behind a small shrine, you can discover the most humorous and suggestive reliefs — vignettes of passionate lovemaking, scenes of gory torments in hell, or such Western-in-spired themes as automobile breakdowns, arm-ed robbery, beer parties, single-prop airplanes, a blossom-wheeled bicycle, and sinking sailing vessels (see page 116). Some of the finest examples of this playful secular sculpture are displayed on the veranda of the Denpasar Mu-seum and on temple gates in North Bali.

With the constant renovation of the island's temples, stone carvings of rustic scenes and rascals continue, but they are markedly sub-ordinated to the architecture. Because of the inflexibility of the material and because they are not easily transportable, free-standing sta-tues are confined in theme to demons and divinities such as those sold in the village of Batubulan, or the small, primitive statues pro-duced in Ubud. The temple, though, remains just as much an eclectic showcase for the Bali-nese spirit—their reverence and ribaldry—as ever. And the more earthy, sensuous temple art, inspired by village life and laughter, is an age-old tradition that continues side by side with the modern movement in woodcarving and painting—a movement opening up a new world of expression to Balinese artists.

203

206

PAINTING. When Balinese painting reached an international audience, it was highly acclaimed as an intriguing and spirited art. Exotic canvases of mysterious jungles harboring imaginary fowl and beasts of prey, of bizarre ceremonies where freakish spooks and vampires accosted people, or where winged maidens hovered above a sleeping prince, mystified viewers in the West. Critics praised these extraordinary pictures with flattering allusions to "the jungles of the douanier Rousseau," "the line of Aubrey Beardsley", or "the hellish fantasies of Hieronymus Bosch". The significance being, of course, that here the inspiration was uniquely Balinese, with no attempt on the part of the painters to imitate foreign or primitive styles. The true merit of these works lay in a creative distillation of the exuberant life on an enchanted island.

These paintings were created when a new spirit of innovation swept through the Balinese art community during the thirties. Before that time, painting was little in evidence as a living art. Aside from painting artifacts of daily use or wooden statues, the Balinese made pictures of only three kinds: *iders-iders,* scroll paintings in the shape of long bands which were suspended along the eaves of temple shrines; *langse,* large rectangular paintings used as hangings or curtains in the pavilions of palace and temple; and painted astrological calendars showing the lucky days in each month. Most of these were narrative paintings with mythological themes. In particular, they illustrated popular episodes from the Hindu epics and classical literature. Always they were executed in the traditional *wayang* style, a formalized mode of painting inspired by the *Wayang Kulit* shadow play, still ardently pursued by many painters.

Everything within a *wayang* painting is governed by a set of rules: the characters portrayed, the scenery, the composition, even the

Preceding pages: The arrival of Western painters ignited an explosion of imagination in Balinese art as is apparent in this early 20th Century painting. Left, detail of the ceiling paintings at Klungkung's Hall of Justice.

colors which are traditionally limited to five hues (red, blue, brown, yellow, a light ochre for flesh), white and black. All available space is covered with patterns, including the white background which is sprinkled with colored clouds. As a narrative painting, it usually contains a number of episodes with the same figure reappearing in several scenes, each scene being partitioned by a conventional border of mountains, flames, or ornamental walls. Battle scenes are crowded and desperate with masses of blood-spattered bodies under a canopy of flying arrows and strange weapons. Scenes where divinities hold council are symmetrically composed in neatly arranged rows, the figure of each deity enclosed by a golden nimbus.

Like the *Wayang Kulit* play, individual characters are denoted by their conventional attributes. Characters of the "refined" type— deities, princes and heroes—are richly clothed in courtly dress, and wear elaborate head-dresses and opulent jewels of a type only found in ancient sculptures. Their gestures are studied and graceful, reminiscent of the formal movements in the classical dance. Their faces always remain serene with a slight smile upon the lips even in the most ferocious battle or gruelling torture. Those belonging to the "rough" type— devils, giants and clowns—have round, bulging eyes, canine teeth, bulbous noses and sometimes small horns sprouting from their temples. Their attitudes are more violent, their colors darker, and their bodies bulky and covered with hair. In all the characters, faces are drawn in a three-quarter view. Rarely does one see a full face and never a profile (see page 206).

Wayang paintings are produced in workshops where the master painter draws the outline of the picture, which is then colored in by his assistants. This tradition of coloring in outlines persists, as Balinese painting, old and new, is basically colored drawing.

Although *wayang* paintings hold to a strict code of conventions, they retain a fine sense of design and purity of style. The beauty in their

Batuan painting of dancing Barong.

rigid formality is reminiscent of Byzantine mosaics or illuminated manuscripts. Just as the narrative art of the Middle Ages in Europe illustrated stories from the New Testament, so these narrative paintings once served as an important expression of a vibrant mythology that was, and still is, deeply ingrained in the hearts of all Indonesians.

Traditional painting was stagnating when the new movement set in. Most of the panels within the temples remained unpainted and artists received few commissions from the palaces. The revival came about during the thirties, stimulated by two foreign artists, Walter Spies and Rudolf Bonnet. The introduction of modern materials—precut pads of paper, ink, watercolors and tempera—and the sudden increase in foreign demand which introduced the novel idea of framing a picture, stimulated painters to experiment in style and media. As a result, there was a change from narrative paintings to canvases restricting their subject matter to a single scene. Gusti Njoman Lempad of Ubud, for example, filled complete drawing pads with individual scenes from the *Ramayana* epic, his sketches often highlighted with specks of gold and red (see page 235).

From the mythical realm of super-heroes, painters increasingly turned to themes of daily life—village streets, harvests, markets, ritual ceremonies and dramatic spectacles—subjects artists had never attempted before. Liberated from a convention-ridden style, painting gained an independence which enabled artists to present freely the beautiful world of Bali.

This new trend in painting flourished in the lively art centers of South Bali. The village of Batuan, just south of Ubud, startled viewers with a surge of creativity. The paintings recalled the artists' own experiences, yet in mood the pictures were dark and foreboding. Canvases were filled to capacity with crowded forms sketched in half-tone against solid black backgrounds. Fragile, stick-like figures of villagers seemed encased in the surging vegetation of weird forests haunted by strange animals and figures of sorcery. Around Ubud, artists took to painting rustic scenes of village life that contained a powerful eclectic vision of festivity. In the coastal village of Sanur, Ida Bagus Rai, an outstanding Balinese painter, devoted his work to themes of the sea—fishermen, turtles, crabs, submarine monsters and ocean birds. His marvellous ink drawings were distinguished by a sharp awareness of the people around him and sheer joy in good witticisms, like a drawing of two anthropomorphic fish conversing underwater. Under the patronage of Australian artist Donald Friend, Ida Bagus Rai began to add selective details of modernity to his work, such as a diligent tourist snapping away with his camera while perched on a chair at a Balinese market place (see page 68).

This birth of individualism rescued the art from its dormant state, but the impetus was short-lived. The outbreak of World War II, followed by the Indonesian Revolution, put a halt to much of the activity in Bali's art centers. By the fifties, a good deal of the original force in the early paintings was lost. Content became weak and insipid: idyllic scenes of cockfights, dancers or harvests which were essentially the work of copyists who produced for tourist consumption.

It was during this general lull in creativity that an entirely new style of painting emerged in Ubud and Sanur which came to be called "The Young Artists School". Boys from thirteen to twenty began making startling canvases noted for their bold simplicity in line and brilliant, aggressive colors. Painter Arie Smit took special interest in this new style. As an experienced art teacher, he taught European painting techniques to the young artists, but left the choice of subject matter, color and composition entirely up to his pupil. The result was a flow of fresh, vivid portrayals of Balinese life and fantasy. Through an enchanting interplay of innocence and insight, the paintings at their best recaptured the spirit of present-day Bali, but sometimes descended to the vulgar. After all, where else but on this island could a witch and an automobile command the same reality?

Magical holdup of a truck, envisioned by a young artist of Ubud.

WOODCARVING. Did you ever sleep easier because your room was guarded by a winged lion perched upon the lintel? In Bali, it happens. Mythological beasts are very much at home in the traditional architecture of the island. Were you to walk into a Balinese palace of bygone days, from the crossbeam would gaze a Garuda bird, on its back would ride the god Vishnu, near the corner would stand a fantastic demon clasping the kris of the king, and in the temple shrine of the royal family would rest two majestic deities covered with gold leaf.

In the olden days, no building of importance was complete without its share of splendid woodcarvings. They appeared in relief on the doors, pedestals and beams of temple shrines and royal pavilions. As free-standing statues, the carvings served as protective figures for the household, or as sacred figurines of divinities honored during ritual ceremonies. Their source of inspiration were the valiant heroes, beasts of magic, and ghoulish villains immortalized in myths and fairy tales. In style, they were traditional Balinese—beautifully carved in robust, volumetric proportions, dressed in classical attire and set in strong angular postures—similar to the ceremonial stone statues in temple art.

Carvers of old also whittled minute figures from wood, bone and horn as bottle-stoppers or the hilts of betel-nut pounders. Carvings of insects, frogs, birds and clever portraits of village folk and noblemen reflected a playful folk art which paralleled the more formal decorative style. But though the carvings of the past were expressive inventions showing exceptional skill, they always served a definite utilitarian purpose. Furthermore, all the carvings were meant to be painted in bright colors, lacquer and gold.

In the 1930s, a dramatic change placed woodcarving in a new perspective. Rather than a decorative craft for enriching the decor of

Preceding pages: a startling pair of finely crafted masks used in topeng *dancing. Left, woodcarving of Singa, a lion, on a Besakih temple door.*

temples, palaces and household objects, woodcarving became an independent art form. Visitors to Bali presented a new market for carvers who had never thought to sell their work before. Woodcarvings for sale suddenly appeared on street corners, in market places, harbors, airports and even in shops in countries far distant from Bali.

Competition encouraged carvers to experiment. From large mythological statues came smaller figures of ordinary people and animals, inspired by familiar scenes of daily life. Statuettes of women seated in prayer, girls bathing, dancers, or an ascetic old man with his dog were all new to Bali. The material used—hardwoods of teak, jackfruit and dark ebony—was left in its natural state, smoothed and polished. In striving for refinement, carvers employed a more simplified line and less adornment than the polychrome traditional sculptures.

The most striking change in rendering form was elongating the torso of a figure. Claire Holt writes of one instance which helped encourage this new style. In 1930, German painter Walter Spies, who loved Indonesia and had settled in Bali, commissioned a carver to make him two statues from a long piece of wood. The carver returned with a single statue of a girl with a particularly lengthened torso, telling Spies that it seemed a shame to cut such a beautiful piece of wood in two. Spies was surprised at such an unusual statue, yet also very pleased, and because he had shown a keen interest in the art community of Bali, his opinion counted.

Not all craftsmen followed suit in making the smooth, attenuated forms created in Mas and Ubud. In the villages of Nyuhkuning and Peliatan, carvers liked to reproduce birds and animals in a distinctly realistic manner, accented by sharp contours and an unerring precision in modeling. In tune with the mischievous love of play among the Balinese, some of these spry creatures bore a remarkable resemblance to certain human personalities. (Certainly, one way to undercut a pompous individual is to carve him as a pompous toad, which a few tricksy carvers did.)

215

The famous carver I Tjokot of the small village of Jati evolved a highly individual "primitive" style. His subjects were born in a visionary sphere of unworldly monsters, ghouls, spooks and enchantresses which he roughly chiseled from huge branches of wood. Often abiding by the utilitarian tradition, Tjokot would artfully design his sculptures as lamp rests, pot supports or even chairs. Today it is easy to recognize a carving in Tjokot's style because so many of them are hollowed tree stumps over one meter high. Some of his original works are preserved in the Ubud museum, and Tjokot's carvings are well worth the visit.

Ida Bagus Njana of Mas, one of the finest woodcarvers in Bali, continued from the thirties through the sixties to create extraordinary carvings—from startling abstractions of the human body into interlacing limbs and curves, to a polished tree stump with knobbed roots, which he transfigured into a surrealistic sylvan ghost. During the fifties, when most carvers were pursuing the fashion of elongated forms, Ida Bagus Njana swung to the opposite extreme by making fat, bulky statues of dozing women. His modeling was superb—only slightly indented lines skimmed the surface of his carvings, letting the waving grain of wood enhance the flow of movement and texturing of form. For decades, Ida Bagus Njana's work commanded the highest prices on the international market. A few of his carvings are still on display in the Ubud Museum and in Mas at the gallery of his son, Ida Bagus Tilem, who is himself an exceptionally gifted carver.

Like painting, contemporary woodcarving flourishes in a variety of unusual styles. Mas remains the center of extremely stylized figures, made from glossy ebony and teak. Incredible themes and compositions and dramatic distortions of the body lend these figures a mood of exoticism and fantasy. Schools of woodcarvers in mountain villages near Ubud fashion crude, primitive figures which recall the mysterious power of magic art in ancient times. Batuan produces statues of boys (mostly young musicians) with round torsos and truncated limbs. And in Denpasar, large workshops are booming in a near-mass production of both smooth unadorned statues and finely detailed miniatures of fantastics, which are sold in galleries throughout the island.

As has usually been the case in Bali, there remain only a few master carvers who produce original work and a host of craftsmen who labor within the set conventions of an established style. Unfortunately in recent years, the art of woodcarving has been increasingly directed to a commercial market, and the desire to experiment has given way to making stereotype statues that sell. Yet although the majority of today's carvings are patterned after a recognizable design, it is easy to overlook their merit. In each style are traits characteristically Balinese—the precision of fine craftsmanship, a strong feeling for nature, a free passage into the world of the imaginary, and most apparent, a love for the material—the richness and beauty of wood.

Because Bali is entering a new era of prosperity, more and more carvers are given the chance to express their talents and to gain the training needed to become master carvers. Bali's artists are extremely skillful at their trade. Even more typical, they approach their work with delightful nonchalance. Seldom is there exaggerated pride in being among the elite of artists. Nor is a new technique carefully guarded in secret. A carver is naturally generous with his ideas. Instead of clinging to his inventions, he immediately teaches his style to his sons or assistants. It is no wonder that Tjokot's entire village is now engaged in producing carvings in his style, or that Ida Bagus Tilem creates pieces as splendid as those of his father. Like everything in the community, works of art are shared and admired by all—friends, family and village.

Right, modern woodcarving of Hanuman protecting Sita in a scene from the Ramayana, executed by I Dojotan of Mas. Following pages: a "Balinese Sistine Chapel" — the treasured ceiling of Kertagasa, Klungkung's Hall of Justice.

CRAFTS. Unlike painting and woodcarving much of the production of which is stimulated by a foreign market, the traditional crafts of Bali serve no other purpose than to provide beauty for the grand occasions and holidays so anticipated by the people.

The Balinese love to dress up in high fashion when attending temple festivals. Women put on their finest jewels, deck their hair with flowers of beaten gold, and wrap themselves in rich, gold-spun materials. Men come crowned in a head-cloth of brocade with a corner cocked high above the forehead. Even tiny babies follow the current fads—a baseball cap, woolen knee socks, knitted boots, a T-shirt with "Paradise Island" written on it, and golden flowers for girls which are dutifully tied around the head if the hair is not yet long enough. Dressing stylishly is not only a sign of respect, but also one of social prestige. During temple ceremonies, you can always tell a noblewoman by glancing at the underskirt which hangs just below her sarong. If she is of a wealthy family, hers will be a train of silk and gold.

Klungkung and Karangasem in East Bali are famous for these silk brocades, patterned with interweaving threads of gold and silver. Often their makers let the imagination guide the hand, resulting in gorgeous tapestries of *wayang* figures, birds and butterflies. One of the rarest kinds of weaving in the world is the art of the women of Tenganan, an ultra-conservative village in East Bali. Here a woman may work for years to fashion one piece of *gringsing,* or "flaming cloth". The technique she uses is an ancient one called *ikat,* "to bind". By carefully binding the threads and then dyeing them, she creates a pattern which will later become a finished design. *Ikat* of the warp, or *ikat* of the weft are weaving techniques common to Indonesia, but the difficult "double" *ikat,* where all the threads are dyed in patterns prior to weaving, is found nowhere else in the country but this one village.

Besides the art of weaving, the Balinese also make a lustrous gilt cloth, *kain prada,* for rituals and dramas. On the village stage, both queens and clowns alike wear brightly colored silks with glittering patterns of gold leaf—the principal motif being the lotus flower.

When a dignified nobleman dresses up for a ceremony, whether it be his marriage or his tooth-filing, he is never without his kris, the traditional dagger of Indonesia. In the past, a man's kris was his most important accessory. It symbolized his family and himself as an individual. Covarrubias tells of an old custom whereby a prince marrying a woman of lower caste sent his kris to the ceremony to represent his presence during the wedding! The eyes of storytellers widen in terror when they relate stories of magic krisses powerful enough to destroy a man when pointed at him.

True, the economic status of a man was determined by the richness of his kris and a good part of his fortune was invested in the gold and jewels adorning it. Metalsmiths labored many a month to perfect the ruby-studded golden demon that formed the kris handle of a king. Sheaths of royal krisses were of the finest polished wood, covered with hammered gold and silver, and topped with a cross-piece of ivory. Sheaths not only protected the kris from external damage (physical or psychic), but insulated its powerful vibrations as well, lest in brought harm to one who ventured too near.

Of all parts of a kris the blade is most sacred. Handle and sheath may be pawned by an owner if in need, but the blade is cherished as an important family heirloom. Kris blades are straight and simple at times, yet often are shaped in vicious tapering curves—a form possibly derived from the mythical serpent *naga,* since on some kris blades there rests a *naga* inlaid in gold.

In olden times, kris-makers belonged to a special guild of metalsmiths called *pande wesi,* who worshipped the fiery volcano Batur and were deemed powerful magicians. Ancient Indonesians considered all metal magically charged and anyone who worked with it must have the art of sorcery at his disposal, otherwise there would be great risks involved. For

Symbolism and significance.

221

this reason metalsmiths were an elite group, regarded as aristocrats by the lower classes. Even the proud Brahmanas had to speak in high Balinese as a sign of respect when addressing a smith with tools in his hands.

One of the most prominent and least recognized forms of artistry among the Balinese is their rich and imaginative "transitory art". Who wouldn't be amazed after spending two weeks in a village where everyone was rushing about to prepare for a cremation, to watch all the sumptuous decorations—tower, sarcophagus, *naga* serpent, everything—go up in smoke just like that? The Balinese, of course. So much of their creative work is made with no thought that it should endure, but that it should only serve. Take offerings, for example. Women spend hours creating lace patterns of palmleaf and pyramids of fruits and flowers to show reverence to the deities during temple feasts. After the offerings have been received in the temple, they are either taken home and eaten, or left in heaps on the ground for hungry dogs to scavenge. Even in the scattered palmleaf ornaments left over from a ceremony one can see the exceptional taste and sense of design that went into their making (see page 113). It is these selfless acts of creativity which remain bound to the original conception of the arts — to beautify life in service to one's religion and community.

Of special interest are the long palm-strip offerings, *lamaks,* that hang from high altars during temple festivals. Women create beautiful mosaics of green leaf in patterns their ancestors used hundreds of years before. Often the designs are variations of the *cili,* an abstract feminine figure identified with the goddess of earth and fertility Dewi Sri. Scholars believe the *cili* figure to be an ancient form native to the island before Hindu times and forerunner of the stylized elongation of the body, so prominent in the figurative art of Bali.

Surprisingly enough, the most influential art form in Bali appears more often than not in shadows. The flickering personalities of the *Wayang Kulit* puppet theatre are beloved by every child growing up on the island, and their

effect upon the Balinese imagination is tremendous. Anthropologist Jane Belo once asked a group of young Balinese children to make drawings and found that most of their figures were unmistakenly puppet-inspired. It is no wonder. The same figures that dance across the screen in silhouette reappear delicately drawn in traditional cloth paintings, preside in stone over the gates of temples, are evoked by the sound of *gamelan* melodies and dramatically come to life in the village plays. In almost any art form one can glimpse a shadow of the shadow theatre. The strong linear trend in Balinese art, the lack of modeling in painting, and the vivid portrayals of fantastics derive from the familiarity of every Balinese with *Wayang Kulit*

As the Indonesian name suggests, *wayang* puppets are fashioned from buffalo parchment for *wayang* means "shadow" and *kulit* means "skin". The figures are cut with a special iron stylus into the most delicate lace and painted (During religious occasions, *Wayang Kulit* may be performed in the daytime in full color with a single string stretched before the puppeteer instead of a screen.) Since all the characters are identified by their appearance, the smallest detail in costume, color and outline each has its significance. A leathersmith who fashions a complete set of *wayang* puppets (over 150 in all) should be commended on a superlative show of dexterous chisel-work After all, a slip of the stylus could deform a giant.

In the casual nonchalance with which the Balinese approach their art one almost forget the extraordinary artistic achievement that is involved in the daily routine of the community Be it an informal rehearsal of a play, the marching rhythm of the *gamelan* at a procession the mastery of a neglected temple carving, o necklaces of bone displayed in sales stands the Balinese instill design and style in all they do. This alone makes their art unique.

At right, swaying penjor decorations, made from palm leaves and flower, adorn the vil lage of Gulungan.

222

songs of adventure

The two great Hindu epics, the *Ramayana* (Story of Prince Rama) and the *Mahabharata* (War of the Bharatas), have been dear to the hearts of Asians for over a thousand years. Translated from Sanskrit into *Kawi*, the old Javanese language of literature, these immortal poems continue to inspire the arts and stimulate the imaginations of Indonesians with a world of heroism and adventure. In Bali, artists reinterpret the epics in stone reliefs, woodcarvings, ink drawings and paintings. Delighted crowds gather to watch the *Wayang Kulit* puppets cast shadows of mystical princes and monsters across the screen, to the chanting of a storyteller. In the classical play *Wayang Wong,* in the contemporary Ramayana Ballet, and in the choral drama of the modern *Kecak*, or Monkey Dance, the tales from these epics are re-enacted with great enthusiasm and appreciated by viewers who find beauty in their many interpretations.

The reason for the popularity of the *Ramayana* and *Mahabharata* goes deeper than mere entertainment. One main theme of Hindu literature in Bali is the symbolic struggle between absolute good and absolute evil. The principal characters and their allies are defined on a moral basis. Rama, hero of the *Ramayana,* is a reincarnation of Vishnu, the Preserver, and embodies the ideal of manly virtues: strength, endurance, love and devotion to truth. His wife, Sita, is the ideal of womanly faithfulness and marital love, while his companion and brother, Laksmana, personifies fraternal courage and loyalty. Rama's antagonist, Rawana, the many-headed demon-king with a retinue of giants, revels in lust, deceit, and hatred. The opposition between hero and fiend could be no more extreme.

Whereas the *Ramayana* illuminates the ethics of human relationships, the *Mahabharata* sings of the glorious exploits and deeds of battle in the war of the Bharatas (an ethnic name for the ancient, warlike races of Northern India). The verses ring of dazzling feats of warriors unconquerable, tournaments of

Stories from the Ramayana and Mahabharata come to life in the Wayang Wong mask drama.

princes, daring escapes from death, and merciless revenge in a bloody feud between two rival royal houses. The heroes of the epic are the noble Pandawas, five brothers of divine birth who are the models of goodness and virtue. They fight against their hundred cousins, the perfidious Korawas. Led by their wicked king Duryodana, the Korawas are the apotheosis of greed and jealousy.

As the adventures of a wandering prince exiled from his kingdom, the *Ramayana* can be likened to the *Odyssey* of ancient Greece; while the *Mahabharata*, as a saga of fiery episodes based upon a great historical war, recalls the *Iliad*. In both Hindu epics is woven a thread of high moral purpose—the ultimate triumph of virtue and subjugation of vice. Every episode performed on stage or portrayed in art is, in a way, a parable relevant to present-day Indonesia. Heroes of the epics are much more than fictional characters to the people. Each defines both a personality and a way of behavior. Many times an Indonesian describes a friend by likening him to a mythological hero, as "he s powerful and strong-willed, like the warrior Bima" (hero of the *Mahabharata*).

The oldest version of the *Ramayana*, attributed to the Indian sage Valmiki, was written around the 3rd or 4th century B.C. The *Mahabharata*, ascribed to the poet Vyasa, probably reached its present form in the 4th century A.D., though parts are many centuries older. Through the ages poets infused the themes of the epics with additions, until they grew to monumental proportions. The present version of the *Ramayana* in India consists of 24,000 verses divided into 500 songs; the *Mahabharata*, probably the longest single poem of world literature, is nearly 90,000 stanzas in its final form. The Indonesian translations written during the Hindu era in Central and East Java are among the most beautiful poems in Old Javanese literature. The following are brief synopses of the epics, in prose. Quotations are from translations by the late Romesh C. Dutt.

The mercurial monkey warrior, Hanuman, carved from satin-wood by Rodja of Mas.

STORY OF PRINCE RAMA. In the kingdom of Kosala, near the Himalayas, reigned King Dasarata who had four sons: Rama, Barata, Laksmana and Saturgna. Raised in wisdom and righteousness, the princes lived always in harmony and were an endless source of happiness to the king and his people. At a great age, Dasarata realized he must give up his throne. He told his subjects to prepare for the coronation of his eldest son, Rama.

The populace joyously embellished the capital with decorations for the momentous occasion. Yet there was one unmoved by the general enthusiasm. Kekayi, Dasarata's second wife and mother of Barata, fostered secret ambitions for her own son. Urged by her wicked servant Muntara, she reminded the king he owed her two, unfulfilled vows. Now she made her demands: that Barata must be king and Rama banished for fourteen years to the forest of Dandaka.

The king, trembling with sorrow and rage, could not revoke his promises and, forthwith, announced Kekayi's requests as royal commands. Rama, respectfully obeying his royal father, prepared to go. As he was leaving, Sita ran to the gate, begging permission to accompany him. Rama refused because of the dangers and hardships of the forest, but Sita replied from her heart:

For my mother often told me
And my father often spake,
That her home the wedded woman
Doth beside her husband make,
As the shadow to the substance,
To her lord is faithful wife;
And she parts not from her consort
'Till she parts with fleeting life.

Laksmana also insisted on following. Finally, Rama consented and the three started for the forest.

The kingdom of Kosala grieved. The king, overcome by sadness, soon fell ill and died. Everyone went into mourning. Kekayi too, mourned, but only in pretence. As soon as time permitted, she approached her son. Much to her dismay, Barata steadfastly refused the crown and ruled the kingdom only as Rama's deputy, with his elder brother's sandals on the throne. Meanwhile, Rama, Sita and Laksmana went deeper into the woods where they found asylum with saints and hermits, one of whom, Agastya, gave Rama a magic bow. In a clearing in the forest they built a simple dwelling where they lived peacefully for thirteen years. Nevertheless, Rama was haunted by a sense of danger and forbade Sita to remain alone; one brother guarded her while the other hunted for food.

Alas, their peace was shattered when the horrible Rawana discovered their hiding place. Captivated by Sita's beauty and grace, he determined to kidnap her, egged on by his sister, Sarpakenaka, whose love and lewd overtures both Rama and Laksmana spurned. Rawana's minister, the giant Marica, was ordered to lure Rama away. Soon a golden deer came to Sita's bower. She begged Rama to fetch it. Hesitating at first, he set off in pursuit. After a while he grew suspicious at being lured so far from the cottage and loosed an arrow at the golden deer. Instantly, where the creature fell dead lay the body of Marica himself. Before he died the giant cried out for help, in Rama's voice. Fearing the worse for her husband, Sita urged Laksmana to go to the rescue. Although acting against his brother's word, Laksmana hurried off to give aid, telling Sita that under no condition should she leave the cottage.

Suddenly, a blast of wind shook the hut and Rawana stood before Sita, in the disguise of a begging Brahmana. With much flattery he persuaded her to open the door. Seeing his blazing eyes, Sita immediately realized her mistake, but too late! The demon caught her in his arms, soared high in the air as he transformed himself back to his original grotesque appearance, and flew to his home in Langka (Sri Lanka). On the way he was attacked by the brave bird Jatayu who vainly tried to rescue Sita, but was mortally wounded and only managed, before dying, to tell Rama of Sita's abduction.

Rama and Laksmana set out into the dangerous woods in search of Sita. One day Rama met the white monkey, Hanuman, servant of the monkey king, Sugriwa, who had been de-

prived of his rightful throne by his wicked brother Subali. Rama regained Sugriwa's kingdom by killing Subali with an arrow while the monkey brothers were fighting. In gratitude, Sugriwa ordered his armies, under the command of Hanuman, to search the whole world for Sita.

After many adventures, they reached the shore opposite Langka. Hanuman leapt across the sea to find Sita in the garden of Rawana's palace. He told her that Rama would rescue her within a month and, in token, gave her Rama's ring. The delighted captive gave him her ring to take to Rama. Before returning, Hanuman created havoc in Rawana's capital. He increased his size a hundredfold and showed

a terrifying warning to the giants. His tail
as set afire by the enemy, but the monkey
neral cleverly used this to burn the town be-
re jumping back across the sea.

The monkey armies prepared their attack,
rming a causeway of boulders across the sea.
ma and his allies invaded Langka and a vio-
it battle ensued, ending with Rawana's death
an arrow from Rama's magic bow. Reunited,
ma, Sita, and Laksmana returned to Kosala
er fourteen years of exile. Barata gladly ceded
s regency. Thereafter Kosala attained new
ights of glory and prosperity under the reign
King Rama.

There is a supplementary book to the epic
th a sadder conclusion. The people of Kosala

*Adventures of Prince Rama are popular
themes of temple reliefs everywhere in Bali.*

suspected that Sita had not resisted her captor's
affections. Rama banished his guiltless wife
who found shelter with sage Valmiki where she
bore Rama two sons, the twins Lawa and Kusa.
Many years later, during the great horse sacrifice in Kosala, the twins came to the capital and
chanted the story of the *Ramayana* as Valmiki
had taught them. Rama suddenly recognized
his sons and sought Sita's forgiveness. Sita returned to Rama, but she had endured too much
of life's sorrows. As she died, she ascended to
heaven on a golden throne that rose from a
cleft in the earth.

WAR OF THE BHARATAS. Once there lived two families of the Kuru clan descended from Bharata: the Pandawas and the Korawas. The Korawas, "wrathful sons of Dretarastra, born of Kuru's royal race", were the hundred sons of the blind king Dretarastra. The five Pandawa brothers, "righteous sons of noble Pandu, god-born men of god-like grace," were the sons of the king's brother Pandu, who ruled the kingdom in his brother's name.

All of Pandu's sons were of semi-divine origin. The eldest son, Yudistira, a man of truth and piety, was descended from Dharma, god of virtue; the dauntless warrior Bima was descended from Bayu, god of the wind; Arjuna, the peerless archer, from Indra, god of the rains; and the twins Nakula and Sahadewa from the celestial Aswin twins. Pandu's wife gave birth to yet another son, Karna, begotten by the sun-god Surya, but his origin remained hidden and he joined the Korawas, becoming their warlord and the chief opponent of his half-brother Arjuna.

While Pandu ruled for his brother, the cousins grew up together. In every contest between the rival families, the Pandawas were victorious. The Korawas grew more jealous and revengeful with the years. When Pandu died, the old blind king appointed Yudistira, his eldest nephew, as heir to the throne. His own enraged sons, headed by the ruthless Duryodana, contrived a plot to destroy the sons of Pandu.

One day the Pandawas and their mother were persuaded to pay a visit to a distant town where a special resting place had been constructed. On the appointed hour the house burst into flames. The brothers and their mother barely escaped through an underground tunnel and fled to the forest. In the wilderness the Pandawas, hearing of a contest for the hand of a princess, journeyed to the kingdom ruled by King Drupada. Arjuna easily defeated all his rivals and won the princess Drupadi. The sons returned to a potter's house where they lodged and told their mother they had received a great

Demon-king Rawana spins a fiery dance in the Ramayana Ballet at Bengkel.

232

gift that day. Not knowing what it was, their mother replied, "Enjoy ye the gift in common." Thus Drupadi became the wife of all the brothers. Later they all had other wives as well. Arjuna married the sister of King Krishna (an incarnation of the god Vishnu).

Meanwhile the devious Duryodana learned of the failure of his plot, and that his cousins had found powerful allies in Drupada and Krishna. Finding that he could not keep the Pandawas from their inheritance, Duryodana retained the richer eastern province of the kingdom; the sons of Pandu were allowed the wilderness to the west. The Pandawas soon cleared the forest and built a new capital, Ngamatra (supposedly the present-day region of Delhi). Yudistira, king of Ngamatra, proclaimed a sacrifice to declare his sovereignty over all kings of India, and his brothers set out in all directions to proclaim his rule. The hundred Korawa brothers and their aging father also attended, but did so in great humiliation and envy.

Duryodana returned from the Imperial Sacrifice burning with jealousy. Determined to secure the ruin of the Pandawas, he gained the assistance of a prince who shared in his hatred —Sukani, an expert at loading dice. They knew Yudistira had one incurable weakness: a love for gambling. Sukani challenged Yudistira who lost game after game. With each loss his recklessness increased and the stakes went higher. Yudistira forfeited everything—wealth, steeds, elephants, his slaves and possessions and, lastly, his kingdom. In a final gamble he staked himself, his brothers, and even the princess Drupadi, against Sukani—and lost!

Duryodana, eager to claim the Pandawas as slaves, was persuaded by his father to soften the claim to banishment. Yet the exile was a harsh one: the Pandawas must go into twelve years of hiding and one year of concealment among the common people. If their identity be discovered in the thirteenth year, they were to be exiled for another twelve years.

The Pandawas then passed twelve years banished in the wilderness. During this time, King Duryodana, still not satisfied with his revenge, decided to appear before them in full regalia and splendor. Unfortunately, along the way, he was taken captive in a skirmish with aerial sprites. The Pandawas heard of his plight, rescued him and allowed him to return to his kingdom; but this act of generosity only deepened Duryodana's hatred and jealousy.

After twelve years, the sons of Pandu went into concealment among the common people by serving a distant king under false names. Yudistira disguised himself as a Brahman courtier and dice expert, Bima became a palace cook, Arjuna put on bangles and earrings and posed as a eunuch, Nakula a stable keeper, and Sahadewa a cowherd. They retained these identities for one year as was their bargain, and then demanded the return of their kingdom. Duryodana refused, saying that no land, "not even a spot which a needle's point can cover", shall be given them.

In council with Krishna, the Pandawas decided to recapture their kingdom by force. The great war of the Bharatas ensued. For eighteen days, the skies were dark with clouds of arrows, and the earth thundered with the clashes of charioteers and cavalry. Arjuna's dialogue with his charioteer and ally Krishna, to whom he turned in anguish, foreseeing the massacre of his kin, is described in the renowned *Bhagavad Gita* in which the agony of war is shown as an inward personal loss. The venerated teachers of both families were killed, as were the younger heroes, Arjuna's and Bima's sons. Then the undefeated rivals, Arjuna and Karna met in mortal combat. Arjuna revenged the death of his son with that of his arch-enemy. Bima and Duryodana, "like two bulls that fight in fury, blind with wounds and oozing blood", fought on until Duryodana fell dead. Later, the women of Kuru visited the battle field to mourn the fallen. The epic ends with the people of Kuru returning home with desolate hearts.

Rama capturing the golden deer, by Gusti Nyoman Lempad of Ubud.
Resembling a gigantic sea anemone, the thunderous Kecak dance unfolds dramas of Rama and his monkey allies. (Following Pages)

sway of the spirit

In a pavilion near the temple, the dancer meticulously adds the finishing touches to his make-up—a curve to the eyebrow, three dots on each temple, a red spot between the eyes. He gives a last glance to the mirror and moves to his place. A signal and the *gamelan* strikes a dynamic chord. Quivering fingers appear from behind the temple gate, until a face emerges with painted eyes and a curious smile. The dancer has already lost his personal identity in the dramatic character who cautiously peers from behind the gate, moves slightly forward with hesitating glances, as if he were passing through an imaginary screen into another existence: the spiritual world of the dance.

For the Balinese, the theatre is not a profession. Aside from those who teach music and dancing, the village creates a theatre for the enjoyment of the community. Those who perform on stage by night lead normal lives in the village by day as farmers, fishermen, goldsmiths, woodcarvers, or whatever their vocations. Theatre is seen as an integral part of life. It is at one with the rituals that fasten society. Birthdays, weddings, temple festivals, processions to the sea, and purification ceremonies are all occasions for dramatic entertainment.

The origin of Balinese theatre is a religious one. Just as a temple offering is food made beautiful to present as a divine feast, so a temple dance offers the motions of daily life made beautiful as a gift to visiting deities during temple festivals. Good music, splendid costumes, fine dancing and drama give pleasure both to divine guests and village audiences. Religious dances serve as ceremonial offering and dedication in the temple. Many forms of contemporary drama, such as the exorcism plays, function also as a bridge between the mundane and the spiritual world.

Because of their religious significance, dances and plays are constantly revived by the community. An adult will have seen a certain

Clothed in the trappings of a clown, an actor adds a final detail to his make-up before a Cupak performance during a temple festival at Pura Panataran Sasih in Pejeng.

play hundreds of times. Therefore, it is not at all important that a drama begins at the beginning and ends at the end. Often an episode enacted is only a small part of a very long story. As soon as the play starts, a Balinese recognizes the story and automatically views it in its proper perspective. If a golden deer appears, he immediately knows the story is from the *Ramayana,* that Sita will soon be kidnapped, but eventually rescued.

Since they know all the tales and dances by heart, the people feel perfectly at home watching a performance. They are not on edge to see what happens next, and may stand for hours without growing tired or impatient. Elaborate props and sets are unnecessary. A conversation between two characters conveys where they happen to be at the moment, whether in the forest, near the seashore, or at the king's palace. By a long familiarity with the theatrical forms and by sheer imaginative force, the mind of the audience creates the pictorial realities of the stage.

Much of the sophistication of the Balinese theatre derives from this extraordinary integration of spectator and action. Action relates to all directions, since the stage is usually a clearing before or near the temple where enthusiastic observers crowd around from all sides. The stage may extend itself if a demonic character lunges too close to the small children who form the front rows, and shrink back to its original size when the children, half frightened and half amused, return to their places. It is not surprising to find, in the middle of a climactic scene, a dog strolling out between an actor's legs. Such relaxed informalities are very much in tune with the Balinese approach to their theatre, and rarely do they hinder the drama.

The theatre appeals to people of all ages. From the smallest children to grandmothers, who usually care for the babies of the family during the show. For the young, the drama is occasion for flirting and courting in the back rows, or at the nearby foodstands where women sell nuts, drinks and sweets—everything to make the night pass agreeably. Experienced dancers view the action from a different angle, scrutinizing the movements of the dance and the quality of the dancers.

The ebullience of Balinese dances gives them an air of spontaneity, yet beneath their finish lies a learned set of motions in a highly stylized dance technique. Each salient gesture has a name which describes its action in terms of a similar one taken from nature, usually from animals. A flurry of turns may bear the name of a tiger defending himself against mosquitoes. A side step may be named after the way a raven jumps. A tilt of the head may be as a duck seeing a bird in the sky. The shimmering of the fingers as two blue birds moving on a slender coconut leaf. Or an upward glance as a monkey looking for fruit in a small tree. The names are essentially descriptive and have no symbolic meaning except in identifying, in terms of metaphor, the exact character and feeling within a set action.

Like many Asiatic dances, the movements of the wrist and fingers vary tremendously giving the dance of the hands a life of its own, and making it an important criterion of judgment as to the quality of the dancer. Great variations of level—leaps, runs, lifts and spins —so familiar in the Western ballet, are seldom seen in classical Balinese dances, where space is usually partitioned in measured steps with the body bent close to the ground. Rarely do two dancers merge in a single form. Traditionally, body contact was not permitted. In the formal dance style, although the motion of the dancers may be highly synchronized, the dancers themselves remain separate entities and relate to each other through the choreography, usually one in formations of lines and rows.

Those exempt from this refined style of dancing are the clowns, who are bound to no strict choreography. The Balinese are so accustomed to the stylized postures, dress, and movements of their actors that when a clown appears who obviously has no style at all, he is extremely funny. Witches, animals and demons, also exempt from the ceremonial behavior of noble humans, have license to adopt hilarious styles of their own and constitute a large part of the comedy.

To everyone introduced to the brilliance of the Balinese stage, costume and headdress seem inseparable from the dance itself. In the capacity of the dancer to identify completely, in attitude and in appearance, with his part, the dance comes alive with a force from within—the "dance dances". Facial make-up is a stylized facade of the character represented. By putting on a mask, the dancer totally adopts the character's appearance. His immobile face seems to have transformed his entire body into a new shape that is one with the abstract world of the mask. The impersonality of Balinese dances—the unfocused stare and closed lips of the dancer—is at first striking to one accustomed to dances in which emotional expression is given free play. In Bali, the personal temperament of the dancer serves only to express the content of the dance, the mood of the melody, and the rhythm of the *gamelan*: to reveal the life of the dance to the audience. For instance, the *Kebyar* dancer, who must be extremely expressive to be good, never discloses his own personality but animates the fluctuating moods of the music, and generates sound in the physical form of the dance.

Dancing is taught by imitation. A young pupil, usually under ten years old, follows every movement of the teacher who leads him through the dance. After he feels assured of the basic motions, the teacher comes behind him and forces his arms and fingers into the correct postures, tilts his head on the proper accents of the drum and adjusts the position of his body. This body-to-body lesson is repeated as often as it takes the pupil to begin to "feel" the dance, for the dance to "enter" him. A pupil always learns a particular dance, such as *Legong, Baris,* or *Janger,* but never dances in general. He follows the beat of the drum which dictates the rhythm of the dance. The drummer is the conductor of the *gamelan* orchestra and leads the changing tempo which guides the movements of the dancer.

Balinese dances and drama cover a wide array of theatrical forms. Most performances are a combination of dance, music, song, and acting. No play is complete without music of some kind, and no dance, even the most abstract, is without story or meaning. Selected here are only a few of over fifty dances active in Bali today. The majority cited are performed regularly for guests, others only during religious ceremonies—and all of them zealously supported by the Balinese.

The dances selected for discussion on pages 244-258 are those highlighting the virtuosity and skill of the dancers. They are regularly presented by touring dance troupes. To execute them well involves years of training, strict co-ordination and technique, and an intricate relation between movement and orchestra. An exceptional dancer, by adding personal modifications of style to the traditional choreography, elevates the dance to new heights and continues his devotion as a teacher. In the second group of dances, entitled "Kings and Comics" (see page 261), the emphasis is upon dramatizing a story. "The Vibrant Ritual" (page 269 describes the ceremonial dance-dramas that actively relate to religious rites.

One of the oldest of Balinese dances is the *Gambuh,* which may be one thousand years old. Many of Bali's most popular dances were derived or influenced by it—among them the *Topeng, Wayang Wong, Cupak, Calon Arang, Legong, Arja,* and *Joged Pingitan.* Most of these dances were created between 1850 and 1900, a period of exceptional vitality for dance, under the patronage of *raja*s and nobles. The *Sanghyang* trance dance influenced such dances as the *Kecak.* Several other dances, such as *Kebyar,* date from the 20th century, created by such great dancers as Mario and Nyoman Kaler.

Dance and drama have given great delight to thousands of tourists, yet have not remained unaffected. Endless commissions to perform have sometimes caused a decline in standards. And the tendency to serve a mixed bag of excerpts, rather than the classic form of a dance, has meant that tourists often do not see the best of this Balinese art form.

Gamelan. In Bali it is easy to know when something is happening. Just listen for the

sounds of the *gamelan* orchestra, generally consisting of brass kettles, gongs and metallophones. Often in the evenings the softened tones of the music float outwards from a distant village, as if accompanying the chirp of crickets and the croaking of frogs in the rice fields. Follow your ears and you are sure to come upon a dance performance, a temple ceremony or a religious procession, for music accompanies every theatrical, religious and social function. On a road at night you may pass five or six music sessions within ten kilometers. The magic of the *gamelan* gives the occasion an aura of vibration with its strange metallic energy.

The word *gamelan* is, strictly speaking, Javanese, though now it has become a general term for the music played by any percussion orchestra, whether Javanese or Balinese. In Bali the word *gong* is used to describe the many kinds of orchestra. Balinese music has undergone considerable change during its history. Beginning in the 1920s and 1930s the old *gong gede* was replaced by the faster *gong kebyar* which is now the commonest form of orchestra.

A basic principle of *gamelan* music is that instruments with a higher range of notes are struck more frequently than those with lower ranges. At given intervals, gongs of various sizes mark off the basic line of the music, the other instruments adding their complicated, shimmering ornamentation. Most of the musicians play a variety of instruments of the *gangsa* metallophone family which consist of bronze bars suspended over bamboo resonators. With one hand the player strikes the keys with a wooden mallet; with the other he dampens the key just struck.

At the heart of the orchestra are the two drums *(kendang)*, one of which, the male, is slightly smaller than the other, the female. The drummers control the tempo of the piece of music. Sometimes using their hands, at other times a round-headed stick, their rhythmic techniques are mind-boggling. The small hand cymbals *(cengceng)* accent the faster warlike music. Helping to keep the orchestra together is the steady beat of the *kempli,* a single small gong struck with a stick. The rich slow tones of the *trompong,* a set of kettles like the *reyong* but played by one man, occurs in certain orchestral pieces and in the *Kebyar* dance.

Other instruments that accompany particular dances or drama performances include bamboo xylophones, flutes *(suling)* and the two-stringed violin *(rebab)*. The shadow play has its own little ensemble consisting of four *genders.*

Archaic ensembles, still played in a few old villages in East Bali, include the *gong selunding* consisting of instruments with iron keys, and the wooden-keyed *gambang*. And finally there is the Jew's harp *(genggong),* one of the world's oldest instruments.

Gamelan instruments are still made in Bali, the leading craftsmen being those of the village of Tihingan near Klungkung, and Blahbatuh.

Most *banjars* have their music club, *sekaa,* a male organization with members ranging from eight-year-old enthusiasts to veterans in their sixties. As with the planting of rice, the upkeep of temples and village government, the orchestra clubs are communal organizations in which everyone has an equal share in the responsibilities. Every practicing musician belongs to a music club of some kind. Frequently, these clubs are a prime source of entertainment to villagers who casually gather around the *bale gong* — pavilion where the village orchestra is kept—to listen to the *gamelan* practice. Some clubs meet only once every five months to brush up on pieces to be used in the coming religious ceremony. Others practice five nights a week, perfecting new and difficult compositions or rehearsing with a dance troupe.

The polyphonic compositions are learned by memory. Musicians seldom use musical notation. The remarkable sense of rhythm in the Balinese people is instilled from childhood. At informal practices, one often sees a baby resting on the lap of his father while he plays. The child remains there, awake or asleep, throughout the session. Experienced musicians say there is no conscious effort to remember learned compositions. They have heard and played them so often their hands work instinctively.

legong

In legends, *Legong* is the heavenly dance of divine nymphs. Of all classical Balinese dances, it remains the quintessence of femininity and grace. Girls from the age of five aspire to be selected to represent the community as *Legong* dancers. Connoisseurs hold the dance in highest esteem and spend hours discussing the merits of various *Legong* groups. The most popular of *Legongs* is the *Legong Kraton, Legong* of the palace. Formerly, the dance was patronized by local *rajas* and held in the *puri*, residence of the royal family of the village. Dancers were recruited from the aptest and prettiest children. Today, the trained dancers are still very young; a girl of fourteen approaches the age of retirement as a *Legong* performer.

The highly stylized *Legong Kraton* enacts a drama of a most purified and abstract kind. The story is performod by three dancers: the *condong*, a female attendant of the court, and two identically dressed *legongs* (dancers), who adopt the roles of royal persons. Originally, a storyteller sat with the orchestra and chanted the narrative, but even this has been refined away in many *Legongs*. Only the suggestive themes of the magnificent *gamelan gong* (the full Balinese orchestra) and the minds of the audience conjure up imaginary changes of scene in the underlying play of *Legong Kraton*.

The story derives from the history of East Java in the 12th and 13th centuries: when on a journey the King of Lasem finds the maiden Rangkesari lost in the forest. He takes her home and locks her in a house of stone. Rangkesari's brother, the Prince of Daha, learns of her captivity and threatens war unless she is set free. Rangkesari begs her captor to avoid war by giving her liberty, but the king prefers to fight. On his way to battle, he is met by a bird of ill omen that predicts his death. In the fight that ensues he is killed.

The dance dramatizes the farewells of the King of Lasem as he departs for the battlefield and his ominous encounter with the bird. It opens with an introductory solo by the *condong*. She moves with infinite suppleness, dipping to the ground and rising in one unbroken motion, her torso poised in an arch with elbows and head held high, while fingers dance circles around her wrists. Slowly, her eyes focus on two fans laid before her and, taking them, she turns to meet the arrival of the *legongs*.

The tiny dancers glitter and dazzle. Bound from head to foot in gold brocade, it is a wonder the *legongs* can move with such fervent agitation. Yet, the tight composure of the body, balanced by dynamic directive gestures—the flash of an eye, the tremble of two fingers—blend in unerring precision. After a short dance, the *condong* retires, leaving the *legongs* to pantomime the story within the dance.

Like a controlled line of an exquisite drawing, the dancers flow from one identity into the next without disrupting the harmony of the dance. They may enter as the double image of one character, their movements marked by tight synchronization and rhythmical verve. Then they may split, each enacting a separatè role, and come together in complementary halves to form a unified pattern, as in the playful love scene in which they "rub noses".

The King of Lasem bids farewell to his queen, and takes leave of Rangkesari. She repels his advances by beating him with her fan and departs in anger. It is then the *condong* reappears as a bird with wild eyes fixed upon the king. Beating its golden wings to a strange flutter of cymbals, it attacks the king in a vain attempt to dissuade him from war. The ancient narrative relates: "... a black bird came flying out of the northeast and swooped down upon the king, who saw it and said, 'Raven, how come you to swoop down on me? In spite of all, I shall go out and fight. This I shall do, oh raven!'" With the king's decision understood, the dance may end; or the other *legong* may return on stage as his prime minister, and in shimmering unison, they whirl the final steps to war.

Tightly bound in gold brocades and crowned with frangipani blossoms, two young dancers pause during the classical Legong Kraton, performed here by A.A. Raka Astuti and Ni Made Puspanurini of Peliatan.

baris

Just as the *Legong* is essentially feminine, *Bâris,* a traditional war dance, glorifies the manhood of the triumphant Balinese warrior. The word *baris* means a line or file, in the sense of a line of soldiers, and referred to the warriors who fought for the kings of Bali. There are numerous kinds of *Baris,* distinguished by the arms borne by the dancers—spear, lance, kris, bow, sword, or shield. Originally, the dance was a religious ritual: the dedication of warriors and their weapons during a temple feast. From the ritualistic *Baris Gede* grew the dramatic *Baris,* a story prefaced by a series of exhibition solo dances which showed a warrior's prowess in battle. It is from these that the present *Baris* solo takes its form.

The Balinese say a good *Baris* dancer is rare. He must undergo rigorous training to obtain the skill and flexibility that typifies the chivalrous elegance of the male. A *Baris* dancer must be supple, able to sit on his heels, keeping his knees spread wide apart in line with his body. His face must be mobile to convey fierceness, disdain, pride, acute alertness, and, equally important, compassion and regret—the characteristics of a warlike noble.

The *Baris* is accompanied by *gamelan gong.* The relation between dancer and orchestra is an intimate one, since the *gamelan* must be entirely attuned to the changing moods of the warrior's imperious will. The dancer enters the stage—a field of action where he will display the sublimity of his commanding presence. At first, his movements are studied and careful, as if he were seeking out foes in an unfamiliar place. When he reaches the middle of the stage, hesitation gives way to self-assurance. He rises on his toes to his full stature, his body motionless with quivering limbs. In a flash, he whirls on one leg, his feet patter the ground to the tumult of the *gamelan*, and his face renders the storm of passions of a quick-tempered warrior. Such a spectacular show of style, mental control and physical dexterity would intimidate any enemy worthy of the *Baris*!

A.A. Oka, a young dancer of Peliatan, performing the Baris.

kebyar

Like the *Baris,* the *Kebyar* is a solo exhibition dance, but of a more individualistic kind. The *Baris* portrays the movements of a generalized Balinese warrior. In *Kebyar,* the accent is upon the dancer himself, who interprets every nuance of the music in powerful facial expressions and movement. *Kebyar* originated in North Bali around 1920, but the man most often credited with its creation is the late Mario, a dancer whose superb performances of *Kebyar* remain unparalleled.

The most popular form of *Kebyar* in South Bali is *Kebyar Duduk,* the "seated" *Kebyar,* where the dancer sits cross-legged throughout most of the dance. By de-emphasizing the legs and decreasing the space to a small sphere, the relation between dancer and *gamelan* is intensified. The dance is concentrated in the flexibility of the wrist and elbow, the magnetic power of the face, and the suppleness of the torso.

The music seems infused in the dancer's body. The fingers bend with singular beauty to catch the light melodies of the metallophones, while the body sways back and forth to the resounding beat of the gong. As the dance progresses, the dancer crosses the floor on the outer edges of his feet and approaches a member of the orchestra, usually the lead drummer. He woos the musician with side glances and smiles, but the drummer is too absorbed in the music to respond. Insulted, the *Kebyar* dancer leaves him and sets out for a new conquest.

The *Kebyar* is the most strenuous and subtle of Balinese dances. It is said that no one can become a great *Kebyar* dancer who cannot play every instrument of the orchestra; for to attain perfection, all the moods of the music—lyrical, idyllic, dark, ominous—must be reflected in the disposition and skill of the dancer. In *Kebyar Trompong,* the dancer actually joins the orchestra by playing a long instrument of circular knobbed kettles called the *trompong,* as he continues to dance and twirl the *trompong* sticks between his fingers.

I Made Sukraka of Bengkel dancing Kebyar Trompong.

248

jauk

As a classical solo performance expressing the movements of a demon, *Jauk* is derived from a traditional play in which all the dancers, wearing frightening masks of the *raksasa* or demon type, enacted episodes from the *Kawi* versions of the *Ramayana* and *Mahabharata.* Like the dramatic *Baris*, the *Jauk* play was prefaced by a series of abstract preludes in which individual dancers could show off their paces. From these solos evolved the present *Jauk* performance.

The harsh stare of the eyes, the thick, black moustache, and frozen smile give the masked *Jauk* dancer an uncanny effect of being from another world, populated by fearsome practitioners of evil. He wears a high, tasseled crown covering a thick mass of tangled hair, and gloves with long transparent fingernails that flitter incessantly to the music. As a mask dance, *Jauk* is considered a high art to execute well. The dancer's aim is to express the character revealed in the appearance of the mask— that of a strong, forceful personality. Unlike the *Baris* dancer, a *Jauk* performer cannot rely on powerful facial expressions to convey feeling. He can dart his artificial looks here and there, but he is obliged to express his demoniac exuberance through his gestures alone. (The round, protruding eyes and tentacle-like fingernails are the marks of identification for a demon.)

The *Jauk* dancer's movements closely resemble those of the *Baris,* but his manner is more exaggerated and violent. He peers out to his audience like a crouching cat ready to leap upon its prey. Suddenly he lunges, the music becomes frenetic with loud, clashing sounds, he spins to reach the perimeter of the stage; then stops, precise and controlled — only the constant shimmering of the tassels and fingernails mirror his intensity. Slowly, he retreats, as if preoccupied by dark, treacherous thoughts. And if his audience in the first rows are little children, they breathe a sigh of relief.

Jauk dancer of Mas leers at his viewers.

kecak

The dark expanse of the banyan tree above the temple gate casts a dense shadow on the courtyard and the carvings that flicker like apparitions in the uneven light. A serpentine stream of bodies coils itself, circle within circle, around a large, branching torch. Two hemispheres of men: one, a pattern of silhouettes; the other, sculptural faces of brown skin caught in a net of torchlight. The half-seen multitude waits in silence. A priest enters with offerings, a blessing of holy water. One piercing voice cracks the suspense; the circle electrifies.

No other dance is so unnerving as the amazing *Kecak*: one hundred and fifty men who, by a regimented counterplay of sounds, simulate the orchestration of the *gamelan*. *Kecak*, a name indicating the "chak-a-chak" sounds, evolved from the male chorus of the ritual *Sanghyang* trance ceremony. By a choreography ingeniously simple, chorus is transfigured into ecstasy. The annihilation of the individual, the cries, the erratic pulse of sound and sublimated violence of the *Kecak* are perfectly contained in the precise use of a few basic motions of head, arms and torso. Through a coordination rehearsed for months prior to a performance, various parts of the dance merge in a startling continuum of grouped motion and voice. Many words and gestures have no meaning other than as derivatives of incantations to drive out evil, as was the original purpose of the *Sanghyang* chorus.

Kecaks include a drama, in which the circle of light around the torch becomes a stage, and its periphery of men, a living theatre with all dramatic effects. Accompanied by the bizarre music of human instruments, the storyteller relates the episode enacted within the performance, usually one drawn from the *Ramayana*. When demon-king Rawana leaps to the center, the chorus simulates his flight with a long hissing sound. When Hanuman enters the mystic circle, the men become an army of chattering monkeys—hence, the nickname "Monkey Dance".

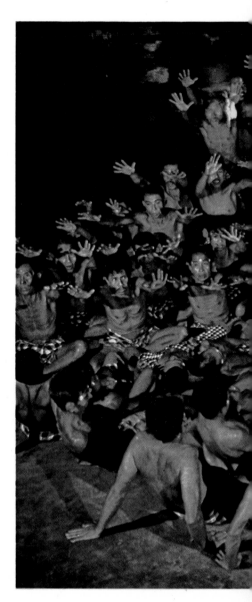

Magic Garuda bird encircles the branched torch during a Kecak performance at Bedulu.

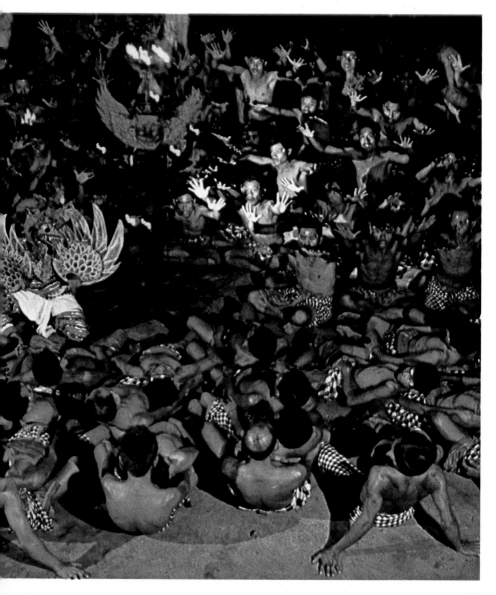

janger

The flute begins an eerie tune, and faraway voices chant a strange song that flows from a loud melody to a nearly inaudible high pitch. Two girl singers appear wearing splendid, floral crowns with multi-colored spikes. They advance, allowing another pair to enter, until twelve girls have filed on stage. Slowly, they kneel opposite each other, cocking their heads and darting their eyes to accent the rhythm of the orchestra.

As the chanting continues, twelve young men silently repeat the girls' entrance. In contrast to feminine delicacy, their movements are deliberate and strong. All wear painted moustaches and bear the self-assured look of a slick courtier. Suddenly, the male formation breaks into frenzied activity of twists, jerks and lunges —all in the tight syncopation of a military drill, with brisk shouts of "*O beh! O beh! Dinga dinga ding janger-ger!*" Instantly, the shock wave ceases, the men freeze in their positions, and the lonely flute carries the dance back to the soft sways and chanting of the girls.

The juxtaposition of the subdued motions of the girls against the dynamic thrusts of the men, the harmonious feminine song against the jagged yells of male voices, makes *Janger* an artful composition of dance, music and chorus. A folk dance introduced to the island in the thirties, *Janger* also has its origin in the *Sanghyang* trance ceremony, in which the women chant the *Sanghyang* song and the men alternate with the gruff sounds of the *Kecak*. When the dance first came into existence, it spread through the *banjars* like fire. Every village had to have a *Janger* group, and the dance became a popular social event between young boys and girls. Within a few years *Janger* lost its paramount place among the dances, and was replaced in popularity by the *Arja* opera. Now, *Drama Gong*, a form of opera which originated only in the mid-60s, is in vogue; which only goes to show innovation is a star attraction among the Balinese and the liveliness of their theatre is in the constant revival of old forms in new styles.

Boys and girls of Bengkel dancing the Janger.

oleg tambulilingan

A modern dance choreographed by the late Mario in 1952, *Oleg Tambulilingan* has become a popular addition to the repertoire of dances included in a *Legong* performance. Originally, it was danced by only one girl and called *Oleg,* a general term meaning the swaying of a dancer. Later, a male part was added to make it a duet, and the dance gained a new theme depicting two bumblebees *(tambulilingan)* flirting in a garden. The female enters first. In light, quick steps she circles the stage, fluttering the long silk scarfs that hang from her sides. If the dancer is a good one, she conveys all the beguiling qualities of a young coquette. At one moment, she is moody and temperamental, her eyes narrow and her lips spread slightly into a seductive smile. The next, she is scornful. She turns, snubbing her viewers—only to return as the most feminine creature with a whimsical air of innocence.

The female's solo is a strenuous one. Her movements must flow from subdued and delicate to tense gestures of haughtiness and disdain. At one point, she dances in the seated position. The sensuous sweeps of her hands, the tremble of her fingers and the fluctuating moods that pass and change, incarnate the idea of woman. The male enters unnoticed, eyes her, and cocks his head with a half-smile of affirmation. He moves forward to make a conquest. At first, they shy away from the moment of contact, yet woo with a display of their graces while pretending to be unaware of the other's fascinating presence. As the circle of flight grows smaller, the flirting increases. The female teases him, he moves forward, she draws back in feigned surprise, yet is secretly pleased with her success. They come together, bringing their faces close in an affectionate caress, then swirl apart in retreat, only to return to one another again. In the end, they fall in love and leave together.

A. A. Bagus woos the charming Ni Gusti Ayu Raka in the flirting dance Oleg Tambulilingan. Raka was the first to perform the dance, composed just before she toured abroad with the Peliatan dance troupe.

ramayana ballet

The *Ramayana* has long been rendered on the Balinese stage through the *Wayang Wong*, a classical dance-drama enacting scenes from the Hindu epic in sequel performances over a period of three or four days. A few years ago, a new dance interpretation of the *Ramayana* was introduced to the island by Kokar, the Conservatory of Instrumental Arts and Dance. Accompanied by the *gamelan gong* orchestra, the *Ramayana Ballet* is a unique mixture of traditional dance technique and modern motifs of slapstick comedy. The story opens in the forest of Dandaka where Rama, Laksmana and Sita have transformed their banishment into a peaceful life in the woods. (For a summary of the *Ramayana* story, see page 229). Because of their ideal beauty, the royal brothers are usually danced by women: Rama wearing a golden crown and Laksmana a black headdress. Their manner is stately and heroic—the refined style of dance reserved for regal personages. In contrast to their noble bearing, the demon king Rawana takes large, dynamic steps—a fiery mode of dance which shows the grandiloquent arrogance of a tyrant.

Frequently, it is the animals of the *Ramayana Ballet* who steal the show. In Balinese theatre, animals have license to improvise fantastic dance styles of their own. One remembers the golden deer that gaily prances before Rama yet always manages to slip from his grasp, the brave Jatayu bird that vainly attempts to rescue Sita, and, of course, the inevitable monkey business. Freed from social propriety, the monkeys may wheel about creating the most comical situations. Hanuman, the monkey general, outwits two horrific giants by cleverly maneuvering out of their way, so that they end up knocking each other out. Aside from delighting in this comic relief, the Balinese are extremely tolerant of their performers. Should a charging monkey, by mistake, fall on his tail, he is all the more hilarious to his attentive audience.

Hanuman triumphantly leads Sita to rejoin Prince Rama at the conclusion of the Ramayana Ballet of Bengkel.

kings and comics

In the following dramas, the accent is upon the unraveling of a story more than the heightened counterpoint between music and dance. The *gamelan* orchestra is always essential, but it is not as commanding as the development of plot and the colorful spectrum of personalities included. Tales of passion, historical romances, love adventures, and military chivalry are popular themes of these dramas. The majority of the stories are drawn from the medieval courts of East Java—a golden age in Javanese history when kingdoms were at the peak of their splendor and of their influence upon Bali. The actors' costumes, language and gestures derive from the grand court style of the past. They speak in the classical language of poetry suitable to well-bred noble families, and dance in the high, refined manner that signifies the stately bearing of the aristocracy.

All the comic interludes the Balinese adore so are provided by the lower members of the court—the retainers and ladies-in-waiting. There are always two male clowns, who are usually servants of the king's prime minister. They function within the drama as interpreters of the narrative, since they translate the difficult poetic language spoken by their regal masters into vernacular Balinese so that everyone in the audience can understand the story.

Like Laurel and Hardy, the clowns are of two types. The first to enter, the *punta*, has the higher position of the two. He struts on stage beaming of self-importance as purveyor of his master's glory. He is followed by his delinquent younger brother, *kartala*, who, in all his attempts to be as pompous as his brother, falters in absurdity. In rowdy witticisms, the two vie against each other: the first incessantly chastising the second for his misbehavior and the second miming the blown-up ego of his superior. This burlesque, sprinkled with off-color jokes, can hold an audience in laughter for hours. Clowns are favorites of the Balinese drama.

A member of I Nyoman Pugra's Topeng troupe plays the faltering clown Kartala.

topeng

Inside the curtain booth, the *topeng* actor places his masks, all neatly covered with white cloth, in their proper order of appearance. After dedicating an offering, he unwraps the first mask, eyeing it for some time as if he were taking into his personality all that is individual about the character reflected in the immobile face. He quickly puts it on and turns. Already his movements are rendered as dance and a transformation is apparent.

The curtain trembles, the *gamelan* builds to a fervent pace of expectation, and dancing feet visible behind the curtain slowly lift and settle to the ground. A stoic-looking man with wide eyes and a questionable smile draws apart the curtain. In swift motions of defiance, he hovers inside the booth, uncertain whether to come out or not. He then begins to march forward, gazing inquisitively, putting a finger to his forehead, taking a bit of his clothing, and, in one delicate gesture, letting it drop from his hand. He resolves to dance, radiating the sound of the *gamelan* in the vibration of his fingertips and pattering feet. After a few moments, he retreats to the curtain and vanishes.

The curtain shakes again. Suddenly, it is pushed aside in the grand gesture of a buxom movie star stepping into the limelight. There before you stands an extremely shy, effeminate young man who draws a limp hand to his mouth and blushes at his abrupt exposure. Languidly he clings to the curtain. Terribly sweet at heart, he cannot bear everyone laughing at him, which of course everyone is. Feeling he should come out for a moment, he coyly moves on stage, swinging to and fro with his hands dangling in the posture of loose noodles. Helplessly, he just stands there looking ridiculous, unable to move except to flutter his eyelashes, while the audience rocks in laughter. Such abusiveness is too much for him. He quickly seeks sanctuary behind the curtain.

Thus was the introductory display of masks for one performance of *Topeng*. Both the stoic and the clown were enacted by one man-the principal *Topeng* actor, who by changing his mask impersonates a series of different characters.

Topeng means something pressed against the face—a mask. *Topeng* masks survive from the 16th century. Today's mask play, commemorating historical exploits of local kings and heroes, was influenced by the traditional *Gambuh* dance. Often called the "chronicle play", *Topeng* stories are drawn from the *babad* literature, genealogical histories of important noble families, set in the villages, kingdoms and temples of Bali.

The medium of a mask play necessarily alters the telling of history. The borderline between fact, legend, and the miraculous has little importance in *Topeng*, in which many episodes include divine intervention or acts of magic. The intent is not to reconstruct exact personalities of the past, but to portray their types: sweet or manly, heroic or simple-minded. The noble characters, usually a king and his family, dance in the refined style. Their stature is so lofty, they do not deign to speak and express themselves only in pantomime. They are accompanied by two clumsy clowns, who wear half-masks which leave their mouths free to talk as interpreters for their dignified masters. Along with the nobility and clowns is always a marvellous display of crude caricatures, whose sole function is decorative and entertaining.

There are many forms of *Topeng*, depending upon the set of masks used and the style of the performers. A popular solo performance is the classical *Topeng Tua*, representing the movements of an old man. In a normal *Topeng* play, three or four actors, usually all men, impersonate all the characters. A full set of *Topeng* masks, numbering from thirty to forty, belongs to the principal *Topeng* actor who is responsible for the series of eccentric personalities that produce the comedy of the play. To watch a good *Topeng* actor is truly inspirational. Through an endless resource of bizarre mannerisms and tones of speech, he manages to concentrate the whole of human folly into one serial panorama of grotesquely masked comics.

At right, the old man of the topeng *dance one of Bali's classic masks.*

cupak

Cupak, a boisterous man possessing a huge belly, is Bali's notorious glutton. Cupak's story, performed as a comic dance, is more like an epic drama: it has a kingdom, a mysterious forest and deep ocean; a villain, princess, witch and hero; disaster, resolution, and great joy.

The issue at stake is the hand of a lost princess. Her father, the King of Kediri, has announced that whoever finds her may become king. Cupak, carrying ambition along with his belly, determines to be her savior. He is accompanied by his handsome younger brother Grantang. A monkey enters to inform the brothers that the princess is being held captive by a witch who likes to eat flesh. Led by their monkey guide, Cupak and Grantang journey deep into the dark forest.

They meet the witch and violence follows. Cupak makes a belated attempt to rescue the princess, but discretion gets the better of his valor and he shimmies up a tree in order to shout directions to his younger brother. In the skirmish, Grantang, the princess and the witch all fall into a well. Grantang defeats the witch, but just as he is about to emerge victorious Cupak yanks the rope, saving the princess but letting his brave brother fall back into the well.

The unscrupulous glutton then goes to Kediri to tell the king how he himself killed the witch and rescued the princess. The joyous king offers Cupak whatever he would like, which, of course, is food: two mounds of rice and one suckling pig! A delightful scene follows when Cupak eats it all himself.

Meanwhile, Grantang manages to climb out of the well on a ladder made from the witch's bones. He seeks Cupak, but his older brother refuses to recognize him and has him thrown into the sea. Grantang is saved by a humble fisherman who nourishes him to health. Before Cupak is about to be crowned king, Grantang challenges him to a fight. He easily defeats the glutton and, much to the relief and joy of the little princess, is given her hand.

Introducing ... Cupak, the unscrupulous glutton! Performed at Bedulu.

arja

A good performance of the folk opera *Arja* is a social event for the entire village. Shortly before midnight, everyone gathers around an open stage to watch a long love story unfold and conclude with the dawn. Sweethearts flirt unnoticed in the back rows. Young men attentively eye their favorite actress, a woman either charmingly beautiful or extremely witty.

Arja developed around 1880 as an all-male dance-drama out of the traditional *Gambuh*; female roles were later added. With more developed plots than other plays, *Arja* stories are mostly drawn from classical romances of the kingdoms of medieval East Java—Kediri, Singasari and Majapahit. The leading characters of the opera are members of the court and move in the highly stylized dance of the nobility, while they sing a low, wailing cadence in poetical Balinese. As usual, their staid countenance is complemented by the unruly knockabouts of the clowns.

Arja plays are packed with sentimentality and melodrama. Like so many great love stories, there is invariably some tragic issue at stake causing the lovers' union to be near impossible —their families prohibit the marriage, a jealous rival makes war on the hero, the princess is captured, the hero falls in love with another woman while under a magic spell. There are always long scenes of heart-rending misery. Fallen from grace, the prince may be misunderstood, beaten, kicked and thrown out of his house. His tragic song reaches the peak of suffering, while angry jeers of the healthy and well-off continue their abuse. After interminable episodes of intrigue and misfortune, the lovers are at last reunited. But by this time, excitement has fled with sorrow, and *Arja* quickly comes to a close.

Although a favorite among the villagers, *Arja* is difficult to follow for those who cannot understand the clowns' translations. Nowadays *Arja* has been replaced as the most popular dance-drama by the drama *gong*, created in the late '60s, in which acting is even more preponderant, music and dance less so.

Late night performance of Arja in Bangli.

the vibrant ritual

These ceremonial dances and dramas directly relate to religious ceremonies by serving as an offering, a prayer, or an exorcism of evil spirits. Presented with the active participation of the *pemangku* (the people's priest and caretaker of the village temple), they are a dramatic form of contact with the spiritual world, and this communicative purpose runs parallel throughout a performance.

As religious dances, they are usually held within or near a temple. *Pendet* may be danced whenever there is occasion to present an offering. In the *Sanghyang*, in which the dancers enter trance prior to dancing, the ceremony begins in the temple and a procession is formed to march to the dance clearing nearby. Because of their association with evil spirits, the *Calon Arang* and Barong plays are generally held near the temple of the dead and the graveyard, which are thought to be favorite meeting places of witches and their disciples.

The masks of the Barong and Rangda also bear a spiritual significance. Because of their relation to the forces of magic and their power to exorcise evil spirits, they are considered *sakti*, magically powerful. Only certain carvers, no matter how exquisite their work, are capable of fashioning a new mask of this kind. A purification ceremony with elaborate offerings is always held to initiate a new Barong or Rangda mask. When they are not being used in the play, the masks are kept in a special pavilion within the temple, where they are displayed amidst heaps of flower and fruit offerings during temple festivals (see page 109). The Rangda mask, capable of emitting dangerous vibrations, is always kept covered by a white cloth as security to contain its magic. The cloth is only removed immediately before the drama, by the Rangda actor as he enters the stage. Some masks considered extremely *sakti* are over a hundred years old, and are followed by large processions whenever they leave the temple.

A young girl from the village of Bona enters trance before performing Sanghyang Dedari, the ceremonial dance of "The Revered Angels".

sanghyang

In the temple, two girls kneel before a brazier of smoking incense. The *pemangku* priest makes offerings to the deity of the temple, requesting protection for the village during the trance ceremony. Behind the girls are seated a group of women who chant the *Sanghyang* song, which asks the celestial nymphs to descend from heaven and dance before the people through the bodies of the girls:

Fragrant is the smoke of incense,
The smoke that coils and coils upward
Toward the home of the three divine ones.
We are cleansed to call the nymphs
To descend from heaven ...
Beautiful in their bodices of gold ...

With eyes closed, the girls rock back and forth above the incense until they fall down fully in trance. The attending women put flowered crowns upon their heads and lift them to the shoulders of male retainers who carry them to the place where they are to dance (see pages 10-11). Set upon the ground between the female choir and male chorus, the little dancers sway listlessly in a dreamy version of the *Legong.* Their movements coincide automatically although their eyes never open during the entire performance. When the chanting ceases, girls fall to the ground in a swoon. They are brought out of trance by the *pemangku,* who prays beside them and blesses them with holy water.

Described here is *Sanghyang Dedari,* a ritual dance where it is believed a divine spirit temporarily descends to a village and reveals itself through the entranced dancers. *Sanghyang* is the title for a deified spirit and means "The Revered One" or "Holiness"; *Dedari* means "Angel".

The girls dancing as "Revered Angels" are always underage, for a virgin child is considered holy. There are other forms of the *Sanghyang* trance dance as well. In *Sanghyang Jaran*, an entranced boy (or priest) dances on a horse, *jaran,* represented by a hobbyhorse. He dances around a bonfire made from coconut husks. If the *Sanghyang* song leads him, he dances through the fire. Mountain villages near Kintamani perform the *Sanghyang Deling,* where puppets dance suspended on a string between two poles manipulated by children.

Sanghyang dances developed from the essential religious function of maintaining the health and well-being of the village. They are performed to exorcise evil spirits that may be infesting the community in the form of sickness or death. The boys and girls selected to be *Sanghyang* dancers are highly regarded by the community and are exempt from certain village responsibilities. The feats they perform while dancing are accepted as a medium of spiritual expression, since the dancer is thought to be possessed by a deity. The *Sanghyang Dedari* dancers have never had any dancing lessons. In normal life, they cannot remember nor repeat the motions they enact while in trance. Nor can a *Sanghyang Jaran* dancer normally walk on fire.

So intriguing to the island visitor, trance, as an elevated state of consciousness, is part of Balinese life and is viewed as quite natural by the people. An entranced person believed communicating with a divine presence is respected as holy and is left free to express himself under a directive influence, usually that of a priest. The Balinese are careful never to let one entranced get out of hand. There are always guardians from the village who stand by during a trance ceremony to exercise control should it be needed.

Although previously there were more variations of the *Sanghyang* than you find today in Bali, this trance dance continues to be influential. The *Kecak* and *Janger* are direct offshoots of the *Sanghyang*, and the notion of a dancer becoming possessed by his role is manifest in a *Topeng* actor "entering" the characters of his masks. That Balinese children from the earliest age instinctively assimilate the movements of the dance is apparent in the *Sanghyang Dedari* girls who, with no dance training, can perform the generalized movements of the *Legong* — in unison!

Riding a hobbyhorse, an entranced Sanghyang Jaran dancer of Bona prances on fire.

barong and rangda

The natural world to the Balinese is one held in balance by two opposing forces: the benign, beneficial to man, and the malign, inimical to humanity. The destructive power of sickness and death is associated with the latter force and the evil influence of black magic. If black magic prevails, a village falls into danger, and extensive purification ceremonies become necessary to restore a proper equilibrium for the health of the community. Dramatic art is also a means of cleansing the village by strengthening its resistance to harmful forces through offerings, prayers and acts of exorcism. Such is the symbolic play of the two remarkable presences—the Barong and Rangda.

Barong, a mystical creature with a long swayback and curved tail, represents the affirmative, the protector of mankind, the glory of the high sun, and the favorable spirits associated with the right and white magic. The widow-witch Rangda is its complement. She rules the evil spirits and witches who haunt the graveyards late at night. Her habitat is darkness and her specialities lie with the practice of black magic, the destructive force of the left. Both figures are of the same earthly substance, possessing strong magical prowess. Somewhere in a mythical past, the Barong was won over to the side of humanity, and, in the play, fights on behalf of the people against the intruding death force of Rangda.

Often the struggle occurs within the framework of a popular story; for instance, an episode from the *Mahabharata*. Yet the essence of the Barong and Rangda play remains the eternal conflict of two cosmic forces symbolized in the two protagonists. Because the play is charged with sorcery and magic charms, extensive offerings are made beforehand to protect the players during the performance.

Usually the Barong enters first, cleverly danced by two men who form the forelegs and hindlegs, the first man manipulating the mask. A Barong's appearance varies with the kind of mask it wears, which may be stylized version of a wild boar, a tiger, a lion, or occasionally an elephant. The most holy mask and the one used in the play is that of the *Barong Keket*, "The Sovereign Lord of the Forest", a beast representing no known animal. In the extreme coordination of the lively Barong, one forgets the fantastic creature isn't acting on its own accord, as it mischievously sidesteps and whirls around, snapping its jaws at the *gamelan*, and swishing flies with its tail.

After the Barong's dance, everyone falls silent. From behind the temple gate appear the splintery fingernails that foreshadow the dreadful vision of Rangda. From her mouth hangs a flaming tongue signifying her consuming fire, and around her neck, a necklace of human entrails falls over her pendulous breasts. Howling a low, gurgling curse she stalks the Barong while waving a white cloth from whence issues her overwhelming magic.

They collide in a desperate clash of witchcraft. In the protection of the Barong lies the preservation of the community, represented by the "kris dancers", men armed with kris daggers. At one point in the fight, when the victory of the Barong is threatened, the kris dancers rush to the Barong's assistance by violently attacking Rangda. The witch's spell reverses their fury back into themselves, and they begin to plunge the blades of their krisses inward against their own bodies. But the Barong, with its own powerful charm, protects the crazed men from inflicting self-harm.

In most plays, this phenomenal self-stabbing is enacted when the kris dancers are in trance. No matter how forcefully they plunge the daggers against their chests, the tips of the blades do not puncture the skin. At the end of the play, the kris dancers are revived by the *pemangku,* who sprinkles them with holy water which has been dipped in the beard of the Barong. (The beard, made of human hair, is considered the most sacred part of the Barong.) A final offering is made to the evil spirits by spilling the blood of a live chicken.

The Barong, a fantastic creature representing no known animal, is a spiritual symbol of virtue and acts in the play as protector of mankind. From Singapadu.

calon arang

It may be the bewitching hour on the first night of the full moon, when long shadows spread like phantoms on the ground, that village crowds gather round a clearing near the temple of the dead to watch the drama of Calon Arang, the widow-witch of Girah. Every Balinese knows the legend of Rangda as Calon Arang, a favorite in local folklore.

Long ago, when Airlangga was king, there lived a widow, Calon Arang, who gave birth to a child in the jungle. The child grew up to be the famed beauty Ratna Menggali. Calon Arang wanted her daughter to marry a prince from Airlangga's palace, but despite her beauty, no prince came. Angered by this, the widow learned the art of black magic and practiced it against the kingdom, causing many people to die. When Airlangga heard of the epidemic in Girah, he consulted his high priest, Mpu Bharadah. The priest sent his son to ask for the hand of Ratna Menggali. Calon Arang was pleased by the offer. The plague subsided, and the couple wed.

Calon Arang had in her possession a *lontar* (palmleaf book) of black magic teachings. Her son-in-law one day found it and gave it to his father, who then deciphered the formulas to the widow's secret powers. When Calon Arang discovered Mpu Bharadah had learned her secrets, she was enraged and declared war upon him. The priest had no choice but to fight and, in a deadly struggle of sorcery, destroyed the widow by casting a spell. Before she died, Calon Arang asked forgiveness. Mpu Bharadah absolved her deeds and showed her the way to heaven.

The story has many variations, and no two Calon Arang plays are exactly the same. Essentially, the play is a drama of magic that serves as a powerful exorcism of evil spirits aligned with the witch-queen Rangda. By dramatizing Calon Arang as Rangda at the height of her magical powers, it is hoped the performance will gain the witch's favor and appease her appetite for destruction.

Rangda is violently attacked by kris dancers during a Calon Arang play at Kerambitan.

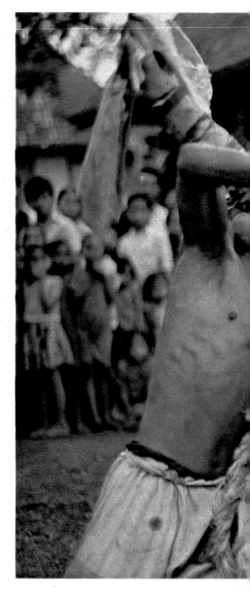

barong landung

On the island of Nusa Penida there lived an incestuous demon, Jero Gede Mecaling, the Tusked Giant. Once he came to Bali, followed by a horde of devils. He landed in South Bali in the form of a Barong and waited there while his henchmen went inland to destroy. The people grew alarmed and consulted a priest who told them they must create another Barong like Jero Gede Mecaling; that alone could scare away the demon. So they made a big Barong and succeeded in frightening the giant back to Nusa. Since then, the Barong has been used for driving away illness and evil spirits.

This folktale gives an origin of the *Barong Landung* ("tall" Barong), a name applying to two giant puppets, a male and a female. Believed to have powers to exorcise harmful influences during times of distress, these puppets are considered sacred and, like the other Barongs, are kept in a special *bale* in the temple. Together they enact a comic opera sung in Balinese, with a story usually taken from history. Jero Gede, the male puppet, is a burly, black giant with puffed cheeks and ruby red lips, who is supposed to resemble the legendary Tusked Giant of Nusa Penida. His consort, Jero Luh, dressed all in white, has a protruding forehead and chin, and a loud, husky voice (that of a man) which she doesn't hesitate to use to its fullest extent.

In many villages of South Bali, the enormous couple is accompanied by puppets with smaller masks, who play the parts of princes and princesses. Often, Jero Gede and Jero Luh act as clowns, rocking about in the most unpredictable fashion to the low resonant drums and shimmering flute. Their remarks can be of the bawdiest humor which go down well with the earthy members of the Balinese audience and draw embarrassed giggles from the shyer ones, especially when the prince and princess show a little affection toward one another.

A Barong Landung play presented before a temple at Sesetan. To the right stands the enormous black puppet Jero Gede who plays the role of a clown and servant to the princess, enacted by the smaller puppet in courtly dress.

277

pendet

Pendet is the presentation of an offering in the form of a ritual dance. Unlike the exhibition dances that demand arduous training, *Pendet* may be danced by everyone: male and female *pemangkus,* women and girls of the village. It is taught simply by imitation and is seldom practiced in the *banjars.* Younger girls follow the movements of the elder women who recognize their responsibility in setting a good example. Proficiency comes with age, and often, it is the grandmothers who possess the most élan of the group. As a religious dance, *Pendet* is usually performed during temple ceremonies. All dancers carry in their right hand a small offering of incense, cakes, water vessels, or flower formations set in palm leaf. With these they dance from shrine to shrine within the temple. *Pendet,* thus may be performed as a serial and continue intermittently throughout the day and late into the night during temple feasts.

In 1968, a huge religious procession in Tabanan produced many versions of *Pendet.* One was danced by a member of the household, who presented the family's offerings in a slow *Pendet* before the approaching wave of thousands of people. In larger villages, a selected group of young girls, bare-shouldered and formally dressed in wraps of gold cloth, carried silver bowls of flowers as they danced a more elaborate *Pendet,* choreographed in interweaving rows and files (see page 103). When the procession settled before a small temple, old women dressed in ordinary clothes began to dance still another form of *Pendet.* They carried no offerings but moved feverishly as if possessed by the music.

Recently, *Pendet* was introduced to open the *Legong.* Here, the young girls are accomplished members of a dance troupe, and their movements are coordinated and exact. Toward the finish of the dance, the girls make praying gestures and throw flowers to the audience—a welcome and blessing to the public.

A Pendet dancer of Sukawati presents an offering.

278

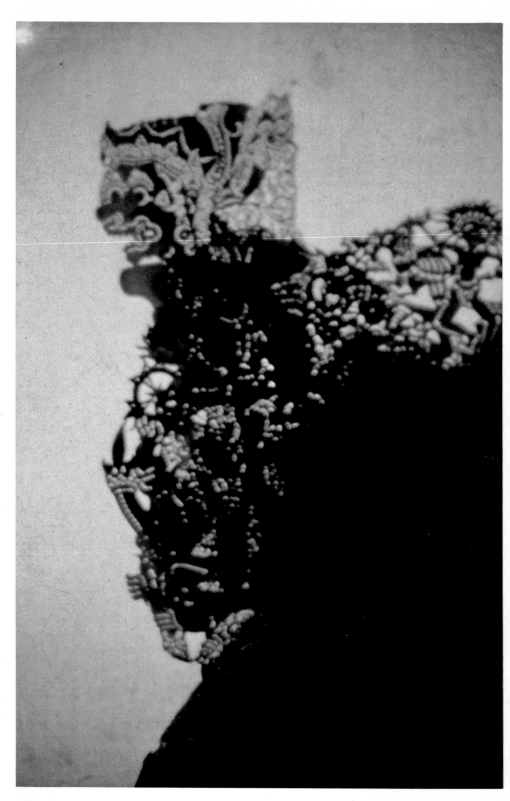

the shadow world

The *Wayang Kulit* shadow play is a dramatic world in itself. Described as "society's teacher", the play is essential to Balinese education since its enormous repertoire of episodes covers all aspects of life, and shows, in silhouettes, the exemplary actions of mankind. *Wayang Kulit* was popular at the court of King Airlangga of East Java in the 11th century, though it is mentioned in a Balinese inscription more than a century before that. Because of the genre's great antiquity and role, too, as a spiritual guide to the people, the shadow play is magically powerful to a high degree and is most frequently performed during religious occasions.

The *dalang*, the mystic storyteller of *Wayang Kulit*, is the true hero of the shadow theatre. His talents are far more encompassing than those of a puppeteer in the Western sense. Aside from directing the drama, he must have exceptional physical endurance to remain seated, continuously chanting for a time span up to six hours. He is both the conductor of the *Gender Wayang* orchestra (the ensemble of four xylophones which accompanies the play) and an experienced musician able to play each instrument he leads. He is a scholar of literature who has spent long years mastering the difficult *Kawi* language. He is an orator with a prodigious memory, enabling him to sing, in dozens of different poetical measures, episodes from the long *Kawi* versions of the *Ramayana* and *Mahabharata*, and occasionally from other stories as well. He is also an ordained priest possessing powers to ward off evil influences, make offerings, protect and bless the people. This role is prominent in the daytime *Wayang* when the screen is replaced by a thread tied between branches of the holy *dapdap* tree. And he is a philosopher who presents a moral truth: good ultimately triumphs and evil meets its ruin.

At night the screen is lit by a primitive oil lamp. (Fire is always used because the flickering effect of the torch enhances the motion of the puppets.) To either side of the *dalang* are his assistants who hand him the puppets during the performance. As is the custom, the *dalang* begins by thrice striking the wooden box containing the puppets, in order to "wake them up". He then hands each puppet to his assistants who put them in their proper place by sticking their supports in the soft trunk of the banana tree at the foot of the screen.

The *Wayang Kulit* stage is a symbolic microcosm representing a spiritual world. The screen denotes the sky; the banana trunk, the earth; the lamp, the sun; the puppets, human beings; and the *dalang*, the deity that conducts them. Set to the right of the *dalang* are puppets representing good characters. Set to his left are the evil antagonists. To indicate the various episodes of the story and to mark the beginning and end, a puppet in the shape of a leaf, which represents the tree of life, is placed in the center of the screen.

When everything is ready and the offerings have been made, the *dalang* begins to chant, accenting the rhythm by tapping a horn he holds between his toes against the wooden box. This tapping also emphasizes the action and conducts the *Gender Wayang* orchestra. One by one, the puppets of the story are introduced; first, an unfocused shade on the screen, then as finely delineated shadows punctured with small holes that define their identity through appearance and dress. Like *Arja*, the characters of courtly stature speak in *Kawi*, while the clowns interpret the story in Balinese. As usual, the clowns provide the most delightful entertainment. There are always four clowns in *Wayang Kulit*. Twalen and his son Merdah are on the side of truth and righteousness. Delem and his sidekick Sangut are allies of the wicked. The clowns flash across the screen, bobbing each other on the head, pushing and biting, and chasing one another. All the while, they exchange crass insults in such rapid succession and with such authenticity that one begins to wonder if the *dalang* isn't a ventriloquist as well.

A shadowy vision of Durga, goddess of death, from a Wayang Kulit play in Mas, left. Bima, mighty hero of Mahabharata, descends in an attack against a demonic giant. (Following Pages)

foods for a feast...

Framed with style and filled with flavor, the Indonesian rice table introduces you to a variety of island specialities. *Nasi goreng* (1), rice fried with shrimps, meats, and spices; and *bakmi goreng* (2), fried noodles, are the basis of a colorful array of side dishes accompanying the Indonesian meal. *Babi guling* (3), roasted suckling pig, and *betutu bebek* (4), duckling broiled in banana leaf, are the favorites at Balinese banquets. Popular dishes of the archipelago are *ikan asem manis* (5), sweet-sour fish; *kare udang* (6), curried shrimp; *babi kecap* (7), pork cooked in sweet soy sauce; lobster (8) (this one caught just off Kuta beach in South Bali); *opor ayam* (9), chicken simmered in coconut milk; *semur sapi* (10), beef stew with tomato; and, of course, *sate* (11), roasted chunks of beef, pork, chicken, or turtle meat served with a delicious, peanut sauce dip (12). Try new tastes with *lontong* (13), rice steamed in banana leaf, and *ketupat* (14), boiled rice wrapped in coconut. No Indonesian meal is complete without a dish of *sambal* (15), hot sauce made from chilli peppers. Finish with a sweet; a tasty rice pudding (16) cooked in palm sugar and coconut milk.

...and fruits for dessert

The customary dessert in Indonesia is an ample serving of fruits. Many of the fruits of Bali come from Karangasem, the easternmost district of the island. Some of the specialties of this region are (1) *salak,* a brown fruit, similar in taste to an apple but with a skin resembling a snake's; (2) dark seeded **grapes;** (3) **mangoes;** (4) **bananas** of numerous sizes and flavors; (5) **tangerines;** (6) **guavas;** and (7) a local variety of grapefruit, *jeruk bali.*

Seen frequently in religious offerings is (8) *sawo,* which looks like a small potato but tastes like a ripe pear. Every family compound grows (9) *blimbing,* a delicious tiny fruit, a favorite of Balinese women. Village markets have (10) the many-seeded pomegranate (11) the furry *rambutan;* (12) *sirsak,* an extremely juicy fruit; (13) jackfruit *(nangka);* (14) **pineapples;** (15) **papayas;** and the famous **mangosteen** — not to mention the infamous smelly (17) **durian.**

TRAVEL TIPS

DESTINATION BALI

GETTING THERE

By Air: Bali's Ngurah Rai International Airport, which straddles the narrow Tuban Isthmus in the south of the island, is served by many daily flights from Jakarta, Yogyakarta, Surabaya and numerous other cities in Indonesia.

International flights operated in conjunction with Garuda, the Indonesian national carrier, arrive directly from Sydney, Melbourne, Darwin, Perth and Port Hedland in Australia, as well as from Singapore, Hong Kong, Tokyo, Amsterdam and Los Angeles. Many other international airlines fly only as far as Jakarta, where you must then transfer to a domestic Garuda flight to reach Bali.

Flights to Bali from Jakarta's Sukarno-Hatta International Airport are frequent throughout the day and you can generally make an on-going connection if you arrive in Jakarta before 6 in the evening. The flight is pleasant and it takes only 90 minutes and includes an incredible view of several volcanos from the starboard windows. (see box for a detailed flight schedule)

By Train: From Jakarta, Bandung or Yogyarkarta, travel first to Surabaya. There are two first-class night trains connecting Jakarta with Surabaya everyday—the *Bima* and the *Mutiara Utara*. Both depart from Jakarta's Kota Station in the late afternoon (at approximately 16:00 and 16:30 hours respectively) and arrive in Surabaya early the next morning. First-class one-way fare is US$33 on the *Bima* (air-conditioned with sleepers) and US$22 on the *Mutiara Utara*.

Carrier	Departure	Arrival	Frequency	Fare
Jakarta-Denpasar				
Garuda	0600	0730	daily	US$83
	1000	1130	daily	
	1400	1530	Sa	
	1445	1615	Th	
	1500	1630	daily	
	1730	1900	daily	
	1930	2100	daily	
Yogyakarta-Denpasar				
Garuda	0820	0935	daily	US$45
	1205	1320	daily	
	1600	1715	daily	
Surabaya-Denpasar				
Garuda	0700	0750	daily	US$34
	1400	1450	daily	
	1730	1820	daily	
Merpati	0610	0720	TuFSu	US$29
	1000	1110	TuWFSaSu	
Bouraq	0600	0705	MTuThFSa	US$29
	0610	0715	MWThSu	

In Surabaya, change over to the *Mutiara Timur*, a non-air-conditioned second and third class train bound for Banyuwangi, a town at Java's easternmost tip. Choose from two daily departures from Surabaya's Gubeng Station, at 11:00 a.m. and 9:30 p.m. Fare is just US$3.50 for first class and US$2.50 for third class. The train travels as far as Banyuwangi (an eight hour journey). In Banyuwangi, a bus picks you up and takes you across the straits to Bali on the ferry, and on to Denpasar (fare: US$1), which is another four hour ride.

By Bus: With improvements in roads and equipment, the *bus malam* ("night bus") from Java to Bali is now much faster and more comfortable than the train. This is the way most Indonesians travel, though in any case your tolerance for cigarette smoke and noise must be high. Do not sit in the very first row, which is dangerous in case of an accident. Be sure to specify AC (air-conditioned) to avoid inhaling the noxious diesel fumes spewed out by trucks and buses enroute. Free meals are included.

One of the best Jakarta-Bali buses is the **Lorena**, which for a little more includes all the deluxe services and a toilet. Contact any travel agent or their office in Jakarta: Jl. K.H. Hasyim Ashari No. 15C-2, Tel: 375662, 358lll, or 353662. You leave Jakarta at 7 a.m. and arrive in Denpasar 24 hours later. Fare is about US$20. The complete route is Bogor-Jakarta-Semarang-Surabaya-Malang-Denpasar.

Non-somnambulists will want to stop-over along the way to Bali. If anywhere, you should stop in Yogya, the cultural center of Java.

The bus from Yogya to Bali (15-16 hours) costs US$9-10. Numerous buses leave daily around 4 p.m. See an agent or try **Jawa Indah Express**, Jl. Mataram 31, Yogyakarta, tel: 2388. This is only one company among many with routes criss-crossing the whole of Java.

Air-conditioned buses from Surabaya to Denpasar (a 10-12 hours trip) cost US$6-8; non-air-condi-

tioned buses are US$5-6. The **Lorena** office in Surabaya is at Jl. Raya Arjuna No. 102; Tel: 42212. Some buses will take you all the way to Kuta or Sanur where you can walk to the nearest hotel room and crash. Otherwise, those with much luggage will need to charter a minibus on arrival, which is readily available. You should refuse to pay over US$3-5 to go to the beach areas from Denpasar.

The same buses leave Denpasar from the **Ubung** terminal for Yogyakarta, Surabaya, or Jakarta at 4 p.m., 7 p.m. or 7 a.m. respectively. Each company has an agent around **Jalan Hasannudin**, and tickets on any bus are available from **Agung Transport**, Jln. Hasanuddin 97, Denpasar, tel: 22663, whose teller is most courteous and speaks some English and Dutch. Airline tickets are also sold here.

Minibuses: Families or small groups can also charter a private minibus ('colt') with driver, between Bali and all cities in Java, at about US$25 per day plus fuel. Going to and from Java this way costs about the same as flying, but you get to see a lot more. Some minibuses are now air-conditioned. Stopovers and side-trips can be planned, and this is the ideal way to see Java.

By Sea: Take a cruise ship if you have the time to spare and want to relax and unwind enroute. Arrangements can be made whereby the traveler with a little less time

can still savor the delights of warm tropical breezes and first-class cuisine, by flying out to Bali and cruising back.

The Grey Line has a cruise schedule to Bali on aboard the *Pearl of Scandinavia*. The two-week cruise starts and ends in Singapore and includes stops in Penang, Belawan, Sibolga, Jakarta, Bali and Surabaya. Sailings are twice a month from December. Passengers can embark and disembark at any port of call with a minimum stay of five nights on board. For the full 14-day cruise, rates range from US$1,960 to US$7,350. Another ship, the Hong Kong-based *Coral Princess*, returns to Singapore in November and it includes cruises to Bali, Jakarta, Penang and Phuket. The Singapore agent for both the ships is Harpers Travel (tel: 250-8118).

Geography: Bali, the first of the Lesser Sunda islands, is one of the smaller islands of Indonesia. Located at 115° East Longitude and 8° South Latitude, it has a land area of 5,632 square km. Bali is part of a volcanic chain that links mainland Southeast Asia with Australia. A mountainous ridge of volcanic origin runs east-west across the island.

The fertile southern slopes of Bali are fanned by rivers, the two major streams being the Pakrisan and the Petanu. These rivers, which run parallel to each other through the district of Gianyar, are regarded as holy. It is on their banks that most of the archaeological remains of

Bali's ancient kingdoms are to be found.

In the west are the almost impenetrable jungles of the province of Jembrana, while in the east is the towering peak of Bali's highest mountain, Gunong Agung, 3,142 meters. Surrounding this mountain is the once-rich regency of Karangasem, which suffered severely when the volcano erupted in 1963 destroying all the ricefields in the area. The work of restoring the land to its former usefulness is now almost complete, though remains of the devastation are still to be seen.

Climate: As Bali is quite close to the Equator, it has an average temperature of 26° and only two seasons—a dry season and a rainy season. The dry season lasts from May to September, with July being the coolest month of the year. The rainy season lasts from October to April, with December being the wettest month of the year.

Clothing: As Bali is divided into beach resorts, temple areas, craft villages and other scenic spots, one must dress to suit the occasion. Tourists coming from the resorts of Sanur, Kuta or the newest spot, Nusa Dua, dress in beachwear during the day. Shorts with halter-tops, or mini-skirts for the ladies, and shorts with sleeveless singlets for the men are usually the "in" thing. Bali has such beautiful beachwear for sale in the shops and boutiques at Sanur and Kuta that there is no necessity to bring too much.

Made-in-Bali outfits of lightweight cotton, in beautiful colors with exotic prints, are not only cool and comfortable to wear but are also extremely fashionable. For air-conditioned hotel-lounges or visits to scenic mountain spots, take along a sweatshirt or sweater. Jacket and tie are seldom worn even on formal occasions. The long-sleeved Indonesian *batik* shirt is customary attire at these times. Sandals are the usual casual footwear and shoes are appropriate for making business calls.

Time Zones: There are three time zones in Indonesia. Bali follows Western Indonesian Standard Time, which is eight hours ahead of Greenwich Mean Time. However, visitors usually find that time soon ceases to be of great importance in Bali and quickly adapt to the rhythm of the sun.

Visa Regulations: Visitors from the other ASEAN countries comprising Singapore, Malaysia, the Philippines, Thailand and Brunei; from all West European countries, Australia, New Zealand, Canada and the United States will be automatically issued a two-month visa. Visitors from all other countries must possess passports valid for at least six months. Tourist, social and business visas can be obtained from any Indonesian embassy or consulate abroad. To obtain a visa submit two application forms with two passport photographs, a return air ticket or other proofs of

onward passage.

An airport tax of Rp 4,000 per person is charged on all international departures from Bali's Ngurah Rai Airport. The charge for domestic flights to other parts of Indonesia is Rp 1,200.

Customs: Regulations prohibit the entry of weapons, narcotics and pornography. Fresh fruits, plants, animals and exposed films may be checked. To prevent rabies, the import of dogs, cats and monkeys is strictly forbidden.

A maximum of two liters of alcohol, 200 cigarettes, 50 cigars or 100 grams of tobacco, and a reasonable amount of perfume may be brought into the country. Photographic equipment, typewriters and radios are admitted provided they are taken out on departure. They must be declared, a customs declaration form must be completed before arrival.

There is no restriction on the import or export of foreign currencies and traveler's checks so long as amounts in excess of US$500 are declared upon arrival. However, the import and export of Indonesian currency exceeding Rp. 50,000 is prohibited. Upon leaving, limited quantities of duty-free purchases and souvenirs are exempt from taxes, but the export of "national treasures" is severely frowned upon.

Currency and Exchange: The *rupiah* is the basic unit, normally abbreviated to 'Rp' followed by the value.

Smaller denominations, Rp 5, 10, 25, 50 and 100, are in the form of coins and larger ones, Rp 100, 500, 1000, 5000, 10000, in the form of notes. The Rp 1000 note carries a portrait of Diponegoro, the famous 19th-century freedom fighter, and a watermark portrait of Gajah Mada.

Values below Rp 50 are rarely seen on the hotel circuit, but are common in the markets and street stalls.

Change or *wang kembali* for high-value notes is often unavailable in smaller shops and stalls, and you may be offered tiny goods-in-kind in lieu of cash. It's a good idea to carry a handful of coins (useful for tipping).

The exchange rate for a US$1 was Rp 995 in early 1984. It is best not to exchange large sums of money if you plan to be in Indonesia for more than a month.

Changing Money: Foreign currency, in bank notes and traveler's checks is best exchanged at major banks or leading hotels (though hotel rates are slightly less favorable than bank rates). There is also a limited number of registered money changers, but avoid unauthorized changers who operate illegally. Always be sure to keep your exchange receipts. Your *rupiah* may be converted to foreign currencies when you are leaving the country.

Traveler's checks are a mixed blessing. Major hotels, banks and some shops will accept them, but even in the cities it can take a long time to collect your money

(in smaller towns, it is impossible). The US dollar is recommended for traveler's checks. Credit cards are usable if you stay in the big hotels. International airline offices, a few big city restaurants and art shops will accept them, but they are useless elsewhere.

B a n k s / M o n e y Changers: Many money changers now operate out of small shops in Sanur and Kuta. Their rates are not very much different from official bank rates. An easy way to tell is by comparing the difference between buying and selling rates, which should be no more than two percent apart. Check the official rates in the newspaper to be sure you are not being cheated. Or else make the trip into Denpasar to one of the following banks.

Bank Indonesia
Jl. Supratman
Denpasar

Bank Rakyat Indonesia
Jl. Gajah Mada
Denpasar

Bank Negara Indonesia
1946, Jl. Gajah Mada
Denpasar

Bank Bumi Daya
Jl. Veteran
Denpasar

Bank Dagang Negara
Jl. Gajah Mada
Denpasar

Bank Export Import Indonesia
Jl. Gajah Mada
Denpasar

Bank Pembangunan
Jl. Surapati
Denpasar

Tipping: At most of the larger hotels a government tax and a service charge of 10 percent each are added to the bill. Although tipping is not traditional, in restaurants where a service charge is not added, a five or 10 percent tip would be appropriate, depending on the establishment and quality of service.

An airport or hotel porter expects Rp 500 to Rp 1000 depending on the size and weight of the bag. Tipping taxi drivers Rp 200 or leaving the change is appreciated but not compulsory. When traveling by taxi, always carry small change with you, as taxi drivers are often short of change.

Weights and Measures: Indonesia employs the metric system of measurement. One kilometer is equal to 0.6214 miles; one meter is equal to 3.2808 feet; one kilogram is equal to 2.2046 pounds; one liter is equal to 0.2642 U.S. gallons or 0.22 imperial gallons.

Business Hours: Indonesians like to get their work done in the morning to avoid working in the heat of the day, so if you need to visit a government office, try to get there between 8 and 11:30 a.m. This also applies to banks and private businesses. Government offices close early on Fridays and Saturdays. Generally, offices are open from 8 a.m.- 2 p.m. Mon. to Thurs., 8 - noon Fri., and 8 a.m. - 1 p.m. Sat.

Places of Worship: There are a number of churches and mosques in Bali. All of them are in Denpasar, except for the Al-Hissan Mosque at the Hotel Bali Beach.

Catholic—Jln. Kepundung
Protestant Maranatha—Jln. Surapati
Seventh Day Adventist—Jln. Surapati
Pentecostal—Jln. Karna
Evangelical—Jln. Melati
Protestant Bali—Jln. Debas
Raya Mosque—Jln. Hasanuddin
An-nuur Mosque—Jln. Diponegoro
Al-Hissan—Hotel Bali Beach

Ask your local travel agent for further information. They can furnish transportation and information regarding times of services.

Security & Crime: Be warned! Bali, once blissfully free of theft and petty crime, is now something of a haven for petty thieves. Carelessness on the part of foreign visitors has a lot to do with this. Points to remember:

Don't leave valuables unattended. Lock up your room securely and make sure that your windows are locked at night. Straight off the plane and the first night in a new losmen are times to be extra careful.

Be extra careful of purses, camera bags and wallets at crowded festivals or in the back of a bemo. It's usually when you are hot and flustered that the pickpocket strikes.

Don't lend money unless you don't mind not getting it back.

Sadly, it has recently become unsafe to walk alone along Kuta Beach at night, and along the Kuta-Legian road. Sanur Beach is still relatively quiet and its hotels are patrolled.

All thefts should be reported immediately to the police, even though there is little chance of recovering stolen belongings. This applies especially to **passports** and other official documents. Without a police report, you will have difficulty obtaining new documents and leaving the country.

All narcotics are illegal in Indonesia. The use, sale or purchase of narcotics results in long prison terms and/or huge fines.

A few hints: To the Balinese, the world is their living-room and its travelers their guests. Decades of tourism have somewhat dimmed this positive attitude, but the Balinese remain remarkably friendly and courteous. They also remain staunchly conservative, for tradition is the backbone of their highly civilized culture. Please do your best to respect their traditions and attitudes.

1. Settle all prices in advance, otherwise you must pay the price demanded for goods and services provided. Don't ask the price or make an offer unless you intend to buy.
2. Dress up rather than down. You are afforded special guest status as a foreigner, so don't abuse it. Old faded or torn clothes, bared thighs and excessively 'native' dress are considered bad form.
3. Keep all valuables out of sight and preferably locked up. The Balinese have a strong sense of pride and consider temptation an affront, suspicion an insult.
4. Wear a sash whenever entering a temple, and expect to pay a token entrance fee to the custodian.

Etiquette: The Balinese are a very polite people and smiles are an island-wide characteristic. Shaking hands on introduction is the usual thing for both men and women. The use of the left hand to give or to receive something, however, is considered taboo and crooking a finger to call someone is considered impolite.

Wear a shirt when not on the beach and don't walk around town in your swim suit. What may seem like a quaint beachside alley may be the courtyard of a house or holy temple. Nude bathing is illegal and impolite. Before entering a private house, leave your shoes outside on the steps. Shoes and a collared shirt must be worn when visiting a government office.

It is compulsory to wear a waist sash when visiting temples. Any material will do, although the Balinese admire colorful brocades or woven cloths. By an ancient law, menstruating women are asked not to enter temples. This is based on a general sanction against blood on holy soil.

Begging is not a tradition

THE PROBLEMS OF A

HEAVY TRAFFIC.

You'll come across massive Thai jumbos at work and play in their natural habitat. In Thailand, elephants are part of everyday rural life.

FALLING MASONRY.

A visit to the ruined cities of Sukhothai o Ayutthaya will remind you of the country's lon; and event-filled history.

EYESTRAIN.

A problem everyone seems to enjoy. The beauty of our exotic land is only matched by the beauty and gentle nature of the Thai people.

GETTING LOST.

From the palm-fringed beaches of Phuket to th highlands of Chiang Mai there are numerou; places to get away from it all.

OLIDAY IN THAILAND.

GETTING TRAPPED.

In bunkers mostly. The fairways, superb club houses and helpful caddies make a golf trap for players of all standards.

HIGH DRAMA.

A performance of the 'Khon' drama, with gods and demons acting out a never-ending battle between good and evil, should not be missed.

EXCESS BAGGAGE.

Thai food is so delicious you'll want to eat more and more of it. Of course, on Thai there's no charge for extra kilos in this area.

MISSING YOUR FLIGHT.

In Thailand, this isn't a problem. Talk to us or your local travel agent about Royal Orchid Holidays in Thailand.

Thai
We reach for the sky.

Discover
the true tropical
BEAUTY

Only Hotel Putri Bali offers all
of the legendary beauty of Bali,
and the standards
of Indonesia's
finest hotel
chain.

Nusa Dua, Bali, Indonesia P.O. Box 1 Nusa Dua
Telephone: 0361- 71020, 71420, Telex 35247 HPB
DPR-IA, Cable NUSABALI, Fax 0361-71139

in Bali. If you freely hand out money you will only be encouraging people to ask again. The only exception is to make a small contribution at the entrance to a temple. This is used to offset the cost of maintenance, so give what you can afford.

At temple festivals or dance performances, the Balinese are relaxed around a camera, providing the photographer does not interfere by standing directly in front of the priest or the kneeling congregation. According to custom, one's head should not be higher than that of a priest or village headman. Therefore, it is rude to climb on the walls of a temple. Likewise, do not remain standing when the people kneel to pray. Move to the back and wait quietly until the blessing has been completed. The same pertains to a procession. If local bystanders kneel in veneration, one should move to the side.

Government and Economy: Bali is one of the 27 provincial regions of the Republic of Indonesia, each of which is ruled by a governor. The Governor of Bali lives in Denpasar. The province is divided into eight *kabupaten* (counties or regencies) each headed by a *bupeti* (regent) under the Governor. There is further sub-division into 564 *kecamatan* (subdistricts) under a *camat*. There are 564 incorporated villages each ruled by a *perbekel* or village head. There are another 1,456 *desa adat* (common villages) sub-divided into 3,397 *banjars* (village wards), each ad-

ministered by a *klian* (village head).

The basic ideology of Indonesia is set out in the five fundamental principles known as "Pancasila," an all-encompassing belief in One Just and Civilized Supreme God, Humanity, Unity of Indonesia, Democracy and Social Justice. Understanding how these five principles of the national philosophy are implemented will help in understanding the complex makeup of the Indonesian society.

Readopted two decades ago, the 1945 constitution vests the highest authority in the People's Consultative Assembly and provides for three independent Supreme State Organs and one Parliament body. According to the constitution, elections for the two highest legislative bodies, the Parliament and the People's Consultative Assembly, are to take place every five years although since 1945 general elections for these offices have been held only four times.

As the Head of State, the President has the right to declare war, make peace, grant pardon, make statutes and conclude treaties with other states but action on all these matters must be ratified by the House, and the President must remain responsible to the assembly. Suharto was voted into his fourth six-year term in March 1983.

Agriculture is the main economic activity of the people in Bali, who grow rice for personal consumption. Their main sources of income are coconuts (for

copra) and the sale of cattle and pigs. Coffee and tobacco are also sold to Chinese middle-men for export. With the development of the tourist industry, some craftsmen derive income from the sale of sculptures, paintings, silverwork, weavings and the like.

Consulates

Australia
Jl. Raya Sanur 146
Tanjung Bungkuk
Denpasar
tel: 25997-8

Japan
Jl. Tanjung Bungkuk 124
Denpasar
tel: 25611

Sweden
Hotel Segara Village
Jl. Segara
Sanur
tel: 8407, 8231

United States
Jl. Segara
Sanur
tel: 8478

Airline Offices

Bouraq
Jl. Kamboja 45
Denpasar
tel: 22252

Cathay Pacific
Hotel Bali Beach
Sanur
tel: 8576

Garuda
Jl. Melati 61
Denpasar
tel: 22028, 24235

Merpati
Jl. Melati
Denpasar
tel: 22159, 24457

Qantas
Hotel Bali Beach
Sanur
tel: 8511

Sempati
Hotel Bali Beach
Sanur
tel: 8511

Thai International
Hotel Bali Beach
Sanur
tel: 8511

Health Precaution: International health certificates of vaccination against smallpox, cholera and yellow fever are required only from travelers coming from infected areas. Typhoid and paratyphoid vaccinations are optional but advisable.

If you intend to stay in Bali for some time, gammaglobulin injections are recommended; they won't stop hepatitis, but many physicians believe that the risk of infection is greatly reduced. Diarrhea may be a problem: it can be prevented by a daily dose of Doxycycline; an antibiotic used to prevent 'traveler diarrhea.' Obtain this from your doctor at home. At the first signs of stomach trouble, try a diet of hot tea and a little patience. Stomach reactions are often a reaction to a change in food and environment. Proprietary brands of tablets such as Lomotil and Imodium are invaluable cures. A supply of malaria-suppressant tablets is also highly recom-

mended. Make sure the suppressants are effective against all the strains of malaria. It was recently discovered that a malaria strain in Bali is resistant to the usual malarial prophylactic (chloroquine). Consult your physician.

Imported pharmaceuticals are expensive. So you may wish to bring some of these along with you: a tube of antihistamine cream for relief of itches (especially mosquito bites), an ointment for fungoid skin infections, a good prickly-heat powder and soap, a cold-suppressant such as Coricidin for the relief of colds and sniffles caused by abrupt changes of temperature, some form of insect repellent, and your favorite brand of aspirin.

All water, including well water, municipal water and water used for making ice, MUST be made safe before consumption. Bringing water to a rolling boil for 10 minutes is an effective method. Iodine (Globoline) and chlorine (Halazone) may also be used to make water potable. All fruits should be carefully peeled before eaten and no raw vegetables should be eaten. By practising good hygiene and good preventive medicine you can be reasonably assured of a healthful tour. Watch what and where you eat, and wash your hands.

Last but not least, protect yourself against the sun. As in all tropical areas, where the sun can be quite intense around noon, it is advisable to wear a hat; straw hats, Balinese-style, are sold everywhere.

Medical Facilities: In this climate a mosquito bite can become a major infection. Any cut or abrasion must be treated immediately. **Betadine**, a powerful non-stinging, non-staining, broad-spectrum antiseptic, is available in solution or ointment at any drugstore.

In event of emergency, you can call an Ambulance by dialing 118. The major hotels in Sanur, such as the Hotel Bali Beach, the Sanur Beach and the Bali Hyatt all have resident doctors and well-stocked clinics. Every village in Bali now has a small government clinic called **Puskesmas**, but for major problems visit one of the hotel clinics or one of the public hospitals in Denpasar, *Rumah Sakit* means hospital.

Rumah Sakit Umum Sanglah
(Public Hospital)
Jl. Diponegoro,
Denpasar
tel: 24141-2
(24 hours)

Rumah Sakit Wangaya
(Public Hospital)
Jl. Kartini, Denpasar
tel: 22142

Rumah Sakit Angatan Darat
(Army Hospital)
Jl. Sudirman, Denpasar
tel: 26521 (24 hours)

Palang Merah Indonesia Badung
(Red Cross)
Jl. Imam Bonjol,
Denpasar
tel: 26305

The following specialists in Denpasar all have open clinics from 4-6 p.m. daily. No appointment is needed.

Dr. Moerdowo
(internist)
Jl. Melati
Denpasar

Dr. Sudaryat
(pediatrician)
Jl, Surapati
Denpasar

Dr. Hamid
(pediatrician)
Jl. Diponegoro
Denpasar

Dr. I.B. Manuaba
(gynecologist)
Jl. Cokroaminoto
Denpasar

Dr. Suwanda Duarsa
(gynecologist)
Jl. Veteran
Denpasar

Dr. Ketut Budha
(surgeon)
Jl. Hasanuddin
Denpasar

Dr. Otong Wirawan
(surgeon)
Jl. Bali
Denpasar

Dr. Indra Guizot
(dentist)
Jl. Patimura lC
Denpasar

Dr. Panteri
(psychiatrist)
Jl. Nakula
Denpasar

Dr. I. Gusti Nyoman Tista
(ophthalmologist)

Jl. Nias
Denpasar

Dr. Wirya Masna
(ear, nose & throat)
Jl. Diponegoro
Denpasar

Prof. Dr. I. Gusti Gede Ngurah
(neurologist)
Jl. Yos Sudarso
Denpasar

Pharmacies (Apotik): Most pharmacies are open daily 8 a.m.-6 p.m. Late at night on Sundays and holidays there is a rotation system in Denpasar. Check the *Bali Post* or ask your hotel to call:

Kimia Farma
Jl, Diponegoro 43
Denpasar
tel: 22376 , 22640

Kosala Farma
Jl. Kartina 106
Denpasar
tel: 22301

Ria Farma
Jl. Veteran 43
Denpasar
tel: 22635, 24154

Bali Farma
Jl. Melati 9
Denpasar
tel: 22878, 22918

Dirga Yusa
Jl. Surapati 23
Denpasar
tel: 22267

Sadha Karya
Jl. Gajah Mada 85
Denpasar
tel: 24009

In **Kuta**, there is an apotik on the main road leading to the airport.

In **Sanur**, try **Farmasari**, Jl. Banjar Taman.

Smaller 'drugstores' are also found on many streets, selling film, toiletries, etc.

COMMUNICA-TIONS

Postal Services: Major hotels handle mail service and telegrams, or you may post letters personally at the Central Post Office, located at the new city administrative center at Jalan Puputan Raya (on the Sanur-Denpasar road). The Post Office is open Monday to Thursday from 8 a.m. to 2 p.m. Friday from 8 a.m. to noon, and Saturday from 8 a.m. to 1 p.m. Poste restante facilities are available at the Central Post Office and the Kuta and Ubud post offices.

Make sure you can see your stamps (especially high values) being "franked" before your letter disappears from sight. Small packets and parcels have a habit of going astray, so it's better to post your souvenirs and treasures in reasonable bulk.

An aerogram to the United States or any European country costs Rp 350; to Asia, Rp 215. Letters by air mail to the U.S.A. and Europe cost Rp 450; and to Asia Rp 300.

Telephone, Telex, Etc.: Telegrams, telex and international telephone call facilities are available at the main international hotels and from the Telecommuni-

297

cations Office (Kantor Telpon), behind the former General Post Office at Jalan Kaliasam in Denpasar.

News Media

Newspaper and Magazines: Three English-language papers are published in Jakarta, the *Indonesian Times*, the *Jakarta Post* and the *Indonesian Observer*. Large hotels and big bookstore chains are the best source of international newspapers and magazines. Prices are steep, but weeklies like *Time* and *Newsweek* are easy to find.

The deluge of Indonesian magazines includes many devoted to the private lives of film stars and pop-culture heroes. But the weekly Indonesian language news magazine *Tempo* (shamelessly similar in format to *Time*) is excellent value as a summary of what has happened, why, and to whom, in the previous week around the world and at home in Indonesia.

Radio and Television: Radio is a vital force in the dissemination of *Bahasa Indonesia* and a vehicle for aural aspects of Indonesia's diverse cultural traditions. Besides the government radio (RRI), there is also a smaller commercial station in Denpasar. The government television station (TVRI) has an English News program at 6 p.m.

IN AND AROUND BALI

GETTING AROUND

Kuta and **Sanur** are your fun spots: swimming, sunbathing, surfing, sailing, shopping, dancing, dining, delighting. Catering for holiday hedonism, the two beach strips are packed with cafes, boutiques, antique shops, discotheques, restaurants and watering holes. Whilst English, French, Italian and Japanese are widely understood, the lingua franca is Australian—the infectious vitality of the Australoid sub-species has taken Bali by storm. See Australia, come to Bali!

Legian is a quieter extension of Kuta, offering a seaside get-away with less hype and hustle, fewer tourist traps, and more elbow room. There are boutiques, antique and cassette shops here as well, but the pace is slower and more peaceful. Here you can find empty stretches of virgin beachfront, and quiet country roads alongside rice padi fields.

Nusa Dua is a new hotel development area on the southern Bukit Peninsula, quite removed from the rest of Bali (though via the new highway it's only 20 minutes from the airport by car, an hour from Ubud). Nusa Dua's spacious white beaches and expansive green lawns are as yet blissfully free of garish billboards, souvenir shops, honky tonks, tour touts and hardsell soft-drink vendors. Nothing here to distract you from the sun, the sand, the sea and the luxury hotel environment.

Denpasar is the capital of Bali, a bustling boom town that most tourists do their best to avoid, except as a place in which to shop, change money, buy air tickets, catch a bus to Java, mail a package, etc. It does have good restaurants, however, and you should stop in at the **Bali Museum**, located on the town square, as well as the **Abian Kapas Art Centre**.

Spice your days in the sun with excursions to temples and to the mountains, or with a sail across the bay to **Nusa Penida**, **Nusa Lembongan** or **Pulau Serangan** ("Turtle Island"), or even with an evening spent at Denpasar's night market for a meal of *sate* and a film. The new Nusa Dua—Kuta—Sanur highway (known as the "by-pass") makes inter-scene travel easy. It's fun to have dinner and see a show on the other side. But don't get trapped in the fast lane. Remember—Bali is out there waiting for you

The arts of holiday

BALIHAI BEACH HOTEL

The Balihai Beach Hotel will have 204 deluxe Rooms and Cottages and be classified as an International first class resort. The location is right on the beach of Kuta. The design of the hotel & cottages will reflect the Balinese style of architecture & maintain the traditional aspects of Balinese culture.

Hotel Address:
Jl. Wana Segara, 33
Kuta Beach - Bali - Indonesia.

nformation & Reservation Office : Jl. Hayam Wuruk 166, Denpasar Bali - Indonesia.
?.O. Box 381 Denpasar Phone : (0361) 37542, 52527, 53035 Telex : 35139 BDB IA Fax : 62 361 88002

One of our most beautiful resort hotels over-
oks the spectacular inland scenery of the
ʋung River Valley at Kedewatan, and is only 5
ɪnutes from the charming village of Ubud
th its artists' studios and choice of interes-
ɪg restaurants.
Each spacious room has its own balcony to
ke advantage of the view.
Our Restaurant serves Western and Indonesi-
ɪ cuisine.
A fine Swimming Pool completes the picture.
ʋr reservation please contact :

> PURI BUNGA VILLAGE
> Kedewatan - Ubud - Bali - Indonesia,
> P.O. Box 381 Phone : (0361) 37542
> Telex : 35139 BDB IA Cable : BDB
> Fax   : 62 361 88002

PURI BUNGA VILLAGE

ON THE MOVE

TRANSPORT

On the road: *"Turis, hallo ris!"* On the road children scream in friendly unison as you pass. In the forecourt of a house a bright-eyed toddler peers from behind the protective folds of his mother's *sarong* as she plaits palm leaves into offerings. A cheeky schoolboy dances an impromptu and uncertain *baris* on the earthern step leading into a house. Bicycles pass piled high with bright pink prawn crackers in plastic bags. A gaggle of ducks waddles to the rice fields for feeding, shepherded by a young girl wielding a long switch. Women file down a village lane, their heads piled high with multi-colored rice cakes for a temple ceremony. A peek through a gateway reveals a mossy courtyard framing an intricate wooden facade and root-wrapped stone statues that glisten in the sun. The din of practicing *gamelan* instruments assaults the ears, as beyond massive temple walls, a panorama of terraced green ricefields and the blue-grey outline of Mount Agung's majestic cone unfolds. The beauty quotient's is extraordinarily high—the experience of it exhilarating. You are on the road in Bali.

Though one can circumnavigate Bali in a day, some claim that you will see more by standing still, allowing the island to come to you. While in principle this is true, not all of us have the time to wait, and the opportunity for serendipitous encounters certainly increases when you are on the move, provided only that you keep your eyes and ears open and your schedule flexible. Don't try to go everywhere. The "real" Bali is all around you, not in some remote village on the other side of the island.

Balinese roads are a parade ground, used for escorting village deities to the sea, for funeral cremation processions, for filing to the local temple in one's 'Sunday best,' or the performances of a trans-island *barong* dance. They are also increasingly crowded. The increase in traffic has been dramatic over the past two decades.

Half-day outings are best, leaving the other half of the day to relax on the beach, stroll through a nearby village or sit in a café and enjoy the view and the company. And if you have the time and energy, plan a two or three day tour of the island—to Ubud, to the mountains, or the north or east coast—stopping over along the way in one of the hotels or losmens that abound at key 'havens' around the island.

In the end, the best way to see Bali is of course by foot. Away from the heavily traveled main roads, along quiet paths and village lanes, the island takes on an entirely different complexion.

Taxis: There is a taxi service from the airport, with fixed one-way fares ranging from US$3 (to nearby Kuta Beach) up to US$10 (to Ubud). To Sanur, Denpasar and Nusa Dua costs US$5-7. Pay the cashier at the desk and receive a coupon that is to be surrendered to your driver. Refuse offers from touts and informal "guides" loitering in the airport.

Note that rather than taking a taxi from the airport, you can just walk out to the road and catch a local bemo to Kuta (Rp 100) or Denpasar (Rp 250).

Taxis and minibuses are for hire at every hotel (and in front of the Hyatt), just with a driver, or with an English-speaking driver/guide. Rates are US$2-4 per hour (two hours minimum) and US$30-40 per day, a bit more for air-conditioning, newer cars and longer journeys. Often there is little difference (other than the price) between simply renting a car with a driver for the day (many drivers speak good English) and going on a professionally guided tour (see below), though some drivers are much more knowledgeable than others. Excursions to various points around the island can be arranged at fixed rates.

Bemo: Mini-buses may be chartered for US$20-25 a day, though generally without air-conditioning or a competent English-speaking guide. Without a guide, however, shopping prices are lower, because shopkeepers are obliged to pay a commission to whomever brings you there. The following is a sampling of rates for simple one-way bemo drop-offs (you will have to negotiate a bit more for round-trip excursions with stops):

Sanur—Denpasar US$3
Sanur—Kintamani US$18
Sanur—Kuta US$4
Sanur—Besakih US$20
Sanur—Ubud US$5
Sanur—Uluwatu US$12

Rental Cars: The best way to get around the island independently is to rent a self-drive car, available in Kuta, Sanur or Denpasar. You must have a valid International Driving Permit. The most commonly rented vehicles are old beat-up VW Safari convertibles (US$25 per day, US$150 per week), although newer (sometimes air-conditioned) Suzuki Jimny's and Toyota Landcruisers are also available for a bit more money (US$30-40 per day). You buy the gas. Buy the extra insurance also (US$5 per day). Book a car through your hotel or from any of the companies listed below. They will deliver the car and pick it up when you are done with it. Test-drive the car before paying in advance.

Bali Wisata
Jl. Imam Bonjol, Kuta
tel: 24479

Bali Car Rental
Jl. By-pass Ngurah Rai
Sanur
tel: 8550,8359

Utama Motors
Jl. Imam Bonjol
Kuta
tel: 22073

Motorcycles: Each year several tourists are killed in motorbike accidents, and many more end up spending their holiday in the hospital. If you do decide to rent a bike, drive slowly and very defensively. This is a very convenient and inexpensive way to get around the island, though be aware that the roads are crowded and the traffic is heavy, so your chances of having an accident are uncomfortably high. Helmets are required by law.

The cost of hiring a motorbike in Bali is quite negotiable, and varies according to the condition of the machine and time of year. The usual price for a 100 cc or 125 cc machine is between US$3 to US$6 per day, or US$20 to US$30 per week (paid in advance). You buy the gas. Any hotel can easily arrange a rental for you, and it is also a good idea to buy insurance, so that you are not responsible for damages in case of an accident. Be sure to test-drive it and see that everything is in good working order before you pay.

You must have an International Driving Permit valid for motorcycles, or else spend a morning at the Denpasar Police Office to get a "Temporary Permit" (valid for one month on Bali only). This entails passing a driving test and paying an administrative fee of about US$4. Bring along your passport and three photos,

plus your own auto driving license from your home country (or a doctor's certificate indicating that you are fit to drive a vehicle). Normally the person who rents you the bike will accompany you to the police station. Getting an International Driving Permit in your own country will save you this hassle.

By Bus or Train To Java

Artha Mas
Jl. Diponegoro 131 A
Denpasar
tel: 25042

Bali Indah
Jl. Hasannudin 78, Denpasar
tel: 22232

Cakrawala
Jl. Hasannudin 4, Denpasar
tel: 24157

Gita Bali
Stasiun Suci, Denpasar
tel: 22349

Jaya Katwang
Jl. Teleng 2, Singaraja

Nilam Indah
Jl. Diponegoro 45, Denpasar
tel: 25538

Puspasari
Jl. Hasannudin 42, Denpasar
tel: 25043

Panca Karya
Jl. Ngurah Rai 23, Singaraja

Ratnasari
Jl. Hasannudin, Denpasar
tel: 22012

Bali Express
Jl. Imam Bonjol 39
Denpasar
tel: 24180

Maju Kembang
Jl. Diponegoro , Denpasar

Jawa Indah
Jl. Hasannudin 69, Denpasar
tel: 22426

Pemudi Express
Jl. Hayam Wuruk 2
Denpasar
tel: 22422

Anugerah
Jl. Diponegoro, Denpasar
tel: 22743

Malang Indah
Jl. Diponegoro 40, Denpasar
tel: 23955

Surya Indra
Jl. Hasannudin 81, Denpasar
tel: 23620

Damri
Jl. Diponegoro 168
Denpasar
tel: 24038

Mutiara PJKA
(Train Office)
Jl. Diponegoro 166
Denpasar
tel: 22336

Public Bemos/Buses: The local system of pick-ups, mini-buses (known as "bemos") and intra-island buses is convenient and inexpensive. You can get from one end of the island to the other for less than US$2. In addition, almost any bemo on the road in Bali may be chartered by the trip or by the day, with the driver, just by telling him where you want to go and then agreeing on a price. Most drivers are willing to go anywhere for about US$25-30 a day (which is what they normally make hauling passengers). Some will ask you to pay extra for the gas if the distances involved are great.

There are four bus/bemo terminals in Denpasar, serving points to the south, west, north and east of the city respectively. Often you will arrive in the city at one end and then have to make your way to another in order to catch a bus/bemo heading out of the city in the direction you are traveling. This is easily accomplished in a three-wheeled inner-city bemo (fare: Rp 75). The following is a list of estimated bemo fares from Denpasar to various points on the island, listed under the terminal where they leave from:

Tegal Terminal
(southwest of Denpasar)

Kuta	Rp 200
Sanur	Rp 250
Airport/Tuban	Rp 250
Nusa Dua	Rp 400

Ubung Terminal
(northwest of Denpasar)

Gilimanuk	Rp 1650
Singaraja	Rp 1050
Sangeh	Rp 350
Mengwi	Rp 200
Tabanan	Rp 300
Tanah Lot	Rp 300

Kereneng Terminal
(east of Denpasar)

Sanur	Rp 250
Ubud	Rp 300
Kintamani	Rp 1200
Klungkung	Rp 600
Bangli	Rp 600
Amlapura	Rp 1200

Suci Terminal
(center of Denpasar)

Benoa Harbour	Rp 200

Inter-City Buses leave for Java from Ubung Terminal, and the bus companies have their offices in town on Jl. Hasannudin near the old Suci Terminal.

FOOD DIGEST

WHAT TO EAT

Centuries of contact with other great civilizations have left their mark on the wonderfully varied cuisine of Indonesia, particularly in Bali. Indian and Arab traders brought not only merchandise, Hinduism and Islam, but also a variety of new spices such as ginger, cardamom and tumeric. Later the Chinese and (to a lesser extent) the Dutch added their own distinctive touch to the cooking pot. The result is a happy blend of the best of each culinary tradition.

Spices abound in Balinese cooking, and are usually partnered by coconut milk (the juice is made by squeezing the grated flesh of the coconut) which adds a rich flavor and creamy texture to dishes containing intriguing tropical vegetables, poultry, meat and fish. Happily for the unaccustomed foreign palate, Balinese cooks are light-handed with both spices and chilies. They are fond of using sugar as well as fragrant roots and leaves, and the final result is food which tastes both subtle and sophisticated.

The basis of a Balinese meal is rice. Each person helps himself to a helping of steaming white rice and then to a little of the three or four dishes of vegetables or meat (known as *lauk*) which are placed in the center of the table for all to share. Balinese do not swamp their plates with food on the first round, but help themselves to a little more of their fancy as the meal progresses. A side dish or *sambal*, made with red-hot chilies ground with dried shrimp paste and other seasonings such as lime juice, should be approached with caution (if you ever scorch your mouth or throat with chilies don't rush for the nearest glass of water to quench it; water aggravates the problem, and cold beer or other fizzy drinks are worse: the quickest relief comes from plain boiled rice, bread, cucumber or a banana). Common side dishes are *tempe*, a protein-rich savory cake of fermented soya-beans, and small crisp cookies (*rempeyek*) made of peanuts. Both are delicious.

The Dutch word *rijsttafel* (rice table) is sometimes associated with Indonesian food. The name was originally given to gargantuan banquets of rice and countless dishes of vegetables and meats accompanied by sa-vory offerings such as *krupuk* (fried prawn or fish crisps), *acar* (cucumber pickles), sliced banana, peanuts, chilies and anything else capable of adding fragrance and flavor to the whole mountainous spread. Full-scale extravaganzas are seldom witnessed (let alone eaten!) these days, although a few hotels make a modest attempt at imitation, and all of the individual dishes of the old *rijsttafel* can still be found and enjoyed.

National favorites include *gado-gado*, a lightly cooked vegetable salad which includes beansprouts, cabbage and potatoes covered with a rich peanut sauce. *Sate*, sometimes regarded as Indonesia's national dish, is a tempting assortment of meat, chicken or seafood grilled on skewers over a charcoal fire and served with a spicy sauce. A tasty, substantial soup known as *soto* is found everywhere.

Chinese influenced noodle dishes such as *mie goreng* (fried wheat-flour noodles) and *bakmi* (rice-flour noodles, either fried or in soup) are also common. *Capcaai* (previously *tjap tjai*) is very popular and tastes much better than its Western name "chop suey" would suggest.

You will, of course, find *nasi goreng* (fried rice) everywhere; topped with a fried egg, it makes a good breakfast. *Nasi rames*, white rice served with a small helping of savory meat and vegetables is also very good.

Some restaurants offer *bistiek*, so-called European food with chips, peas and all.

It's frightful!

Like all Indonesians, Balinese are very fond of snacks. Wherever you go, you'll find someone selling sticky cakes, crunchy peanut biscuits, strange salted nuts and lentils, steamed sweetmeats wrapped in banana leaf, and a host of other extraordinary but thoroughly delicious goodies. Although ice-creams and other iced confections are sold in most places, it's wise (for health reasons) to avoid those sold by street vendors.

The tropical fruits of Bali are excellent: pineapples, bananas (ranging from tiny finger-sized *pisang mas* up to the foot-long *pisang raja*), papayas and mangoes are joined by even more unusual seasonal fruits. Some of the most outstanding are *rambutan* (hairy red skins enclosing sweet white meat), *mangosteen* (purplish black skins with a very sweet juicy white fruit inside) and *jeruk Bali* (pomelos). The huge spiky *durian* has (to most people) a revolting rotten smell, but its buttery-rich fruit is adored by local people and a few adventurous visitors.

Thirst Quenchers: Most familiar Western drinks are available in Bali, though some of them take on an exciting new dimension. Tea is usually very fragrant, and similar to Chinese tea in flavor. Served hot or cold, *manis* (with sugar) or *pahit* (without), it is delicate and refreshing. Coffee is a delight to real coffee lovers, being served almost Turkish-style with a few grounds

PACUNG COTTAGES .....
LUXURY MOUNTAIN RESORT

For a different view of Bali, and for some cool fresh mountain air, come and stay with us.

Our luxury suites and cottages come with modern services including Hot Water, and 24 hour Room Service.

Other facilities include a Swimming Pool, Safety Deposit Box, and a Conference Room for 100 persons.

Our restaurant serves Seafood, Chinese, Indonesian and Western food.

You will find us just 9 km from scenic Lake Bratan, which is close to the famous Bali Handara Golf Course, and also to many other beauty spots of Central Bali.

For further information and reservation please contact your Travel Agent or telephone our Representative in Bali at :
Jl. Supratman 23 A, Denpasar, Bali.
Telephone : **(0361) 25824, 25746.** Fax : 62 361 37638

floating around (known as *kopi tobruk*). Locally manufactured beer (Anker and Bintang) is similar to European lager beer. It's moderately priced and available everywhere, but as it is seldom kept chilled, you may be faced with the choice of warm beer, beer *pakai es* (with ice) or no beer at all.

Fresh fruit juices are popular. *Air jeruk*, as orange juice is called, is served either hot or cold: be sure to specify what you want. There are also juices made from pineapple, apple and other common fruits. Westerners accustomed to regarding avacado as a vegetable will probably be amazed at the *apokat* drink, but it's worth trying: avocado, rum or coffee essence, palm sugar and tinned milk are blended to make a thick, rich liquid that leaves most milkshakes for dead.

Cordials are known as *stroop*: among the best are *zirzak,* made from soursop and *markisa,* made from passionfruit. *Es kopyor* is a favorite concoction of rose syrup, ice, scoops of jelly-like flesh from the inside of the *kopyor* coconut. *Es campur,* mixture of shaved ice with fruits and jelly (also known as *cendol*), *es tape* and *dawat santen* are all absolutely delicious. See individual heading for detailed listing of Bali restaurants.

SHOPPING

Bali is a great place to shop. Hundreds of boutiques and roadside stalls have set up all over the island, and thousands of artisans, craftsmen, seamstresses, woodcarvers, painters, etc. are kept busy supplying the tourist demand. Swarms of vendors crowd the beaches, plying you with trinkets and colorful textiles. Many shopkeepers have developed a hard-sell sales pitch reminiscent of Hong Kong or New York. Sometimes it is a bit overwhelming, but rare is the visitor who comes away without at least one bag full of souvenirs. The variety is literally endless. See listings under each area of the island for more detailed information about specialities.

Woodcarvings: You are sure to find good woodcarvings in the shops along the main road of **Mas**, (particularly well-known is Ida Bagus Tilem's Gallery and Museum). Also try the villages of **Pujung** (past Tegalalang north of Ubud), **Batuan** and **Jati**. All types of indigenous wood, ranging from the butter-colored jackwood to inexpensive bespeckled coconut, are sculpted here in bold designs which set the standards for carvers elsewhere on the island. Woods imported from other islands—buff hibiscus, rich brown Javanese teak and black Sulawesian ebony are also hewn into delicate forms by Balinese craftsmen. Hunt for elaborate antique woodcarvings that once adorned gilded temple pavilions or royal palaces, in shops in **Kuta, Sanur** and on the main street of **Klungkung.** But always beware that fakes abound.

Paintings: The artist's center is **Ubud,** including the surrounding villages of **Pengosekan, Penestanan, Sanggingan, Peliatan, Mas** and **Batuan**. The famous **Neka Gallery & Museum** and the **Puri Lukisan Museum**, both in Ubud, will give you an idea of the range of styles and the artistry achieved by the best painters. Then visit some of the other galleries in the area: **Gallery Manut, Gallery Agung**, and the gallery of the **Pengosekan Community of Artists**. Examples from every school of painting active in Bali are found here as well as canvasses of young artists portraying festivals and dancers. For bargains try the smaller galleries and artshops in Ubud: **Puspa's Gallery** is always well-stocked and reasonably priced.

For quality works of art, seek out the gallery-homes of well-known artists in Ubud such as **Antonio Blanco, Hans Snel, Wayan Rendi, Arie Smit** and the late, great **I Gusti Nyoman Lempad.** This is a fascinating journey into the private world of artist, whose studio is usually at the back of his shop. Many private galleries here afford you the privilege of meeting the painters and seeing them at work.

In other villages, seek out **Mokoh** and **I Made Budi** in **Batuan**. **Sanur** is chock-full of little shops with unusual paintings by lesser-known or unknown artists, including **Misran** who has a studio on Jl. Tanjung Sari near Sari's Cafe.

For traditional astrological calendars, "*ider-ider*" (strips of cotton a foot wide and 15 feet long which are suspended from the eaves of shrines during temple ceremonies) and paintings in the so-called *wayang* style, visit **Kamasan** just south of **Klungkung**. This style has been around for many centuries, though real antiques are hard to come by. Some examples may be found in Klungkung and in antique shops elsewhere on Bali.

Stone Carvings: For traditional sand-stone carvings, stop at the workshops in **Batubulan**. And **Wayan Cemul**, an Ubud stone carver with an international following, has a house full of his weird and wonderful creations.

Textiles: The spiraling designs and geometric patterns of Javanese "batik" are seen everywhere on the islands as part of the daily dress of the Balinese. Buffaloes, birds, masks and puppet figures are some of the motives entwined in characteristic compositions. For "batik" clothing, try the many boutiques in **Kuta Beach**. Brocades that gleam like gold lamé, and also the simpler, handloomed *sarong* cloths, are sold in every village. **Gianyar** is the home of the handloom industry, but the villages of **Blayu**, **Sideman**, **Mengwi**, **Batuan**, **Gelgel**, **Tengganan** and **Ubud** all produce their own style of weavings. All can be bought now in the scores of fabric and clothing boutiques found in **Kuta**. Bali now has one of the biggest garment industries in Southeast Asia. There are perhaps 500 designers and exporters working in **Kuta** and **Legian**. Textiles from other islands, such as Sumbanese *hinggi* and Batak *ulos* may also be bought in many shops in **Kuta** and **Denpasar**.

Gold and Silver: Inventive Balinese jewelers smelt, cast, forge and spin delicate flowers, offering bowls and images of demons studded with semi-precious stones. The centers for metal working are **Celuk** and **Kamasan**, where all such ornaments are on sale at reasonable prices. These craftsmen will also of course produce pieces and settings to order, just bring them a drawing or a sample to copy. If you don't like it, they'll smelt it down and start over. **Kuta** is another center for exporting gold and silver ware. For traditional Balinese jewelry, visit the shops at **Jl. Sulawesi** and **Jl. Kartini** in **Denpasar**.

Handicrafts: Bamboo implements, *wayang kulit* figures and ornaments made of coconut shell and teakwood are sold at most souvenir shops. Bone carvings can be bought at good prices at **Tampaksiring**, while plaited hats and baskets are the specialty of the women of **Bedulu** and **Bona**. **Suka Wati** market and the row of stands opposite **Gua Gajah** (the 'Elephant Cave') are the best places to buy baskets. **Klungkung** market also has some finely worked traditional wares.

For detailed descriptions of the endless variety of fine and unusual gift shops in **South Bali**, see under "**shopping**" for **Denpasar**, **Kuta**, and **Sanur** in that section.

The **Handicrafts Centre** ('Sanggraha Karya Hasta') in Tohpati, **Denpasar**, has a collection of the handicrafts from Bali and the other islands of Indonesia, such as baskets and weavings. This center is not really a museum, but a government-sponsored cooperative selling Indonesian and Balinese handicrafts. Open 8 a.m.-5 p.m. daily, closed Mondays.

In **Sanur**, the beach markets in front of the Segara Beach Hotel, south of the Bali Hyatt, and along the road into the Sanur Beach Hotel, are the best spots for gift-shopping at reasonable prices. There is also a row of small shops hidden in an alley behind **Museum Le Mayeur**, where the women assemble exquisite shirts and blouses by attaching Sumbanese *ikat* dyed fabric with crochet.

The morning **Pasar Badung** market in

Denpasar is also an eye-opener. Coral-lined alleys lead to a ceremonial knick-knacks section selling baskets of every imaginable shape and size. **Kuta** has an endless variety of trinkets at the lowest prices, including wind chimes that play *gamelan* music and brightly-painted model banana trees of various sizes (see under "**Kuta**" for directions).

Antiques: Bali has elaborately carved furniture, doorways, huge ornate wedding beds, wavy ceremonial *kris*, baskets, *lontar* palm-leaf books, hand-woven fabrics, old Dutch lamps, masks, Chinese ceramics and sculptures from many parts of Indonesia, as well as China and Japan. If actual Balinese antiques interest you, head north and east to the towns of **Klungkung** and **Singaraja**. Here you are likely to find interesting remnants of Bali's past mercantile relations with the Arabs, Dutch, Portuguese and Chinese.

The antique shops, adjacent to the Kerta Gosa in **Klungkung** house collections of rare Chinese porcelains, old Kamasan *wayang* style paintings, antique jewelry and Balinese weavings. Prices are reasonable. **Singaraja** has some of the best antique shops in Bali. They are all on the main streets of this northern port town.

Other than this, as always, **Kuta** is the place to shop for anything and everything. **Denpasar** also has some good stores, and many less fancy ones, which in fact often have more variety at half the price. (See listings under these cities for details on individual shops.) For a look at high-quality antiques (at high-quality prices), try the shopping arcades of major hotels.

Do not buy until you are sure you know you are getting a genuine antique. There are many imitations which are both charming and inexpensive, such as the wooden ducks and *garudas* sold in practically every trinket shop. They often have a sign saying 'antique,' but the term is used very loosely.

The way to be sure is shop around and price similar items. Then at least if you don't get an antique, chances are you won't pay for any either.

Pottery: Some unusual pottery is manufactured in the village of **Pejaten** about 12 miles (20 km) west of Denpasar. Here, the villagers create striking figurines with twisted limbs and grotesque bodies out of terracotta, as they have done for many generations. Beautiful glazed ceramics are also being produced now in Batu Jimbar, **Sanur**, by a young crew of craftsmen under the direction of Brent Hesslyn. Inquire at the shop in the Bali Hyatt shopping arcade.

Photographic Supplies: The **Bali Foto Centre** on the main highway in Kuta (right near the bend in the road), and the **Sanur Foto Centre** just in front of the Tanjung Sari Hotel in Sanur are the most complete shops near the beach areas. The latter also has a new branch in Nusa Dua, the **Nusa Dua Foto Centre**. In Denpasar, go to **Prima** on Jl. Gajah Made 41 (tel 25031 or 25038), or **Tati Photo** on Jl. Sumatra 10-14 (tel 26912 or 24578). All these shops have sales agents all over Bali, with frequent pick-ups and two-hour processing. Film is available in most hotel shopping arcades, drug stores, and in Ubud at **Murni's Warung.**

Shipping: Shipping your purchases home from Bali is now reliable, fast and insurable. For small items no more than three feet (one meter) long and 22 pounds (10 kg) per package, you can post them yourself at Denpasar. Or for about double the cost, the packing and mailing will be done for you by any one of many "Shipping Agents" whose offices are to be found near every major hotel and shopping area. They all claim never to have lost a package, but insurance is recommended.

For more serious buyers, it is not only practical but more reasonable to ship by air or sea cargo. Air cargo is by the kilo (with a 10 kg minimum) and is quite expensive for heavy items, whose weight is also increased by the crate.

Sea cargo is around US$350 for the minimum of 33 cubic feet (one cubic meter) all the way to the United States, which takes only a month, and into which you can get just about everything including yourself. Insurance is seven percent of whatever value you claim.

The beauty of this method is that all the packing, even the individual cartoning of delicate objects or paintings, is done. The difficulty is you must buy enough to justify the minimum size and expense, and arrange transportation to your home from the nearest sea port. Air shipping goes to the nearest international airport, and parcel post to your door,

If cargo is necessary, try to purchase the bulk of your items from one shop owner who has connections with a reliable shipping agent. Chances are he will get you a small discount, and be an additional safeguard against any blunders by the agent, to help with your complaints.

Aside from this, you need only take the common-sense precautions of carefully list-

ing prices and descriptions of your merchandise, demanding written guarantees and receipts, and if you like are welcome to watch how the items are packed. They will even pick them up from the shop or come to your hotel room. What remains is to be aware of what problems you might encounter in your home country.

MUSEUMS AND GALLERIES

Bali has many museums with fine collections of traditional and modern art. The **Bali Museum** in Denpasar offers a vivid picture of Balinese life and art from prehistoric times up to the 20th century, with emphasis on the antique. The new art center at **Abian Kapas** in an eastern suburb of the city has a permanent exhibition of modern Balinese art. **Museum Le Mayeur**, just north of the Hotel Bali Beach in Sanur, houses the private collection of the late Belgian impressionist painter, Le Mayeur.

Museum Puri Lukisan in Ubud displays works dating from the late 1920s, when Balinese painters first began to break away from the formality of traditional paintings styles, up until the present. Many were gathered by Dutch painter Rudolph Bonnet with the assistance of Ubud's prince. It contains excellent contemporary paintings and carvings, most created during the past 20

years by artists living in or around Ubud. Recently, a new gallery has been added where selected works of arts are on sale. Open daily, 8 a.m.-5 p.m.

The **Archaeological Museum** by the main road in Pejeng, less than a mile (one kilometer) north of Bedulu on the Tampaksiring road, contains an excellent collection of Megalithic and Bronze Age remains found in this area, including huge stone sarcophagi and tiny Hindu votary lamps. Open every day, 8 a.m.-1:30 p.m.

The **Gedung Kirtya** in Singaraja is a unique library of old *lontar* (palm leaf) manuscripts and scholarly Dutch books. It was founded by the colonial government in the 1930s and most of the manuscripts were collected by Dr. C. Hooykaas. Open daily 8 a.m.-12:30 p.m. except Sundays.

The **Museum Manusia Yadna** in Mengwi, just

across the moat from the Puri Taman Ayun Temple, was founded several years ago with the admirable idea of preserving in a single collection, examples of the arts of Balinese temple offerings. Unfortunately, the museum has not been well kept and receives few visitors, but if you are fascinated by Balinese ritual life, this collection is a must. Exhibited are all sorts of offerings used for various rites of passage and temple ceremonies. Open everyday (but often left unattended).

The **Neka Gallery & Museum**, several kilometers to the west of Ubud, contains the finest collection of paintings on Bali, better than the Puri Lukisan. Neka is a Balinese art dealer who has personally known all the great painters of Bali over the years, and this is his private collection. Paintings are sold in an adjoining gallery. Neka also runs another gallery on the main street in Ubud. Open daily 8 a.m.-5 p.m.

Visit also the many private galleries in the homes of artists. One of the most lavish is the gallery/home of American **Mario Blanco** up on the left after the bridge in Campuan (Ubud). This old building is a well-preserved example of Balinese architecture. Inside you can meet the artist's family, and view his private collection of erotic paintings and collages. Open daily 8 a.m.-5 p.m.

Hans Snel is another well-known foreign artist living in Ubud, a Dutchman painting in the Gauguin/Spies/ Bonnet tradition of native-modern art. His gallery has recently been expanded to include a guest house, bar and restaurant, so that after viewing his work you can sit and have a cozy drink.

Ida Bagus Tilem was the most famous wood-carver of Mas. His house is on the main road just to the south of Ubud, and his son, himself a talented carver, now manages a large gallery here exhibiting his father's work. Many contemporary carvings are also sold in the adjoining showrooms. Open daily 8 a.m.-5 p.m.

PERFORMING ARTS

The best way to see Balinese dances, *wayang kulit* puppet shows and *gamelan* orchestras is to attend a village temple festival. There is one going on somewhere on the island almost every day. Ask at your hotel, or consult the **Bali Post Calendar**, available in most shops. In the fine print beneath are listed the names of villages having ceremonies and the type of celebration (but it is not 100 percent accurate).

For visitors whose time in Bali is more precious, public performances are given at various central locations all over the island. These are mainly for the benefit of tourists, but that doesn't mean they are inferior to genuine temple performances. Some of Bali's best dancers and musicians participate in tourist performances, and for many of them it is a good outside source of income.

The times and locations change constantly, so check with your hotel or with any travel agent to be sure, but the following are fairly well-established venues and schedules.

Kecak Dance

Ayoda Pura
Tanjung Bungkak
(6-7 p.m. daily)

Banjar Taman
Sanur
(6-7 p.m. daily)

Banjar Legian Kelod
Legian
(8-9 p.m. Tuesdays)

Banjar Buni
Kuta
(6-7 p.m. Sundays)

Bona
Gianyar
(8-10 p.m. Mondays)

Abian Kapas Art Centre
Denpasar
(6-7 p.m. daily)

Ramayana Ballet

Ayoda Pura
Tanjung Bungkak

(8-9 p.m. Saturdays & Sundays)

Pemecutan Palace Hotel
Denpasar
(6-7 p.m. Mondays)

Banjar Pengaretan
Kuta
(8-9 p.m. Saturdays)

Indra Prasta
Kuta
(8-9 p.m. Saturdays)

Barong Dance

Saha Dewa
Batubulan
(9-10 p.m. daily)

Banjar Seminyak
Legian
(10-11 a.m. daily)

Legong Dance

Puri Agung
Peliatan
(6-7 p.m. Saturdays)

Ayoda Pura
Tanjung Bungkak
(8-9 p.m. Thursdays)

Pemecutan Palace Hotel
Denpasar
(7-8 p.m. Mondays)

Indra Prasta
Kuta
(8-9 p.m. Saturdays)

Wayang Kulit

Pemecutan Palace Hotel
Denpasar
(6-7 p.m. Mondays &
Thursdays)

**Trance Dance and
Fire-walking**

Bona
Gianyar
(6-7 p.m. Mondays, Wednesdays & Fridays)

The following hotels also have regular evening dinner shows:

Bali Hyatt Hotel
Sanur

Hotel Bali Beach
Sanur

Bali Seaside Cottage
Sanur

Nusa Dua Hotel
Nusa Dua

Sanur Beach Hotel
Sanur

It is possible to hire dance performances individually, such as the *Legong, Frog Dance, Topeng, Janger, Joged,* etc. Also visit the Balinese dance academies in Denpasar, **Kokar**, and **Asti**, both on Jl. Ratna. They have frequent student performances and the best young dancers are found here.

Movies
Larger cinemas are all in Denpasar and feature Indonesian as well as foreign films. For Indian movies, visit the smaller cinemas outside Denpasar; these also feature Indonesian movies and videos.

Denpasar Theatre at 41 Jalan Diponegoro has three shows daily at 3, 5 and 7 p.m.
Tickets are from Rp 500 to Rp 1000 or more, depending on the movie.
On Sundays there is a show at 10 a.m.

Nirwana Theatre at 50/52 Jalan Hasanudin (tel: 2699) has three shows daily at 5.30, 7.30 and 9.30 p.m.
Tickets are from Rp 500 to Rp 1000 or more.

Indra Theatre at 7 Jalan Gajah Mada (tel: 6152) has four shows daily at 3, 5, 7 and 9 p.m. Tickets are from Rp 1000 to Rp 3000.

Kusumasari Theatre at Kasumasari Shopping Complex, Jalan Gajah Mada.
Four shows daily at 5, 7, 9, 11 p.m. Tickets from Rp 1000 to Rp 2000 or more.

SPORTS

Aquatic Sports: Over the last five years surfing, snorkeling, scuba diving, spearfishing, wind-surfing and deep-sea fishing have all become very popular in Bali. **Nusa Lembongan**, the small island directly opposite Sanur has developed into a haven for surfers and divers alike. Group charters and safari tours are available, together with equipment and instruction if needed. A complete scuba outfit and a ride out to the reef at Sanur can be had for as little as US$20 a person for a group of five or more (US$40 for just one).
P.T. Baruna Water Sports. Jl. Seruni 29, Denpasar, tel: 24610 or 26647, has a kiosk at the Bali Beach, Bali Hyatt, and Bali Nusa Dua Hotels in **Sanur.** They offer tours to all the main scuba diving attractions on the island, as described in their brochure: (rates listed are based on one day trips for a party of five).

Sanur and Nusa Dua
Dives at six to 39 feet (two to 12 meters) depth will be rewarded by beautiful underwater panoramas. Gigantic table and trophy shaped coral and sponge grow for miles on her barrier reef. Thousands of colorful fish swim by in kaleidoscopic profusion (US$30)

Padangbai and The Gili Tepekong Islands
Located about 37 miles (60 km) northeast of Sanur.

This picturesque bay is surrounded by majestic cliffs and hills ideal for dives at nine to 66 feet (three to 20 meter) depths. Her waters are strewn with a full growth of coral and fish which will guarantee an impressive underwater adventure. (US$37.50)

Lembongan Island

Located about 12 miles (20 km) due east of Sanur and two hours by motor boat, is actually one of the three sister islands of Bali. White sandy bottom and crystal clear, exceptionally cool water present you with assorted fish and marine vegetation. Underwater grottos are the wonders of this area. (US$42.50)

Tulamben

Located about 330 miles (100 km) northeast of Sanur, you drive through idyllic Balinese countryside. On location you will see remnants of the U.S. merchantman *Liberty* sunk during World War II. The wreck is fully grown with all kinds of anemone, gorgonia, sponge, and coral. Docile fish accompany you and welcome you to visit their rusty home. (US$42.50)

Singaraja

Located about 49 miles (80 km) due north of Sanur, where the calm waters of the Bali Sea create pool-like conditions ideal for snorkeling. The best spots are around Lovina beach, suitable for beginners, and Gondol beach having slight currents from 16 to 49 feet (five to 15 meter) depths. (US$45)

Menjangan Island National Park

The tiny adjoining island 74 miles (120 km) northwest of Sanur is accessible by boat, only 30 minutes from the mainland. This area is suitable for all-season diving where magnificent underwater vistas will surprise even the most seasoned diver. It is rich with all kinds of sponges, sea plants, coral, and fish for miles on end. The area is considered the diver's paradise in Bali and words cannot describe its true beauty. (US$67.50)

Tabuhan Islands

Coral reefs, tropical fish and shark sites are the main diving draws. (US$67.50)

These same tours are offered by numerous agencies throughout the island. In **Sanur**, contact the following travel agents for these and other sports tours: **BIL** or **Natrabu**. The **Segara Village Hotel** offers water skiing and windsurfing. Most of the hotels in Sanur rent wind-surfers, and the fishermen chartering sailboats across the Sanur lagoon to Nusa Lembongan are hard to avoid.

In **Kuta** contact Nyoman at **Bali Aquatic Sports** (in La Barong Bar). Also in Kuta, try **Gloria Maris** (Jl. Airport) and **Nusa Lembongan Tours** (at the Happy Restaurant). Many shops in Kuta rent surfboards. For the best surfing on Bali, make your way to **Ulu Watu** on the western shore of the southern Bukit Peninsula.

Hotel Bualu in **Nusa Dua** is the only PADI (Professional Association of Diving Instructors) resort in Indonesia. For hotel guests, boats and diving guides are free and you pay only US$10 for two tanks and all the equipment. A range of sports, from bicycling to horseback riding, is also available free of charge to hotel guests. **Hotel Nusa Dua**, in addition to tennis and scuba diving, offers squash, water-skiing and aqua-planing, plus free transportation for golfers to the Bali Beach course in Sanur. Look under "**Nusa Dua**" for more details on both of the above.

Billiards: At the Segara Leisure Club, Segara Hotel, for US$0.50 per hour, or the Hotel Bali Beach for US$3.

Bowling: At the Bali Beach Hotel in Sanur, for US$1 per game.

Golf: There are two courses on the island. The **Hotel Bali Beach** in Sanur has a small 9-hole course that can be used for US$12; $24 for 18 holes or full day. Equipment and caddies are available, all with discounts for hotel guests. A Mini Golf course is also available for US$1 per hour. Tel 8511 ext 594, for reservations. See individual hotel listing.

The serious golfer will want to visit the **Bali Handara Country Club** at Bedugul. This 18-hole championship course was designed by Peter Thompson and is the only course in the world set inside a volcano. It is also gazetted among the top 50 professional courses in the world. Green fees are US$45 per day on the weekends, US$30 during the week. An adjoining hotel has double rooms for US$55 (plus 21 percent), and if you stay here you get a 50 percent reduction on green fees. Contact the booking office in Sanur for reservations: **Bali Handara Country Club,** Jl. Raya Sanur 131, P.O. Box 324, Denpasar, tel: 26419, 23046, tlx: 35141 DENPASAR.

Squash: For guests at the Hotel Bali Nusa Dua.

Swimming: For a fee ranging from US$1.50-5 per day, the pools at most of the larger hotels may be used by non-guests. The Hotel Bali Beach has the largest pool in Sanur, though the Bali Hyatt, Sanur Beach, Bali Seaside Cottages, La Taverna and the Tandjung Sari all have small ones. On the Kuta side, Pertamina Cottages, Legian Beach Hotel, Kuta Beach Club, the Kuta Beach Hotel and the Bali Oberoi also have pools. The Bali Hotel in Denpasar and the Hotel Campuan in Ubud have pools too, as of course do all the hotels in Nusa Dua.

Tennis: Courts are available at the Bali Hyatt, Segara Village, and the Bali Beach hotels in Sanur, at Hotel Bualu in Nusa Dua, and at the Pertamina Cottages in Tuban by the airport. Costs range from free (for hotel guests), to US$5, including ball boys. Equipment and partners are available. Private courts can be rented in Denpasar on Jalan Kamboja, on Jalan M.T. Maryono, in Tanjung Bungkak and at Putung Karanga.

TOURS

Expert daily bus tours, with well-informed multilingual guides are run by many travel agencies. They range in prices from US$6-7 for a half-day jaunt to Ubud or Sangeh/Mengwi, up to US$15-20 for a full-day cross-island trip up to Kintamani or Besakih, including a Barong Dance in Batubulan, lunch and several stops at shops and temples.

You can also design your own private guided tour, in an air-conditioned car with a chauffeur/guide, which allows you to establish the itinerary and the amount of time spent at each place. The prices ranges from US$30 up to US$60 per day, all inclusive. For either type of tour, contact one of the agents below or inquire at the travel desk in your hotel. The most experienced agents for the English-speaking traveler are **Bil** and **Pacto**. **Celong** and **Rama** cater to Japanese tourists. **Perama**'s in Kuta is highly recommended for the budget traveler.

In addition to specialties mentioned, all of the agents mentioned below offer variations on the following:

Denpasar Tour (museums, galleries, markets, etc)
Tampaksiring Tour, including art shops of Celuk, Mas, and Ubud; longer tours continuing the above to **Besakih** or **Kintamani,** a **Monkey Forest Tour** and a **Tanah Lot Tour**. Also a "Turtle Island" tour, Bratan Lake tour, "Bali Island" tour covering major cities, Kuta Beach tour, "Bat Cave" tour.
Bali Holiday, Tanjung Bungkak, Denpasar, tel: 24000.
Bali Indonesia Ltd. (B.I.L.) Hotel Tanjung, Denpasar, tel: 22634. Or Travel Desk, Bali Hyatt Hotel, Sanur, tel: 8463-4, 8434.
Bualu Hotel, Nusa Dua, tel: 71310-71311, offers all the standard tours plus extensive diving tours and facilities.
Carefree Bali Holiday, Jl. Bakung Sari, Kuta, tel: 8781 ext. 80.
Golden Bali Tour, Bali Beach Hotel Arcade, Sanur, tel: 26401 ext 128.
Golden Kris Tour, Jl. Veteran 33, Denpasar, 26388.
Ida's Tour, Ida Beach Inn, Kuta, tel: 8781 ext 44.
Jan's Tour, Jl. Bayusuta, Denpasar, tel: 24595.
P.T. Genta Bali Tours, Tourist Beach Inn, Jl. Segara, Sanur, tel: 8418. Offers four to five day safari tours to Komodo, Flores, or Borneo.
Natour, Jl. Veteran 1, Denpasar, tel: 24161, 22619, 22408.

SOMETIMES REALITY CAN BE BETTER THAN DREAMS

W hen your clients ask for paradise, – a tropical isle where time passes slowly and where luxurious vegetation borders the long secluded beaches – they are asking for Bali. A place where reality is better than dreams. Here, on the Nusa Dua Beach, hidden amongst the exotic plants and palm trees you'll find the *Meliá Bali Sol* With its five restaurants, two bars, disco, squash and tennis courts, swimming pool and outdoor theatre. Yours clients dreams will become reality.

INSIGHT
GUIDES

Indonesia

Available at all leading bookshops.

APA PUBLICATIONS

Natrabu, Jl. Kecubung, Denpasar, tel: 23452, 25448, 25449. Bali Beach Hotel Office: Lobby arcade. Also a "Bali Behind the Wall" tour, introducing you to the social life of the people.

Nitour, Jl. Veteran 3, Denpasar, tel: 22849, 22593.

Pacto, Jl. Sanur, Sanur, tel: 8247-8. Or Bali Beach Hotel, Sanur, tel: 8511. Also a Bedugul golfing tour, and one to four night excursions to Lombok, Sulawesi, Mt. Bromo and Surabaya, Yogyakarta and Borobudur.

Rama Tours, Jl. Raya Sanur 159, Tanjung Bungkak, Denpasar, tel: 4972, 3285. Also a counter at the Bali Beach Hotel, Sanur.

Satriavi, Jl. Veteran 5, Denpasar, tel: 24339.

Tunas Indonesia, Bali Beach Hotel Arcade, Sanur, tel: 84015.

Exotic wildlife safaris for US$60 up to around US$400, which includes airfare to see the "Komodo Dragon," to the Buluran Wild Game Reserve in East Java, and the Sukomade tour, continuing the above to "Turtle Bay" renowned for surfing, diving, and the impenetrable jungle of the Meru Betiri National Park where the Rafflesia, world's largest parasitic bloom can be seen, and the six remaining "Javan tigers." Also a "Bali Barat National Park" tour, where lives the "Rothschild Starling," an extremely rare blue-faced white starling found nowhere else in the world. Plus all the standard tours of Bali offered by other guides, including cultural events such as Legong or Kecak dances.

Vayatour, Tanjung Bungkak, Denpasar. One of the best agents for discount airline tickets.

FESTIVITIES

HOLIDAYS

Public Holidays: Religion is a way of life in Indonesia, and throughout the entire archipelago people enjoy and celebrate Buddhist, Hindu, Muslim and Christian holidays. The first national holiday is **New Year's Day** observed throughout the country. Although celebrations vary from area to area, it is often celebrated with street carnivals, fireworks, special entertainment and shows. **Chinese New Year's Day**, timed on the lunar calendar, continues for 15 days until the night of *Chap Go Meh*. The Balinese New Year **Nyepi** (Day of Silence) is also a national holiday. It is a Hindu holiday of retreat and spiritual purification.

The most important Muslim celebration is **Idul Fitri** (Grebeg Sjawal) on the first day of the 10th month (Sjawal) of the Islamic calendar symbolizing the end of the fasting month of Ramadan. All over the country mass prayers are held in mosques and town squares and everyone wears new clothes and visits relatives seeking forgiveness for past transgressions. It is a two-day public holiday. Also on the Islamic calendar is **Maulud Nabi** (or Grebeg Mulud) in commemoration of the birthday of the Prohpet Mohammed preceded by the Sekaten festival. The day of the **Ascension of the Prophet Mohammed** falls on the 27th day of the seventh month on the Muslim calendar and **Idul Adah** (Grebeg Besar) on the 10th day of the 11th Muslim month is the Muslim day of sacrifice where goats and cattle are slaughtered and meat is given to the poor and needy.

Good Friday is a national holiday as is the **Ascension of Christ** (Kenaikan Isa Almasih), the 14th day after the resurrection.

April 21 is **Kartini Day**, a national holiday commemorating the birthday of the late Raden Ajeng Kartini, the pioneer for the emancipation of Indonesian women at the turn of the Century. Everywhere women appear in national dress.

August 17 is the Indonesian national **Independence Day** (Hari Proklamasi) celebrated throughout the country with organized sports events, puppet and shadow plays, traditional cultural performances, carnivals and festivals.

October 5 is **Armed Forces Day**, the anniversary of the founding of the Indonesian Armed Forces with military parades and demonstrations of the latest achievements of the army, navy, air force and police.

Christmas Eve is celebrated by Christians in Bali with church services and mass. A joyous national public holiday, **Christmas** is celebrated with candlelight gatherings and religious ceremonies.

Be sure to check the schedules for holidays during the period of your visit: the lunar, Islamic and Hindu holidays fall on different days each year of the solar or western calendar.

The Balinese Calendar: Intricate paintings of the Balinese calendar contain a number of squares, each corresponding to a certain day and week in the year. Within each square is painted a scene depicting a profitable action or event that relates to that particular day. One day may be devoted to religious duties, another to human endeavors, another to responsibilities concerning cows, fish, fowl or coconut. The calendar not only regulates the lives of the Balinese, but indicates the most favorable dates to undertake such ordinary tasks of daily life as blessing a house, building a bed, or selling cattle.

The Balinese follow two time systems simultaneously: the Hindu *saka* calendar in which the years are numbered, and the Balinese *wuku* calendar which does not register the years. The *saka* solar-lunar year is divided into 12 months or "moons," with full moon and dark moon important for ceremonies. Every month contains 29 or 30 solar days, similar to the West, except the years are numbered 78 years earlier; so A.D. 1976 was the *saka* year 1898. The majority of Balinese use of *wuku* calendar, a complex time system consisting of 10 simultaneous weeks, ranging from a one-day week to a 10-day week, which is called *wuku* and begins on Sunday, with each day named after a planet in the solar system. The five-day week is as important. A *wuku* year is made up of 210 days, or 37-day weeks, *wukus*, with each *wuku* having its own name.

Nyepi

"New Year" by the *saka* calendar falls on the day after the new moon of the ninth month. It is celebrated by a day of stillness, *Nyepi*, when no fires may be lit, no transport taken, and no work done. On the day before *Nyepi*, the last day of the year and one marking the end of the rainy season, a great purification offering is made by all the villages to cleanse the country of evil. Laid on the ground at every crossroad are huge offerings of wines and flesh from very wild and domestic animal. These are to feed the evil spirits, while from a raised platform, high priests recite powerful magic formulas to exorcise them. That night, everyone is out in the streets sounding gongs, cymbals and other noise makers to chase them away. In Denpasar, thousands of boys gather in the town square for a parade through the capital with fire torches to sweep the town of all impish spirits.

Galungan

Every 210th day by the *wuku* calendar, the Balinese hold a great feast commemorating the victory of the people over the legendary demon-king Mayadanawa. According to myths, this king strictly forbade his subjects' worship of their ancestors and deities. Assisted by the god Indra and his divine allies, the people revolted and, in a great battle, defeated the demon-king. Thus, they were free again to worship according to their own beliefs—those of their religion *Agama Hindu*. On *Galungan*, it is believed that the supreme God Sanghyang Widi, followed by other deities and ancestral spirits, descends from heavens to their temples on earth to feast. For 10 days, they receive many offerings and continuous entertainment of processions, dances and songs. All the *barong* are marched from the temples and paraded from village to village, often stopping at the roadside and dancing on the spot. The tenth day, *Kuningan*, is the last day of their sojourn on earth.

Independence Day

One holiday the Balinese

share with all Indonesians is Independence Day, on Aug. 17. The courage of Indonesia's early leaders and revolutionaries is remembered as the national colors fly from all the avenues, and parades of school children — some of them dressed in the rugged jungle gear of freedom fighters, others in the regional costumes of many islands united in nationhood—march through the city streets.

For many Balinese dancers and musicians, Independence Day is the culmination of hours of training. Once in every four years, an islandwide gong competition is held to select the village who has the best *gamelan* orchestra. The stage holds two *gamelans* as final contestants, each trying to outdo the other by new compositions and remarkable precision playing. Dancers, too, are at their peak, captivating their viewers with the power of an interpretive style and surprising them with daring innovations. The auditorium is always crowded, and the appreciation of the audience is as revealing as the performers themselves, for here the Balinese masters are the judges of their arts.

Temple Festivals (Odalans)

Each temple holds a festival on its "birthday," the anniversary of its consecration, either every 210th day or every lunar year. To villagers it means an all day, all night celebration. From early morning, the *pemangku* priest is on duty to receive and bless the offerings the women bring. By afternoon, a cock-fight is in full swing, vendors have set up their refreshments, a medicine man is laying out his paraphernalia for demonstrating cure-alls, processions of people in festival dress are arriving...and so it continues—from sundown until dawn.

Days of Honor

Besides national holidays and festivals, the Balinese set certain days aside to honor individual deities who are guardians of special disciplines. Once a year by the *wuku* calendar, a day is devoted to **Saraswati,** goddess of wisdom. Offerings are made to *lontar* manuscripts (Bali's early books) and no one is allowed to read or write on that day. Another day is dedicated to **Batara Sangkara,** the lord of all crops. Offerings are presented to coconut trees which are "dressed up" in wrappings of fine cloth; climbing them is prohibited. On the day devoted to the **divinity of prosperity and financial success,** no business is done. The day honoring **weapons** forbids the use of any sharp objects. There is also a day of the **"golden blessing"** when offerings are made to all objects of gold, silver and precious stones, and to the lord of gold, Mahadewa, guardian of the West. Little of nature or of the tools that serve the people is left unattended. One day is reserved for all **offerings to domestic animals,** another for all **utensils and equipment** used in rice farming (during which time no rice may be husked or sold), and still another for all **musical instruments, dance costumes and puppets.**

In Bali, there are no off-seasons. Every day brings celebrations and no matter when you arrive you are bound to encounter one celebration on the island. Perhaps it is because the Balinese are never forgetful of all that have given them a prosperous and healthy life.

The Festival Cycle

Galungan and *Kuningan* and many temple festivals follow the fixed 210-day *wuku* cycle, and therefore their occurrence can be determined well in advance. However, *Nyepi* and many other temple festivals (including those at such major temples as *Pura Besakih* and *Pura Batar*) follow the lunar calendar, and the dates on which they fall are determined by the religious authorities only at the end of each year.

Major temple festivals are listed under each month in the printed Balinese calendars that are found hanging in almost every house, hotel and office in the island. The best way to know what is going on is to consult that calendar. But do not rely on that alone; always ask around, for in that way will you hear about cremations, tooth-filings, and other interesting ceremonies.

Many important temple festivals fall at much the same time as *Galungan* and *Kuningan*.

Pura Luhur, Batukau: Galungan + 1 day "Perang Pandan" Tenganan: Kuningan (Noon) "Perang Dewa" Desa Sattyra, Klungkung: Kuningan (4 p.m.) Pura Dasar, Gel Gel: Galungan + 5 days Pura Taman Pule, Mas: Kuningan Pura Sada, Kapal:

Kuningan Pura Sada, Kapal: Kuningan Pura Sakenan, Serangan: Kuningan, and Kuningan + 1 day Pura Tanah Lot: Kuningan + 4 days Pura Petilan/ Pengerebongan, Kesiman: Kuningan + 8 days Pura Luhur, Uluwatu: Kuningan + 10 days Pura Goa Lawah: Kuningan + 10 days Pura Goa Lawah: Kuningan + 10 days Pura Taman Ayun,

Mengwi: Kuningan + 10 days

Although the occurrence of festivals based on the lunar calendar cannot be predetermined exactly, they tend to fall at much the same time each year. *Nyepi* usually falls towards the end of March or beginning of April. Many important temples have festivals on the full moon of the fourth month (end of September-early October) or on the full moon of the tenth month (early-middle April).

SANUR

Sanur is for gracious living, peaceful and quiet. More "international" but somehow far less cosmopolitan than frenetic Kuta. Foreigners have been staying in Sanur since the 1920s, and they know how to take care of you here. Strictly first-class, with very few places for budget travelers. Seek out the lovely Sanur temples, particularly when they are having their anniversary ceremonies (*odalan*), every seven months.

WHERE TO STAY

There are so many excellent hotels in Sanur that you can scarcely go wrong. The main choice is between the convenience and luxury of the large 4-star establishments (the **Bali Beach**, the **Bali Hyatt** and the **Sanur Beach**), or the quietude and personality of a private bungalow by the sea. Reservations are advisable during the peak tourist seasons (July-Sept and Dec-Jan). Prices quoted below do not include the obligatory 21 percent tax and service surcharge. During the low seasons (between Jan 15-July 15 and Sept 1-Dec 15) a 10-20 percent discount from the published rates is available at many hotels just for the asking.

First Class
(US$35 per night and up)

For a large luxury hotel, the **Bali Hyatt** offers a remarkably breezy, spacious "Royal Hawaiian" feeling, with public areas, clay tennis courts and hanging Babylonian gardens. The venerable **Hotel Bali Beach** (con-

structed as a war reparation by the Japanese in the 60s) looks more like a traditional "Miami Beach" luxury hotel—a 10-story concrete block by the sea, set amidst a golf course, bowling alleys, and two swimming pools. It has assumed, over the years, the stature of a major Balinese institution, training chefs and staff through its hotel school and providing bread and pastries from its bakery to other hotels.

Last but not least of the three 4-star establishments, the smaller **Sanur Beach Hotel**, owned by Garuda, claims to be the friendliest large hotel in Sanur, with thorough service, a handsome staff and Rudy Vallee-style concerts.

Of the smaller "bungalow" resorts, the **Tandjung Sari** is the hands down favorite of frequent visitors.

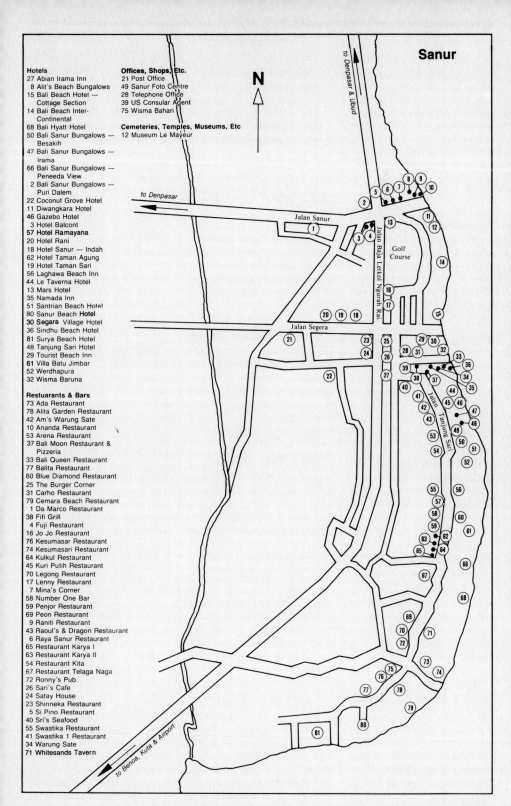

Sanur

N

to Denpasar & Ubud

Hotels
27 Abian Irama Inn
8 Alit's Beach Bungalows
15 Bali Beach Hotel —
    Cottage Section
14 Bali Beach Inter-
    Continental
68 Bali Hyatt Hotel
50 Bali Sanur Bungalows —
    Besakih
47 Bali Sanur Bungalows —
    Irama
66 Bali Sanur Bungalows —
    Peneeda View
2 Bali Sanur Bungalows —
    Puri Dalem
22 Coconut Grove Hotel
11 Diwangkara Hotel
46 Gazebo Hotel
3 Hotel Balcont
57 **Hotel Ramayana**
20 Hotel Rani
18 Hotel Sanur — Indah
62 Hotel Taman Agung
19 Hotel Taman Sari
56 Laghawa Beach Inn
44 Le Taverna Hotel
13 Mars Hotel
35 Namada Inn
51 Santrian Beach Hotel
80 Sanur Beach **Hotel**
30 **Segara** Village Hotel
36 Sindhu Beach Hotel
81 Surya Beach Hotel
48 Tanjung Sari Hotel
29 Tourist Beach Inn
61 **Villa Batu Jimbar**
52 Werdhapura
32 Wisma Baruna

Restuarants & Bars
73 Ada Restaurant
78 Alita Garden Restaurant
42 Am's Warung Sate
10 Ananda Restaurant
53 Arena Restaurant
37 Bali Moon Restaurant &
    Pizzeria
33 Bali Queen Restaurant
77 Balita Restaurant
60 Blue Diamond Restaurant
25 The Burger Corner
31 Carho Restaurant
79 Cemara Beach Restaurant
1 Da Marco Restaurant
38 Fifi Grill
4 Fuji Restaurant
16 Jo Jo Restaurant
76 Kesumasar Restaurant
74 Kesumasari Restaurant
64 Kulkul Restaurant
45 Kuri Putih Restaurant
70 Legong Restaurant
17 Lenny Restaurant
7 Mina's Corner
58 Number One Bar
59 Penjor Restaurant
69 Peon Restaurant
9 Raniti Restaurant
43 Raoul's & Dragon Restaurant
6 Raya Sanur Restaurant
65 Restaurant Karya I
63 Restaurant Karya II
54 Restaurant Kita
67 Restaurant Telaga Naga
72 Ronny's Pub.
26 Sari's Cafe
24 Satay House
23 Shinneka Restaurant
5 Si Pino Restaurant
40 Sri's Seafood
55 Swastika Restaurant
41 Swastika 1 Restaurant
34 Warung Sate
71 **Whitesands Tavern**

Offices, Shops, Etc.
21 Post Office
49 Sanur Foto Centre
28 Telephone Office
39 US Consular Agent
75 Wisma Bahari

Cemeteries, Temples, Museums, Etc
12 Museum Le Mayeur

to Denpasar

Jalan Sanur

Golf
Course

Jalan Baja Letkol Ngurah Rai

Jalan Segera

Jalan Tanjung Sari

to Benoa, Kuta & Airport

Run by Wija Wawo-Runtu and his wife, Tati, this was one of the island's first beach bungalow establishments and is still the most charming and efficient. Every nook and cranny of this Shangrila is decorated in the manner of pleasure gardens for Bali's rajas. Wia's latest addition (since the hotel's vintage Ford bus was attacked by a band of Balinese painters) is a nightclub, Rumours, which feaures backgammon and a well-stocked video loft.

Among the many other bungalow-style hotels, the **Segara Village** deserves mention for its snazzy and congenial Indonesian atmosphere. Each of the hotel's five "villages" has a distinctive character and its "Leisure Club" provides a variety of activities for everyone in the family including small children.

And the **La Taverna** gets kudos for its Italian Balinesian and attractive beach restaurant-pizzeria.

Bali Hyatt Hotel (348 rooms), Sanur, P.O. Box 392, Denpasar, phone: 8271, tlx: 35127. A/c rooms and suites overlooking the sea. Several restaurants, swimming pool, discotheque, convention facilities, broad beach. US$72 to $400 a night.

Bali Sanur Bungalows (Unit Besakih Bungalows) (44 rooms), Jl. Tanjungsari, Sanur, Denpasar, phone: 8423-4, tlx: 35178 GRIYA BSB. Each hotel is set in a meandering garden that winds its way to the sea. A pool and two restaurants. All bungalows with a/c, western baths and hot water. US$36/$42 a night.

Bali Sanur Bungalows (Unit Penida View) (44 rooms), Jl. Tanjungsari, Sanur, Denpasar, phone: 8425, tlx: 35178 GRIYA BSB. Cable "Peneeda Bali". Part of the large "Bali Sanur Bungalows" group. A bungalow-style hotel right on Sanur beach. A pool and two restaurants. All bungalows with a/c, western baths and hot water. US$36/$42 a night.

Gazebo Beach Cottages (60 rooms), Jl. Tanjung Sari, Sanur, P.O. Box 134, Denpasar, phone: 8300. Private beach with cool 2-story bungalows in a garden. All with a/c and hot water. US$30 to $40 a night.

Hotel Bali Beach (577 rooms), Sanur, P.O. Box 275, Denpasar, phone: 8511-7, tlx: 35133, 35129. Ten-storey Inter-Continental hotel with a new 2-story wing. Private beach, three swimming pools, four restaurants, bowling alleys, tennis courts, a golf course, water skiing, scuba diving and wind-surfing. Convention facilities. All rooms with a/c, carpeting, hot water. Rooms for US$60-$245 a night.

La Taverna Bungalows (44 rooms), Jl. Tanjungsari, Sanur, Denpasar, phone: 8497. Delightful thatched bungalows with Italian stucco walls and elegantly-styled rooms set in a meandering Balinese garden. Private beach, swimming pool and pizzeria. All rooms with a/c and hot water from US$50/$55. Four person family units and suites for US$75 and $85.

Peneeda View Bungalows (44 rooms), Jl. Tanjung Sari, Sanur, P.O. Box 306, Denpasar, phone: 8421-2, tlx: 35178 GRIYA BSB. Located on the beach right next to the Bali Hyatt. Similar to Besakih Beach but with one restaurant, the Nusa Penida. All with a/c and hot water. Rooms from US$35/$40 with $100 suites.

Santrian Beach Hotel (80 rooms), Jl. Tanjungsari, Sanur, P.O. Box 55, Denpasar, phone: 8181-5, tlx: 35169. Private seaside bungalows in a spacious garden, some of which open into a garden and others with a view of the ocean. All rooms with a private terrace. One pool, two restaurants, one opens for 24 hours, traditional dance performances Saturday night and a barbeque on Wednesday night. Rooms from US$36/$40 to US$32/$35 not including tax and service charge.

Sanur Beach Hotel (320 rooms), Sanur, P.O. Box 279, Denpasar, phone: 8011-5, tlx: 35135. Garuda-owned 4-story international hotel, with 26 bungalows attached. All rooms with carpeting, a/c and hot water. Four restaurants, swimming pool, ocean sports facilities, tennis courts, mini-golf and a video viewing room with video cassette rental available. Rooms and bungalows for US$50/$55 to US$60/$70 a night. Suites for US$90 to $200 a night.

Segara Village Hotel (93 rooms), Jl. Segara, Sanur, P.O. Box 91, Denpasar, phone: 8407-8, 8231, tlx: 35143 SEGARA DPR. A variety of charming, private bungalows, some patterned after traditional rice granaries, arranged in tiny gardened "villages" bordering the sea. Two swimming pools, complete water sports facilities, traditional Balinese dance classes, a children's recreation room, gym, tennis courts and lots of personal attention from the staff. All rooms with hot water and a/c. Rooms US$30/$42 and bungalows US$50/$55 to $60/$65. Suites US$80/$100 a night.

Sindu Beach Hotel (50 rooms), Jl. Sindu, Sanur, P.O. Box 181, Denpasar, phone: 8351-2, tlx: 35166-35141 DPS. Bungalow hotel right on the beach, with a swimming pool. All with a/c and hot water. Rooms cost between US$39 to $65 a night. Inquire about the 25%-40% discount in the low season.

Tanjung Sari Hotel (24 rooms), Jl. Tanjungsari, Sanur, P.O. Box 25, Denpasar, phone: 8441, tlx: 35257 TANSARI. Name means "Cape of Flowers." Serene and stylish, with private bungalows by the sea and lovely gardens. Excellent service and food. All rooms a/c with hot water. US$65 to $170 a night.

Village Club Bungalows formerly the "Puri Dalem," (44 rooms), Jl. Raya Sanur, P.O. Box 306, Denpasar, phone: 8421-2, tlx: 35187. Located on the main road to Denpasar, it is just a 5-minute walk from the beach. Simply furnished bungalows in a lush garden setting. All with a/c and hot water. US$32 to 45 a night.

Intermediate Range
(US$15-35 a night)

We recommend the **Irama Bungalows** ("casual but cozy") at the upper end of the scale. **Baruna Beach Inn**, the smallest and one of the oldest bungalow hotels in Sanur is also very personal and cozy, with a superb breakfast pavilion overlooking the lagoon. All of the other bungalow establishments in this category are of excellent value and generally quite pleasant, the major difference being that some have a beachfront and air-conditioning, while rooms at the lower end of the scale have only a fan and no private beach. Prices do not include the 21 percent tax and service charge unless otherwise stated.

Abian Srama Inn [42 rooms] Jl. Brig. Ngurah Rai, Sanur, phone:8415. Ten minutes from the beach. Pleasant and reasonable rooms, some with a/c and hot water, all with laundry service and free hotel transportation. Rooms US$9/$12 to $20/$25 a night.

Alit's Beach Bungalow (25 rooms), Jl. Hang Tuah

Sanur, P.O. Box 102, Denpasar, phone: 8567, 8560 tlx: 35165 ALIT DPR. At the north end and two minutes from the beach. Cottages in a garden that borders a small road, and a beachfront packed with brightly-painted sailing craft. A/c and hot water. US$35 to $37 a night.

Bali Sanur "Irama" Bungalows (23 rooms), Jl. Tanjung Sari, Sanur, P.O. Box 306, Denpasar, phone: 8421-2, tlx: 35178. The nicest of the "standard class". Bali Sanur Bungalows. All rooms with a/c and hot water, surrounding a spacious, manicured garden. Small pool but no beachfront. Excellent and inexpensive restaurant, the "Kuri Putih" (see WHERE TO EAT section). US$25/$30 a night.

Bali Sanur "Respati Beach" Bungalows (20 rooms), Sanur, P.O. Box 306, Denpasar, phone: 8421-2. A narrow string of duplex bungalows with white tiled floors, twin beds, a/c, bathtub and shower. Comfortable but basic. Narrow beach front, restaurant and small swimming pool. US$25/$30 a night.

Baruna Beach Inn (7 rooms), Jl. Sindu, Sanur, Denpasar, phone: 8546. Oldest hotel on the beach. Traditional thatched rooms furnished with Balinese antiques open onto a wide court-yard bordering the sea. Balinese archways open into a garden. Small and personal. All with a/c and hot water. Rooms US$35/$40 a night including breakfast, tax and service. Cheaper during off season.

Diwangkara Beach Hotel (36 rooms), Jl. Pantai Sanur, Sanur, P.O. Box 120, Denpasar, phone: 8577, 8412. Private bungalows in a secluded compound just behind the Le Mayeur museum at the north end of the beach strip. Some with a/c and hot water. Swimming pool. One minute from the beach. Rooms are between US$20 to $32 .

Hotel Belcont (14 rooms) Jl. Hang Tuah, Sanur, phone: 8250, Denpasar. Seven minutes from the beach. Some rooms with a/c from US$15/$20 to $30/$35. Additional charge for extra bed or triple.

Hotel Ramayana (10 rooms) Jl. Tanjungsari, Sanur, Batu Jimbar, P.O. Box 66, Denpasar, phone: 8429. Clean rooms, five minutes from the beach. This hotel takes pride in catering to the individual traveler's needs. Rooms US$16 with a fan, $20 with a/c and $25 for a private bungalow.

Laghawa Beach Inn (12 rooms), Jl. Tanjung Sari, Sanur, Denpasar, phone: 8494, 8214. Simple cottages with a/c and hot water in a garden. Five minutes from the beach. Rooms from US$15/$25 to $20/$30 a night. Triplets available and family suites for $40.

Mars Hotel (18 rooms), Jl. Raya Sanur, Sanur, P.O. Box 68, Denpasar, phone: 8236. Bungalows in a gar-den, 5-minutes from beach. All with a/c and hot water. Rooms US$20/$24. During the high season, room price does not include the 15 per cent tax and service charge which is included in the low season. US$32/35.

Puri Mas Hotel (16 rooms), Jl. Raya Sanur, Tanjung Bungkak, Denpasar. About 3.5 km from Sanur Beach on the main road to Denpasar. Simple accommodations in a bungalow complex. Some with a/c and hot water. US$22 to $30 a night.

Queen Bali Hotel (17 bungalows), Jl. Sindu, Sanur, P.O. Box 119, Denpasar, Phone: 8054, 8035. Simple bungalows; all with a/c and hot water. Restaurant, bar and discotheque. Quiet gardens two minutes from the beach. US$32/$35 a night.

Sanur Village Club (40 rooms) Jl. Hang Tuah, Sanur, P.O. Box 306, Denpasar, phone: 8421-2, tlx:35178 GRIYA BSB. All rooms surround a central garden with a pool, seven minutes from the beach. Rooms with both twin and double beds US$20/$25.

Shanti Village (10 rooms) Next door to Santrian Beach Hotel on Jl. Tanjung Sari, P.O. Box 460, Denpasar, phone: 8060. Simple hotel with some family suites. Guests can use the Santrian Beach pool and beach access. Rooms US$25/$30. Inquire about discount during low season.

Surya Beach Hotel. Down past the Sanur Beach Hotel, at the very southern end of the strip. Quiet and secluded.

Budget
(under US$15 a night)

Cheapest room in Sanur is US$6 a night. Even budget places provide laundry service and some offer guided tours and transportation to the airport. Inquire at the front desk. The **Tourist Beach Inn** is closest to the water, but the three bungalow establishments across from the Post Office are a bit cleaner and more spacious. The **Taman Sari** has some inexpensive rooms with air-conditioning.

The **Taman Agung** in Batujimbar is the nicest budget place in the Sanur area, with well-kept gardens and very quiet. If serenity is not required, budget travelers get better value for money in Kuta, however.

Hotel Rani (25 rooms) Jl. Segara, Sanur, Denpasar. Opposite the Post Office, 10 minutes from the beach. These losmen-style rooms are clean and quiet. There are no rooms with a/c but all have cold water showers and western toilets. Rooms from US$7 to $8 including tax and service, and an additional dollar for breakfast.

Sanur Indah (10 rooms) Jl. Segara, Sanur, Denpasar. Several losmen-style rooms with a fan, 10 minutes from the beach. US$7-10 including tax and service.

Taman Agung Beach Inn (20 rooms), Jl. Tanjungsari, Sanur, Denpasar, phone: 8549, 8006. Very pleasant, losmen-style rooms with fan, and facing a well-kept garden. Five minutes from the beach. US$8 to $15 a night, including tax, service and breakfast.

Taman Sari (22 rooms) Jl. Segara, Sanur, Denpasar. Next door to the Rani and the Sanur Indah, and the nicest of the three. Some rooms with a/c. All rooms with cold water baths and western toilets from US$7 to $15 including tax and service.

Tourist Beach Inn (10 rooms), Jl. Segara, Sanur, P.O. Box 42, Denpasar, phone: 8418. Losmen-style rooms with a fan, cold water showers and western toilets, built around a central garden. Very close to the beach and quiet. Rooms US$8 to $12 including breakfast, tax and service.

WHAT TO EAT

For elegant as well as informal western dining, Sanur's **Bali Hyatt**, **Bali Beach** and **Sanur Beach** hotels offer a wide choice of poolside lunches, buffets, barbeques, coffee shops and supper clubs with or without evening dance performances and/or live musical entertainment. The kitchens are operated under the direction of European chefs, whilst the menus are predominantly Western, Indonesian, Chinese and Japanese dishes are also available. Many coffee shops are open 24 hours.

The **Tanjung Sari Hotel** restaurant has a formidable reputation for Indonesian "rijsttafel" and a sublime atmosphere. A bamboo "tingklink" orchestra provides the ideal accompaniment to dinner in a cosy, antique-filled dining area by the beach. The restaurant's new menu has a more creative "nouvelle Bali" slant, and the bar, designed by Australian artist Donald Friend, is an elevated pavilion overlooking the sea.

At **Kuri Putih**, in the Bali Sanur "Irama" Bungalows, chef Nyoman Sana of Ubud has at last brought his kitchen to Sanur. Try the barbequed specials from the grill and choose from a wide range of salads and juice drinks. Reasonably priced, with a complimentary welcome drink made with real Bali brem in the evening.

The **Kul Kul Restaurant** near the Hyatt has an elegant bar and serves good western, Indonesian and Chinese cuisine in its handsome garden pavilion. Book for the dinner-dance night (Batuan's famous "Frog Dance" troupe).

The nearby **Swastika Gardens** is also a great favorite with those who are tired of paying hotel prices. The food is fair and the menu varied enough to satisfy most tastes—try the Balinese speciality, curried duck ("bebek tutu").

The **Telaga Naga** ("Dragon Lake") opposite the Bali Hyatt is a spectacu-

larly stylish Szechuan restaurant under the stars overlooking a lotus pond, designed by Hyatt architect Kerry Hill. The food is good and the prices are non-hotel, though the restaurant is owned and operated by the Bali Hyatt. The chef is from Singapore. Try the "Chicken With Dried Chilli Peppers," the "King Prawn" and the duck dishes.

The "Best Italian food on Bali" is available at **Trattoria "Da Marco"**, where Reno and Diddit da Marco have guarded their reputation and clientele for 15 years now. Try the grilled fish, spaghetti carbonara, bean salad and delicious steaks—truly the best in Bali.

La Taverna is part of a Hong Kong-based chain of Italian restaurants in Asia. The Sanur branch is a charming bar and open dining area on the beach, with a menu that features imported cheeses, French pepper steak, seafood and pizza from a real brick pizza oven.

For a meal by the seaside, try the inexpensive **Sanur Beach Market** (on Jl. Segara right at the beach), a little outdoor restaurant run as a cooperative by Sanur's mayor. Great for lunch (*sate, nasi goreng* and fresh grilled fish) or dinner (grilled lobster), with delicious Balinese desserts, all at reasonable prices. Every Wednesday and Saturday night they have a dance performance and a special set dinner, though there is no cover charge and you may order from the regular menu.

Rumah Makan "Mini" on the by-pass has good budget meals—*nasi cap cay* and *sate* for less than US$1. And the last "warung" (Mak Beng's) on the left on Jl. Raya Sanur by the beach (just past the entrance to the Hotel Bali Beach) has fantastic grilled fish.

Finally, **Meme Disco** and her basket of "turtle sate" are parked in front of the old Sanur Police Station every evening from 4-8 p.m. And despite considerable bad press during the World Wildlife Fund's recent conference here, a packet of these grilled morsels with a gin and tonic is still one of the island's best kept culinary secrets.

SHOPPING

If you don't mind a surcharge for the comfort and convenience of shopping in an air-conditioned arcade, the **Bali Hyatt**, **Bali Beach** and the **Sanur Beach** hotels all have well-stocked shopping malls. In fact they have some of the best antiques on the island (at international prices).

The **Sari Bali** boutique in the Bali Hyatt and the **Barbarella** in the Hotel Bali Beach also have some locally-produced demi-haute couture bargains. Have a look too at the **Sari Bumi** shop in the Bali Hyatt, for locally-produced pottery and ceramics.

For inexpensive handicrafts and souvenirs, the **Sanur Beach Market** behind the Segara Village Hotel (on Jl. Segara at the beach) and the shops on the main road leading to the Sanur Beach Hotel are the best spots, packed with small shops selling gift items at reasonable prices. There is also a row of small shops hidden in an alley behind the **Museum Le Mayeur**, where women assemble exquisite shirts and blouses by attaching Sumbanese *ikat* dyed fabric with crochet.

The main Sanur road, **Jl. Tanjungsari**, is lined with artshops selling carvings, batiks, paintings and handicrafts. **Misran** has a studio open to the public on Jl. Tanjung Sari, right near Sari's Cafe. You can recognize him by the roll of canvas stretched out to dry, which he meticulously primes using a traditional method.

For magazines and newspapers, the lobby drugstore at the Bali Hyatt has the island's most comprehensive selection, including fashion glossies.

Sailing from Sanur: The fleet of native outrigger canoes (*jukung*) lining Sanur's beach, with their brightly-coloured "Bir Bintang" sails, are obviously no longer used for fishing, now that the tourists have taken to chartering them for cruises across the water. The fishermen have wisely banded together into a cooperative to regularize their rates and give everybody an equal chance to get passengers. Each boat owner may now only go out once a day. After that, he furls his sail and goes home. The standard fee, for a sail around the lagoon, is US$7 for one hour. Sometimes, late in the afternoon, you can bargain a bit and get a slightly reduced rate, but normally they stick to this price.

To **Pulau Serangan** ("Turtle Island") and back costs about US$16, a voyage of about 2 hours each way. Across to **Nusa Penida** or **Nusa Lembongan** costs US$18 one-way, US$20 round-trip, and takes about 4-5 hours each way. At certain times of the year, however, the straits are full of strong currents and whirlpools and this voyage is not advised in a *jukung*. Check with your hotel.

MUSEUMS

Museum Le Mayeur, on the beach just north of the Hotel Bali Beach in Sanur, houses the collection of paintings of the late Belgian painter, Le Mayeur, who moved to Bali in 1932 and lived here for 26 years. His house was bequeathed to the government after Le Mayeur's death, and his collection was then looked after by the painter's lovely wife, Ni Polok, once Bali's most famous "legong" dancer. She has now passed away, too, but the museum is still open daily.

A few hundred feet from the Telephone Office, on a rutted dirt side-road, is **Pura Agung**, a Balinese temple. Visitors come here to witness what ancient worship is like, untrodden by tourists.

In front is a small soccer field with children making a goalpost of the main entrance, but inside the flowers and incense reassure you the moss-covered ruins are in use. Ancient banyan trees, though hollow with age and offerings yet miraculously alive, serve even more than the man-made structure to produce an aura of timelessness. Although it is but a walled-in square, floored with dirt and centered around a symbolic doorway capped by a tall spire, the feeling of a cathedral cannot be mistaken. This is obscured by the profusion of bilbulous gargoyles, which rather than flourishes as in the medieval or primitive sense, lacking delicacy and restraint, seem to counteract the silence. Whereas these decorations came from a later time, it is in the architectural purity that is still to be found the strength and fertility of the original soil. You have here a projection of the Balinese mind.

KUTA

Kuta in the 80s is a malignant seaside Carnaby Street of the 60s. Chaotic, noisy, lots of hype, but a great playground. Originally what drew visitors to Kuta was the wide beach and the surf, and it still has the best seafront on the island, though now cluttered with hundreds of homestays, restaurants, bars, boutiques, travel agencies, artshops, car and bike rentals, banks, cassette shops and scores of tourists, domestic and foreign. Though there are now many first-class hotels, the five km strip still caters best to the economy traveler who likes to be in the thick of things. The Legian end of the beach is the best place to stay for any period of time—much quieter and more relaxed. Stay in Sanur, though, if you really want peace of mind and solitude.

GETTING ACQUAINTED

Upon your arrival in Kuta, you may wish to visit the **Bali Government Tourism Office** on Jl. Bakung Sari (near the corner of Jl. Airport Ngurah Rai) where you can get information about hotels, restaurants, performances and entertainment. There is a post office and teleTel/telex service, as well as a window where you may make hotel reservations.

A walk down the beach will give you a taste of the "Kuta scene." You will be besieged by eager young girls offering coconut oil massages. Be prepared to either barter (Rp 1000 is the going price), or sternly avoid them. You can also have your hair braided with beads for as much as Rp 10,000 per plait. Ladies selling tee shirts, bikinis, and the popular g-string bathing suits for the men will also approach you. They are used to getting a high price and will not accept less. Do not feel ashamed if you must be stern as there is often no other way to avert their advances.

To rent bicycles, cars, or motorcycles, visit the hotels or keep an eye out for one of the many shops offering the cheapest prices. Feel free to barter. A reasonable price for a bicycle is Rp 1000/day, and Rp 3000/day for a motorcycle. Auto prices depend upon the condition and the model, but can run anywhere from Rp 25,000-35,000/day.

Surfboards and equipment are available for rent and/or purchase at **Bali Barrel** (two locations) on Jl. Legian.

WHERE TO STAY

Kuta Beach has so many bungalows, hotels and homestays (called *losmen*, a term derived from the French word *logement*) that no list could ever be complete, nor is a list really needed. Drop in and shop around. The difference between Kuta and Sanur is that one has far more choices in the lower price range here. Reservations are recommended for the larger hotels during August and around Christmas-New Year.

First Class
($35 and up)

First Class bungalow resorts line the beach, providing the traveler with a number of excellent choices. The

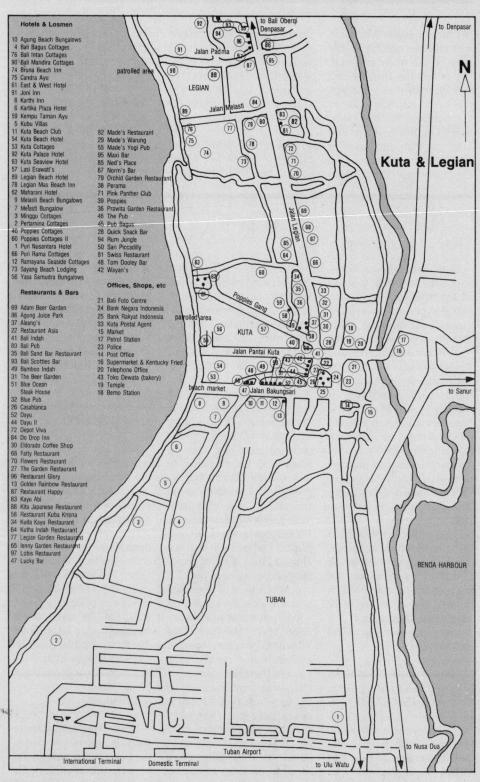

Hotels & Losmen

10 Agung Beach Bungalows
4 Bali Bagus Cottages
76 Bali Intan Cottages
90 Bali Mandira Cottages
74 Bruna Beach Inn
75 Candra Ayu
61 East & West Hotel
91 Joni Inn
8 Karthi Inn
6 Kartika Plaza Hotel
59 Kempu Taman Ayu
5 Kubu Villas
11 Kuta Beach Club
54 Kuta Beach Hotel
53 Kuta Cottages
92 Kuta Palace Hotel
63 Kuta Seaview Hotel
57 Lasi Erawati's
89 Legian Beach Hotel
58 Legian Mas Beach Inn
62 Maharani Hotel
9 Melasti Beach Bungalows
7 Melasti Bungalow
3 Minggu Cottages
2 Pertamina Cottages
40 Poppies Cottages
60 Poppies Cottages II
1 Puri Nusantara Hotel
66 Puri Rama Cottages
12 Ramayana Seaside Cottages
73 Sayang Beach Lodging
56 Yasa Samudra Bungalows

Restaurants & Bars

69 Adam Beer Garden
86 Agung Juice Park
37 Aleang's
22 Restaurant Asia
41 Bali Indah
80 Bali Pub
35 Bali Sand Bar Restaurant
93 Bali Scotties Bar
49 Bamboo Indah
31 The Beer Garden
5 Blue Ocean
  Steak House
32 Blue Pub
26 Casablanca
52 Dayu
44 Dayu II
72 Depot Viva
84 Do Drop Inn
30 Eldorado Coffee Shop
68 Fatty Restaurant
70 Flowers Restaurant
27 The Garden Restaurant
96 Restaurant Glory
13 Golden Rainbow Restaurant
87 Restaurant Happy
83 Kayu Abi
88 Kita Japanese Restaurant
58 Restaurant Kuba Krisna
34 Kuda Kayu Restaurant
64 Kutha Indah Restaurant
77 Legian Garden Restaurant
65 Jenny Garden Restaurant
97 Lobis Restaurant
47 Lucky Bar

82 Made's Restaurant
29 Made's Warung
55 Made's Yogi Pub
95 Maxi Bar
85 Ned's Place
57 Norm's Bar
79 Orchid Garden Restaurant
38 Perama
71 Pink Panther Club
39 Poppies
36 Prawita Garden Restaurant
46 The Pub
45 Pub Bagus
28 Quick Snack Bar
94 Rum Jungle
50 Sari Piccadilly
81 Swiss Restaurant
48 Tom Dooley Bar
42 Wayan's

Offices, Shops, etc

21 Bali Foto Centre
24 Bank Negara Indonesia
25 Bank Rakyat Indonesia
33 Kuta Postal Agent
15 Market
17 Petrol Station
23 Police
14 Post Office
16 Supermarket & Kentucky Fried
20 Telephone Office
43 Toko Dewata (bakery)
19 Temple
18 Bemo Station

Kuta & Legian

to Bali Oberoi
Denpasar

to Denpasar

LEGIAN

Jalan Padma

Jalan Melasti

Jalan Legian

patrolled area

Poppies Gang

KUTA

patrolled area

Jalan Pantai Kuta

Jalan Bakungsari

beach market

to Sanur

BENOA HARBOUR

TUBAN

to Nusa Dua

Tuban Airport

International Terminal   Domestic Terminal   to Ulu Watu

322

following are listed in order of location, south to north. Rates include breakfast unless noted otherwise, but not government tax or service charges.

Pertamina Cottages (178 rooms), close to the airport, P.O. Box 121, Kuta, Tel: 51161, tlx: 35131, cable: PERCOT Bali Indonesia. Located five minutes from the airport. This luxurious hotel was first built as a convention center by the state oil monopoly, Pertamina, and then opened to the general public in 1975. Facilities include several restaurants, banquet and convention halls, tennis courts, 3-hole golf course, badminton, boating, water skiing, wind surfing, and a swimming pool. Services available include laundry service, barber and beauty salon, drugstore, shopping arcade, bank, postal service, massage parlour, and medical service. All rooms with airconditioning, carpeting, and hot water, refrigerator, telephone, radio, and in-house movies. Standard US$65-75; deluxe cottages US$76-86; executive cottages: US$86-96; suites US$104-US$600.

Santika Beach Hotel (94), on Jl. Kartika, P.O. Box 1008 Tuban, Denpasar, Tel: 51267-8, tlx: 3527. An exquisite hotel with three swimming pools, coffee shop, restaurant, bar, tennis courts, and in-house video. All rooms are air-conditioned, and have refrigerators and taped-in music. Convention facilities seating

250 are available. Standard: US$50. Superior: US$60. Deluxe: US$70. Family Room: US$80. Sunset Suite: US$150.

Bali Rani Hotel (36), on Jl. Kartika, P.O. Box 1034 Tuban, Denpasar, Tel: 51369, tlx: 35279 BRANI DPR. Across the street from the beach, beautiful two-story buildings in traditional Balinese style, overlooking a central garden area with swimming pool. All rooms have air-conditioning, hot water, music, intercom, and private balcony or veranda. Restaurant serves Indonesian, Chinese, and Western food. Standard: US$32-36. Superior: US$36-40. Extra bed: US$10. Rates do not include breakfast.

Beach Hotel Kartika Plaza (120 rooms), Kuta Beach, P.O. Box 84, Denpasar, Tel: 51067-9, tlx: 35102 KAZA DPR. Beachside rooms and bungalows in a large garden. All with a/c and hot water. Table tennis, tennis court, and swimming pool. Convention facilities with seating capacity of 100. Garden View: US$34-40. Ocean View: US$36-44. Suite: US$60-80. Rates do not include breakfast.

Natour's Kuta Beach Hotel (83 rooms), Jl. Bakungsari, P.O. Box 226, Kuta, Tel: 51461-2, tlx: 35166. A bungalow-style hotel 150 metres from the beach. Air-conditioning or fan, hot water, refrigerator, color TV, private balcony or garden veranda. Standard: US$45-50. Suite: US$55-

60. Family Suite: US$110. Extra bed: US$15.

Intermediate Range (US$15-$35)

Intermediate Range accommodations are to be found everywhere in Kuta. Walk along the beach, or on the inland lanes if there are no vacancies on Jl. Legian. The following are at the northern end of the beach, and are excellent values.

Yasa Samudra Bungalows (65 rooms), on Jl. Pantai Kuta. P.O. Box 53, Denpasar, Tel: 51562, tlx: 35303 TLXBOOTH. Wonderful, quiet setting right in the middle of Kuta. Dining room famed for fresh seafood. Hot water, swimming pool, postal and laundry service. Fan-cooled Rooms: US$15-18. Air-conditioned Rooms: US$22-25. Family Room: US$35. Extra bed: US$6.

Kuta Seaview Cottage (37 rooms) at the north end of the beach, P.O. Box 36, Denpasar, Tel: 51961, tlx: 35208 SEAVIEW. Air-conditioning, hot shower, teleTel, in-room music, swimming pool, and restaurant. US$25-30.

Kuta Beach Club (96 rooms), Jl. Bakung Sari, P.O. Box 226, Kuta, Tel: 51261-2, tlx: 35138 KUTA CLUB. In the middle of Kuta, quiet bungalows and rooms surround a patio garden. All with air-conditioning and hot water. Mini tennis, badminton, swimming pool, and restaurant.

Standard: US$34-38. Bungalow: US$38-40.

Suite: US$60-75. Rates include government tax and service charge.

Kuta Cottages (40 rooms), Jl. Bakung Sari, P.O. Box 300, Kuta, Tel: 51101, 51406. Small bungalows at back of beach. Swimming pool, bar, and restaurant. Rates include breakfast. Fan-cooled cottages: US$12-18. Air-conditioned cottages: US$16-30.

Poppies Cottages I (Rooms #1-21), Poppies Gang I, Kuta (near Jl. Pantai Kuta and Jl. Legian) P.O. Box 378, Tel: 51059, 51149 tlx: 35516 POPCOT IA Attn: Poppies. Well-designed cottages in a beautiful garden, with hot water and refrigerator. The newest of two Poppies lodgings, only 300 metres from the beach. Frequently filled to capacity. Fan-cooled room: US$24. Air-conditioned room: US$29. Air-conditioned room with kitchen: US$35.

Poppies Cottages II (Rooms #22-25), Poppies Gang II, Kuta (north of Poppies II between beach and Jl. Legian) P.O. Box 378, Tel: 51059, 51149 tlx: 35516 POPCOT IA Attn: Poppies. Quite popular, but smaller than Poppies I, but it is still necessary to make reservations in advance. Same rates as Poppies I.

Ramayana Seaside Cottages (45 rooms), Jl. Bakung Sari, Kuta, P.O. Box 334, Denpasar, Tel: 51864-6, tlx: 35149. 150 meters from the beach. Fan-cooled room: US$20-$25. A/c room: US$25-32.

Budget
(under US$15 a night)

There are more than 300 "losmen" or homestays in the Kuta area, where rooms rent for only $2-5 a night. These vary greatly in quality, cleanliness and service, depending on the family who runs them. Often you'll be approached at the airport or at the bus terminal on arrival in Bali, and it will do you no harm to go along to have a look (be sure only that the price suits you beforehand). Frequently the place turns out to be quite nice. The best way to find a room, though, is just to walk around in any area that you fancy— whether near the beach or tucked back in the coconut groves, away from the crowds. Stop in at every house. Chances are they have rooms for rent and you can have a look and ask the price, which is negotiable in the off-season. Make your decision based on the people as much as the room, but once you have made a commitment, stick to it.

Rock-bottom rooms are available for US$1.50-2 a night, just a bed and four walls, with a shared splash bath and outhouse. For US$5-6 you get a private bath and a few frills.

WHAT TO EAT

New restaurants seem to open daily in Kuta, from small fruit salad and yoghurt stands by the beach, to large Chinese, French, Mexican or seafood and steak establishments. The quality of the food goes up and down as cooks come and go, so we list here only a few old standbys where you can hardly ever go wrong. Ask around though for tips on the latest "in" restaurant.

Made's Warung on Jl. Pantai Kuta hasn't missed a beat in its metamorphosis from one of only two foodstalls on the main street of a sleepy fishing village, to a hip "Cafe Voltaire" in this St. Tropez of the East. It has great food (spare ribs, Thai salads, escargots, turtle steaks, home-made ice cream and yogurt, chocolate-mint cake, capuccino, freshly squeezed orange and carrot juices, breakfast specials), great music and always a host of the bright young international Balinese demi-monde. Made also serves a fabulous Rijstaffel on Saturday night.

Poppies Restaurant on Poppies Gang I, a narrow lane parallel to Jl. Pantai, is another Kuta fixture. Avocado seafood salads, sashimi, chicken liver paté, tacos, grilled lobster, steaks, kabobs and tall mixed drinks pack this garden idyll to capacity during the peak tourist seasons. Get there early to be assured a table.

Nearby **TJ's Mexican Restaurant** serves the best enchiladas, tacos, tostadas and nachos this side of the Pacific. Try the eggplant or tahu/bean dip with chips, great with a cold beer.

Bali Indah and **Lenny's** are both first-rate for Chinese cuisine and seafood. Try the "crab in black bean sauce" and "Gung Bao chicken" at Bali Indah. And for fresh lobster or fried tuna fish steaks, go over to the **Yasa Samudra Hotel** (at the end of Jl. Pantai Kuta) and dine under the stars by the sea. **George & Dragon** on Jl. Legian serves elegant Indian samosas, tandoori chicken, and curry; truly one of the best cuisines in Kuta. For a special treat, start your meal with the chicken paté. Bali's only serious Japanese restaurant, **Yashi**, is located in the Pertamina Cottages, several kilometers south of Kuta at Tuban by the airport, where two Japanese chefs prepare a full range of dishes from sushi to tempura.

SHOPPING

Kuta is a fun place to browse. Bali now has one of the biggest garment industries in Southeast Asia. There are perhaps 500 designers and exporters working out of Kuta and Legian (including many young Italians and Japanese). The clothes are ideal for casual summer wear in warm climes. The island's inherent partiality towards the shiny and the glittering has inspired a mini industry of flashy jumpsuits and dazzling footwear. The best way to find a store that specializes in designs to your liking is to walk along Jl. Legian, or down Jl. Bakung Sari.

You will find a great number of "antique" stores in Kuta, but not all of these sell the real thing. Beware of contemporary masks, batik, and wood-carving. They are plentiful and poorly made, and can often be sold at unreasonably high prices to the unwary visitor. Authentic batik is at least two or three times more expensive than the machine-printed imitations, and unique wood carving is detectable by close scrutiny. Usually, the most telling sign is a willingness on the part of the shopkeeper to come down quickly from his original price.

Baharuddin's, on Jl. Bakung Sari in Kuta, specializes in *ikat* dyed fabrics from Sumba, Flores, Sawa, and Kalimantan; *ragi hidup* and *limar* from Sumatra; and many beads, baskets, and curios from various islands. The **Borneo Art Shop** on Jl. Legian makes nifty rattan and leather bags which are not only handsome, but handy for carrying towels, cameras, and tennis shoes. The same bag sells for almost twice as much in Singapore, so take a look here first. Antique silver, ivory, and textiles primarily from Borneo are the shop specialty. The **Kaliuda Art Shop on** on Jl. Legian has a large and whimsical collection of wood carvings and ikat from Timor, Sumba, and Flores. Even more antiques are available at **Anang's**, **East West Artshop**, and **Uddin's** (on Jl. Buni Sari, an alleyway off Jl. Legian near Jl. Bakung Sari).

If you are in the mood for lightweight shopping, visit the "Art" Market at the end of Jl. Bakung Sari where you can barter for tee shirts and inexpensive wood carvings. It was originally a government-sponsored affair, this new market is an indication of the modern trend toward mass production that is replacing the intricate, careful handwork of yesterday. Here you may find an endless variety of handicrafts at the lowest prices—for example, wind chimes that play *gamelan* music, and model banana trees of all shapes and sizes. Paintings and carvings are also available in Kuta, but it is best to shop for these items in Ubud, Mas and Batuan.

Kuta also has a supermarket, **Gelael**, where you can get lots of imported foodstuffs, toiletries and bottled drinks at reasonable prices. It's next to the petrol station on the road to Denpasar. The **Bali Photo Center** on the main road, has the most modern processing lab on the island and stocks a full range of film and photo accessories. They also sell books, maps, postcards and ice cream, and the travel agency next door is one of the most reliable.

Nightlife: Disco fever has hit Kuta with a vengeance. If your feet feel like dancing, visit **Peanuts** and **Cheaters** on Jl. Legian. It has elevated dancefloors with mirrors, strobe, and swirling colored lights. A great place to get your blood moving, let off some steam, and watch the idiosyncratic styles of several cultures come crashing together in a heady cacophony of physical expression.

LEGIAN

The village of Legian lies at the north end of the Kuta Beach strip. This is the place to stay if you want the best of both worlds. Conveniently located within 15 minutes from the center of Kuta, yet safely removed from the nerve-wrecking intensity and hype, Legian is perfect for extended vacations.

TRANSPORT

The main road of Legian is a vehicular maelstrom linking Legian to Kuta and parts north. To get yourself around and about the town, you can rent a motorcycle, car, or bicycle at any one of many rental shops. They are also easily available at:

Bali Mandira Cottages (end of Jl. Padma) Car: US$25 per day; Jeep: US$30; Mini Bus: US$35 per day.

Bali Purnama (on Jl. Melasti at corner where it meets Jl. Legian) Tel: 51901, 51792, tlx: 35303. Car: US$25 per day, $175 for 2 weeks; Jeep: US$25-30/day, $175-210 for 2 weeks; Motorbike: US$3.50 -4.50 per day, $24-30 for 2 weeks; Bicycle: US$1.50 per day, $10 for 2 weeks.

WHERE TO STAY

There are several first class hotels in Legian, a great number of intermediate-range bungalows, and a plethora of inexpensive "losmen". As is true in Kuta, you will find what suits you best by shopping around.

First Class
(US$35 a night and up)

First class hotels are on the beach, fully air-conditioned with hot water, restaurants, and swimming pools. Spacious lobbies, gift shops, travel and tour services and free transportation make your stay as pleasant as possible. Prices do not include tax or service charges.

Bali Intan Cottages (at the end of Jl. Melasti) Jl. Melasti 1, P.O. Box 1002, Legian, Kuta, Tel: 51770, tlx: 35200 BINCO DPS. Closest first class hotel to Kuta. Tennis court, coffee shop, snack bar, and seafood restaurant. Standard Room (70): wall-to-wall carpet, teleTel, color TV, private balcony. US$50-55. Cottage (48): shower, individual cottage terrace. US$56-60. Suite (4): US$125 plus $10 per extra person. Includes two children under 12 years old free of charge.

Bali Mandira Cottages (at the end of Jl. Padma) Jl. Padma, Box 1003, Denpasar, Tel: 51363-4, tlx: 35215 MANDIRA DPS. Built in 1982, this friendly and immaculate hotel provides tennis and squash courts, tours for skin-diving and snorkeling, and an open view of the ocean. Standard Cottage (46): one-story, with refrigerator. US$30-40. Deluxe Cottage (48): two-stories, close to beach. US$30-40. Suite (2): sitting/dining room. US$60.

Kuta Palace Hotel (at the end of Jl. Pura Bagus Teruna) Jl. Pura Bagus Taruna, Legian, Kuta, P.O. Box 244, Denpasar, Tel: 51461-2, tlx: 35234 KPH DPR. A pleasant atmosphere which caters to the young, complete with volleyball court, and an open-air theater with weekly performances of Balinese dance. Standard: US$40-45, Superior: US$45-50, Deluxe: $50-55, Family Room: US$75, Kuta Palace Suite: US$85.

Bali Oberoi (at the end of Jl. Kayu Ayu, on the northern end of the beach) Jl. Kayu Ayu, P.O. Box 351, Denpasar, Tel: 51061, tlx: 35125 OBHOTELDPR. Designed by Australian architect Peter Muller, the hotel's coral-rock lanais and villas are adaptations of classic Balinese "puri" palace designs. Private and secluded beach, luxurious accommodations. Lanai Cottage: US$75-85. Private Villa: US$155. Presidential Villa with private swimming pool: US$255. Price includes surfboards, in-house movies, shuttle to and from airport. Services available include massage and sauna, beauty parlor, dry cleaning, and medical doctor.

Intermediate Range
(US$15 to $35 a night)

Intermediate Range accommodations are plentiful in Legian. Although most do not have the convenience of air-conditioning, they are all very comfortable and affordable. The alphabetical listing below is only a partial one. You will easily locate more by strolling through the streets or along the beachfront. New places are being built constantly, as Legian moves ahead to take its place among the noteable beach resorts.

Kuta Kumala Bungalows (on the road between Jl. Blue Ocean and Jl. Pura Bagus Teruna) P.O. Box 451, Denpasar. Newly built in 1984, featuring a quiet location away from the beach, swimming pool, and small restaurant. Cottage: fan, bathtub, US$16. Bungalow: air-conditioning, shower. US$13-16.

Legian Beach Hotel (near the end of Jl. Melasti, very close to beach) Jl. Melasti, P.O. Box 308, Denpasar, Bali Tel: 51365-6. tlx: 35104 LEBE HOTEL DPS. Large facility wrapped in a relaxed atmosphere, the hotel offers free airport transport, hot water, and a restaurant.
Rooms with air-conditioning: US$34-45.
Room with fan: USS$20-22.

Legian Cottages (on Jl. Blue Ocean, near the beach), Jl. Blue Ocean, P.O. Box 1020, Denpasar, Tel: 51876-7, tlx: 35168. Air-conditioned or fan-cooled rooms, a modest restaurant, and a

meticulous garden setting. US$21-25.

Legian Village Hotel (on Jl. Padma in the center of town) Adjacent restaurant serves wide variety of Indonesian and Western dishes. Swimming pool, laundry service. Rooms with air-conditioning or fan, hot water: US$15-20. Rooms with fan: US$12-15.

Orchid Garden Restaurant (near end of Jl. Pura Bagus Teruna) Tel: 51802. Not to be confused with Orchid Garden Bar and Restaurant on Jl. Melasti, this intimate establishment offers clean rooms and some of the best food in Legian. US$8-10.

Purnama Garden Cottages (on Jl. Melasti II, north of Jl., Pura Bagus Teruna) P.O. Box 1051, Tuban, Tel: 51792 or 51901, tlx: 35303. Hot water, fan-cooled.
Cottage: US$7-15.Bungalow: US$12-22.
Family Room with kitchen and extra room: US$35.

Rama Garden Cottages (on Jl. Padma, near the beach) Jl. Padma, P.O. Box 334, Tel: 51971-2, tlx: 35263 RAMACO IA RAMA GARDEN. Modern in style and comfort, this small hotel offers refrigerators in every roon, tiled bathrooms with hot water, air-conditioning, and teleTel. Swimming pool with restaurant. US$29-32.

Especially noteworthy in

Legian are the inexpensive, beachfront hotels which can best be seen and evaluated by a walking tour along the beach. The following are listed in order of location, south to north:

Sari Beach Inn (between Jl. Padma and Jl. Pura Bagus Teruna) Clean, pleasant, fan-cooled rooms in a beautiful garden setting. More expensive rooms are upstairs with balcony. US$8-US$12.

Legian Sunset Beach Hotel (between Jl. Pura Bagus Teruna and Jl. Blue Ocean) Secluded and peaceful. Right next to the Blue Ocean Bar and Restaurant which caters to the ex-60s sun-seekers and searchers. US$10-15.

Evergreen Bungalows (to the north of the Blue Ocean). It has two-story, thatched-roof and spacious bungalows. Hot water and fan. US$15-25.

WHAT TO EAT

Most of the eateries in Legian offer similiar bills of fare which range from the Indonesian *nasi goreng* and *satay* to Western-style breakfasts and omelettes. A number of hotels have excellent restaurants, such as the Bali Oberoi and Bali Mandira. In addition, there are a handful of distinctive restaurants in Legian which deserve mention.

Kura Kura (at the Bali Oberoi) is perfect for a special occasion. Try to get there before the sun sets for a romantic cocktail hour. Bouillabaise de l'ocean Indonesian, grilled lobster, and smoked salmon are all well-prepared and delicious.

Bali Mandira offers an extensive menu at reasonable prices. A special Balinese dinner on Tuesday, and live traditional music on Friday make dinner there a delightful experience.

Bali Aussie and **Bali Too Bar and Restaurant** (Jl. Melasti) were designed with the Australian traveler in mind. On Monday night at Bali Too you can get an Aussie meal consisting of minestrone, roast beef, pork, or chicken, potato, vegetables, gravy, bread, and fruit all for only about US$4. Dinner is served at 7 p.m.

Nightlife in Legian is quiet by Kuta standards. The **Anchorage** and **Waltzing Matilda** on Jl. Legian, and **Chez Gado Gado** at the end of Jl. Seminyak cater to those who like to go out after dinner, but would rather avoid the disco scene. **Bobbie's** on Jl. Melasti is another popular nightspot with a low profile.

EXCURSIONS

Tours can be arranged through any of the larger hotels, or smaller businesses in town. The following daily sightseeing coach tours, coded by color for your convenience, are made available for you:
Kintamani (Red):
7 hours US$6-7

Besakih Temple (Blue):
8 hours US$6-7

Monkey Forest & Bedugul (Green):
8 hours US$6-7

For these and more extensive tours, visit the **SURYA WISATA** office on Jl. Melasti, Tel: 51673 or 51786, tlx: 35258. You may also book airplane flights from this office.

SHOPPING

In Legian, as in Kuta, you may purchase any number of contemporary outfits in bright, sometimes garish, silk-screened and painted patterns. These are sadly replacing the traditional *ikat* and *batik* fabrics which are increasingly harder to find. There are a few antique shops along Jl. Legian where you can find examples of the beautiful and stunning natural arts and crafts. Noteable amongst them is the **Timor Art Shop** (Jl. Legian, Tel: 51537) where you can have vests or jackets made to order from hand-picked ikat fabric.

NUSA DUA

As the newcomer on the scene, Nusa Dua is at a bit of a disadvantage because it is rather isolated from the rest of Bali. On the other hand, the new hotels here have made up for this by providing a "total" hotel environment—everything you could possibly ask for is available on the premises. A few restaurants and souvenir shops are sprouting up at the edges of Nusa Dua, and in a few years this area may become another Sanur. But in the meantime, Nusa Dua is a remarkably peaceful place.

The brand new **Nusa Dua Beach Hotel** offers the ultimate in opulence—a palatial Balinese setting, health club, squash courts, three restaurants and a discotheque. And the newly revamped **Hotel Bualu** offers a comprehensive sports package, lush gardens and horse-drawn buggies (*dokar*) for romantic, tropical-evening rides up and down "hotel row."

Two new luxury hotels have opened—the **Bali Sol** and the **Putri Bali**, and the new **Club Mediterranée**.

Hotel Bualu (50 rooms), Nusa Dua, Tel: 713-10, 713-20, tlx: 35231 BUALU. Lush tropical gardens, a swimming pool and very private, deluxe rooms about 100 meters from the beach. Tours and transportation within Nusa Dua, tennis courts with equipment and ball boys, horse riding, windsurfing, surfing, snorkeling, and outrigger sailing, are all available with or without instructors free of charge to hotel guests. Scuba diving equipment available for a nominal charge, free guide, free boat transportation, and lessons available by the only P.A.D.I. (Professional Association of Diving Instructors) certified instructor on the island. US$45 to $85 a night.

Bali Sol (500 rooms), Nusa Dua, Tel: 71510-11. Watersports facilities, five restaurants, swimming pool, gym and tennis courts. US$84-US$550.

Hotel Putri Bali (425 rooms), P.O. Box 301 Nusa Dua,Bali, Tel: 710-20, 714-20 tlx: 35247 HBN DPR. Seven miles from Ngurah Rai International Airport. All rooms with a/c, balcony, tv with two in-house video programs, four restaurants, two bars, pool, tennis courts, golf, water sports and recreation room. Rooms cost between US$76 to US$84. Cottages from US$90 to $120 a night. Suites from US$180 to $500 a night.

Nusa Dua Beach Hotel (450 rooms) P.O. Box 1028, Denpasar, Bali, Tel:712-10, tlx: 35206 NDBH DPR. A hotel on a scale of grandeur that even Bali's rajas never conceived of in their wildest dreams. Huge pool, three restaurants, squash courts, tennis courts, health club with weight room, discotheque and large beach front. Rooms from US$65/$70 to US$75/$80 a night. Suites from US$150 to $500 a night.

DENPASAR

WHERE TO STAY

If you really must stay in Denpasar, the old **Bali Hotel** on Jl. Veteran or the **Pemecutan Palace Hotel** are the only places to consider. The Bali Hotel was built in the early 1930s and was once the colonial oasis in Bali—the *rijsttafel* is still good and the swimming pool courtyard charming. The Pemecutan Palace is actually located in the Badung palace and one has the feeling, at least, of hobnobbing with Balinese royalty here in the extensive courtyards.

There are scores of other hotels in the US$3-20 category, most of them catering to domestic Indonesian tourists. Many are located on Jl. Diponegoro around the **Hotel Denpasar**. Two that are popular with foreigners are the **Adyasa** and the **Two Brothers Inn**.

Adyasa (20 rooms), Jl. Nakula 23, Denpasar, Tel: 2679. Losmen-style rooms arranged around a central garden. US$4 to $8 including breakfast.

Hotel Denpasar (78 rooms), Jl. Diponegoro 103,. P.O. Box 111, Denpasar, Tel: 26336, 26363. Half of the rooms have a/c and hot water, the other half are quite spartan. A favorite of large Indonesian tour groups from Java. US$6 to $30 a night.

Hotel Pemecutan Palace (44 rooms), Jl. Thamrin 2, Denpasar, Tel: 23491. This hotel takes one side of the extensive Badung palace, where day to day palace life continues all around you. Some rooms with a/c and hot water. US$15 to $24 a night.

Natour's Bali Hotel (71 rooms), Jl. Veteran 2, P.O. Box 3, Denpasar, Tel: 25681-5. Centrally located in Denpasar, just a block from the main intersection and town square. Good restaurant and bar. Many rooms with a/c and hot water. US$20 to $40 a night.

Two Brothers Inn, Jl. Imam Bonjol, Gang VII/5, Denpasar. Friendly losmen for budget travelers. Near the Tegal Bemo terminal. US$2 to $3 a night.

WHAT TO EAT

Denpasar has the best Chinese and Indonesian restaurants on Bali, so if you are passing through or have errands to run here, be sure to stop in for a meal, too.

For local fare, the expatriate's favorite is **Rumah Makan "Betty"** on

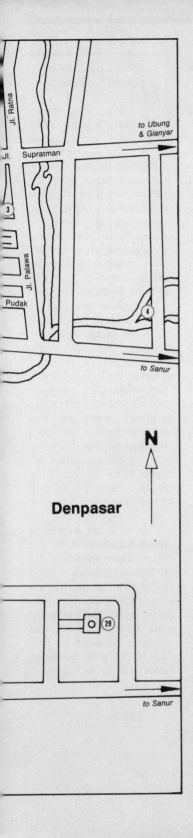

Denpasar

Hotels & Losmen
16 Adi Yasa
12 Bali Hotel
26 Hotel Denpasar
24 Two Brothers Losmen
3 Wisma Taruna — YHA

Restaurants & Bars
17 Restaurant Atoom Baru
15 Restaurant Delicious
14 Restaurant Gajah Mada
13 Restaurant Puri Selera

Offices, Shops, Etc.
9 Badung Tourist Office
7 Garuda Office
28 General Post Office
27 Immigration Office
20 Kusumasari Shopping Centre
29 Office of the Governor
6 Radio Station
8 Telephone & Telegram Office
18 Zamrud Office

Cemeteries, Temples, Museums, Cinemas, Etc.
4 Art Centre
10 Bali Museum
25 Cockfights
19 Cinema
21 Cinema
1 KOKAR — Art School
11 Puputan Square
2 Stadium

Bemo/Bus Stations
5 Kereneng Bus Station (to Central & East Bali)
22 Suci Bus Station (to Java)
23 Tegal Bus Station (to Kuta & Airport)

Jl. Kartini, which has a not-so-spicy menu of Javanese and Chinese dishes. Try the *tahu goreng kentang* (bean-curd and potato curry), *bubur ayam* (rice porridge with chicken) and their *nasi campur*. Also excellent juices and mixed ice drinks.

The Balinese favorite, meanwhile, is the **Rumah Makan Wardini** in Tapakgangsul, a modest diner serving traditional dishes (daytime only). For a full range of Indonesian chicken dishes—soups, fried chicken legs, liver *sate*, curries—visit the ever-popular **Kartini Restaurant**, diagonally opposite the Indra Cinema near the petrol pump.

The **Gajah Mada Restaurant** near the traffic lights on Jl. Gajah Mada also serves top-notch Javanese food. Their *ayam lontong* and curry dishes are a gourmet's delight.

Kalasan Baru on Jl. Suropati, near the bandjar at Abian Kapas (by the Art Centre) has the warrant from Denpasar's upper echelon bureaucrats. *Hati ampla goreng* (deep-fried giblets), *ayam goreng kalasan* (Yogya-style fried chicken) and *sayur asem* (tamarind vegetable soup) are their specialities.

SHOPPING

The morning market at **Pasar Badung** in Denpasar is the island's largest emporium. A real eye-opener, coral-lined alleys lead to a ceremonial knick-knack section selling a thousand and one ceremonial offerings, baskets, spices and knick-knacks. Avoid the meat department.

Balinese coffee is famous the world over. Buy a kilo of the gourmet blend at a coffee shop on Jl. Gajah Mada by the main intersection (next to Mekar Jaya). Five doors down is a shop specializing in the beautiful blankets of eastern Indonesia. Jl. Sumatra is thick with fabric merchants—beat back the rag traders in Kuta, buy a few meters and have your favorite shirt copied by a local tailor (about US$4).

Denpasar's main street (Jl. Gajah Mada) and a few salesrooms on the outskirts of town at **Tohpati** are the only places on Bali to buy top quality hand-drawn "tulis" Javanese batiks. **Antique** shops are along Jl. Gajah Mada up near the town square end. Also on Jl. Arjuna, Jl. Dresna, Jl. Veteran and Jl. Gianyar.

Be aware that most shops in Denpasar open at 8 a.m., close for a siesta from 2-5 p.m., and then re-open in the evening until 9 p.m. The night markets by the river are a great place to shop for kinky Indonesian tee shirts and childrens wear.

Money changers and **Banks** are located all along the main road, Jl. Gajah Mada.

MUSEUMS AND GALLERIES

The **Bali Museum** on the eastern edge of the town square offers a vivid picture of Balinese life and art from prehistoric times up to the 20th century, with emphasis on the antique. The museum was built by the Dutch and opened in 1932; its collection was lovingly assembled with advice from German painter and long-time Bali resident, Walter Spies. Particularly informative are the scale models of such rites as the tooth-filing ceremony, weddings and cremations. The museum also houses a valuable collection of old "topeng" masks, weapons, textiles, Ming ceramics, paintings, wood carvings and betel nut sets that once belonged to Balinese royalty. Open everyday between 8 a.m. to 12:30 p.m. (Friday until 11:30 p.m.); closed Mon.

The new art center at **Abian Kapas** in an eastern suburb has a permanent exhibition of modern art. There is also an arena for frequent evening dance performances, and a shop where artworks are sold. A calendar of events is available (or call: 227-76). Open everyday between 8 a.m. to 5 p.m.

UBUD

The beauty and artistry of Ubud have attracted visitors from all over the world ever since the 1930s, when painters Walter Spies and Rudolph Bonnet first came to this mountain village and made it their home. Finding an abundance of local painting, dance and woodcraft in the traditional style, they founded the *Pita Maha*, a society which introduced local artists to European techniques. Since that time many more western artists have settled here. Dutch-born Hans Snel and American Antonio Blanco now maintain homes and galleries in Ubud and many Ubud painters—like I Gusti Nyoman Lempad, Ida Bagus Made Poleng and I Gusti Ketut Kobot—have become internationally reknown.

Although the Ubud of today is no longer the serene and traditional place that it once was, it is still a relatively quiet alternative to the bustle and hustle of the beach resorts. Many visitors to Bali make this their "home base," taking short one or two-day excursions from Ubud to the other points on the island. Here you can find charming thatched-roof bungalows overlooking verdant rice paddies, fall asleep amidst a cacaphony of croaking frogs, and awaken to the crowing of roosters at dawn. Yet also in Ubud are to be found several excellent restaurants serving a wide variety of Indonesian and western food, as well as enough fellow foreigners to provide congenial company in the quiet evenings.

Spend your days strolling along the main street of Ubud browsing in the village's numerous art galleries, chatting or reading in an open-air cafe and wandering the backlanes outside of Ubud, where you may catch glimpses of Balinese village life as it has been for centuries. Ubud is also excellent for shopping—you will find everything here from traditional wood carvings to contemporary paintings in the latest acrylic hues.

GETTING ACQUAINTED

There are several landmarks in Ubud that are useful to know about, although it is such a small place that after a few hours, you will know your way around like a native.

Tourist Information Center "Bina Wisata" (in the center of town on the main road) is a new, "volunteer" organization that strives to maintain and nurture Ubud's traditional values, including friendliness to outsiders. "For love and spirit," as the sign says. But in many ways this is just like an all-purpose travel agency. They offer maps, newspapers, tours, car and bike rentals, a message board, postcards, cigarettes and helpful advice. The map of Ubud sold here is loaded with native lore and remedies for common tourist ailments.

Surya Cargo and Travel Service (on the south side of the main road, next to Nomad Restaurant) is a new branch of the Legian business. Here you can book flights to any place in the world—Jakarta, Singapore, or Bangkok. Prices are not bad—just a bit higher than Jakarta or Bangkok. Still, for the traveler who likes to make plans while on the go, it is a useful service. Open 8-4 p.m., Sunday and holidays 9 a.m.-12 noon. (Telex 35258 SURYA IN) **Unit Pelayanan Telekomunikasi** (Telecommunication Service) is the only place you can send a telex or telegram or make a phone call from Ubud. Prices are subject to change.

TELEPHONE (3 mins.)
Denpasar	Rp 2.625
Australia	Rp 17.400
USA	Rp 19.350
Europe	Rp 22.800

TELEX (per word)
Australia	Rp 460
USA	Rp 530
Europe	Rp 530
Denpasar	Rp 20

Tino Drugstore (on the main road next to Tourist Information) is Ubud's general store, providing the tourist with all the necessities of modern life. Cosmetics, drugs, imported sweets, canned foods, shoes, books, postcards and umbrellas make up only a portion of their offerings.

Ubud Post Office (at the eastern edge of Ubud). Note

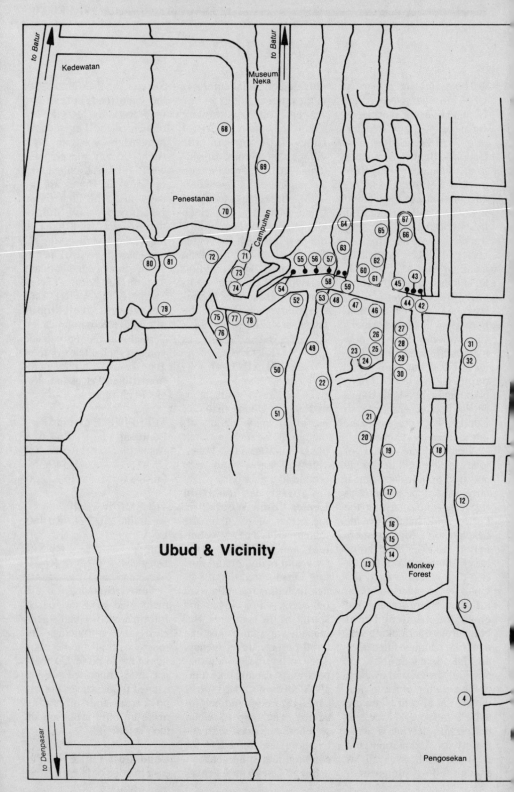

Ubud & Vicinity

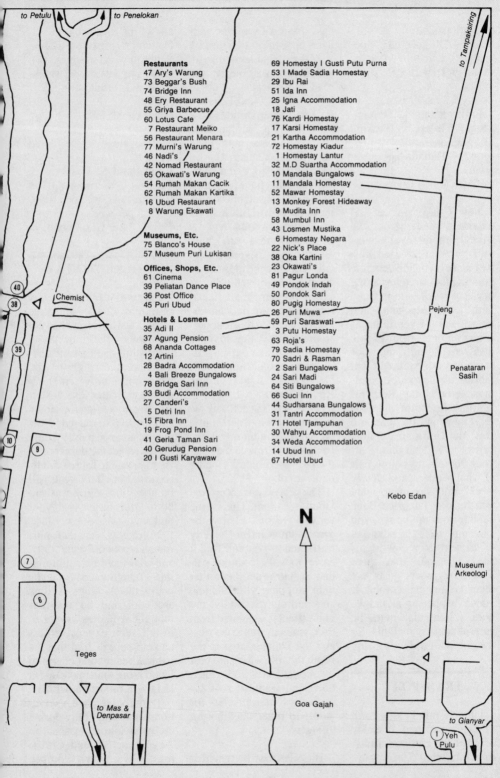

to Petulu   to Penelokan   to Tampaksiring

Restaurants
47 Ary's Warung
73 Beggar's Bush
74 Bridge Inn
48 Ery Restaurant
55 Griya Barbecue
60 Lotus Cafe
7 Restaurant Meiko
56 Restaurant Menara
77 Murni's Warung
46 Nadi's
42 Nomad Restaurant
65 Okawati's Warung
54 Rumah Makan Cacik
62 Rumah Makan Kartika
16 Ubud Restaurant
8 Warung Ekawati

Museums, Etc.
75 Blanco's House
57 Museum Puri Lukisan

Offices, Shops, Etc.
61 Cinema
39 Peliatan Dance Place
36 Post Office
45 Puri Ubud

Hotels & Losmen
35 Adi II
37 Agung Pension
68 Ananda Cottages
12 Artini
28 Badra Accommodation
4 Bali Breeze Bungalows
78 Bridge Sari Inn
33 Budi Accommodation
27 Canderi's
5 Detri Inn
15 Fibra Inn
19 Frog Pond Inn
41 Geria Taman Sari
40 Gerudug Pension
20 I Gusti Karyawaw

69 Homestay I Gusti Putu Purna
53 I Made Sadia Homestay
29 Ibu Rai
51 Ida Inn
25 Igna Accommodation
18 Jati
76 Kardi Homestay
17 Karsi Homestay
21 Kartha Accommodation
72 Homestay Kiadur
1 Homestay Lantur
32 M.D Suartha Accommodation
10 Mandala Bungalows
11 Mandala Homestay
52 Mawar Homestay
13 Monkey Forest Hideaway
9 Mudita Inn
58 Mumbul Inn
43 Losmen Mustika
6 Homestay Negara
22 Nick's Place
38 Oka Kartini
23 Okawati's
81 Pagur Londa
49 Pondok Indah
50 Pondok Sari
80 Pugig Homestay
26 Puri Muwa
59 Puri Saraswati
3 Putu Homestay
63 Roja's
79 Sadia Homestay
70 Sadri & Rasman
2 Sari Bungalows
24 Sari Madi
64 Siti Bungalows
66 Suci Inn
44 Sudharsana Bungalows
31 Tantri Accommodation
71 Hotel Tjampuhan
30 Wahyu Accommodation
34 Weda Accommodation
14 Ubud Inn
67 Hotel Ubud

Chemist

40
38
39
10
9
7
6

Pejeng

Penataran Sasih

Kebo Edan

Museum Arkeologi

N

Teges

to Mas & Denpasar

Goa Gajah

to Gianyar

1 Yeh Pulu

the various hours:
Stamps / Registered / Special Delivery
Monday-Thursday 8 a.m.-4 p.m.
Friday 8 a.m.-11 p.m.
Saturday 8 a.m.-12:30 p.m.
Money Orders / Banking Transactions
Monday-Thursday 8 a.m.-noon.
Friday 8 a.m.-11 p.m.

New Ubud Market (on the main road, across the street from the royal palace, Puri Saren) is housed in a two-story brick and concrete building that stretches along one city block, and is filled with local merchants and their wares. Everything is available here, from plastic dishware to craft items of carved wood, batik and ikat fabrics, fresh produce, paintings, and clothing. Remember that prices of all non-food items are flexible, and that the local merchants expect you to bargain. Start your bargaining below half of what is asked, and slowly work your way up to what you think is a fair price. If the vendor does not budge, you can come back the next day or go next door. Few items are so unique that there won't be others just like them around the corner. If you do happen to fall in love with a particular item, be careful not to reveal this, for the price will certainly go up.

TRANSPORT

Ubud is only 17 kms north of Denpasar, and is easily reached by car, motorbike, or public bemo. The new by-pass around Denpasar connects up to the east of the city with the main Gianyar road, and further on a smaller side-road north leads on up to Ubud via Mas and Peliatan. By private car Ubud is now only about a half an hour from Sanur, an hour from Kuta or Nusa Dua.

Arriving by bemo, you will normally have to change over in Denpasar, but may be lucky enough to find a driver in Sanur or Kuta who is heading all the way to Ubud. Note: bemo drivers expect and encourage tourists to charter their vehicles at much higher than usual rates. If you are not chartering, be sure that this is understood and that the driver is picking up other passengers. A reasonable fare from Denpasar to Ubud is around Rp500 one way. Expect to pay US$4 to $5 each way for a chartered bemo, depending on your bargaining skills. Bemos to Denpasar can easily be hailed along Ubud's main street.

The best way to get around Ubud is on foot. This is true for two reasons. Firstly, the town is small and not heavily trafficked —you will find it easier to walk from one gallery or stall to another rather than stopping your vehicle and parking. Secondly, the main street is separated from the Campuan area to the west and the Peliatan area to the south by hills which are best overcome on foot. You may, however, want to rent bicycles or motorcycles for jaunts to other neighboring villages.

Bicycles may be rented at any of the following:
Robiyana (next to Bahan Seni Lukis, art supply store): US$1 per day, $8 per week.
Tourist Information: US$1 per day
Hotel Ubud: US$1 per day

Motorcycles may be rented from:
Robiyana: US$3 per day
Tourist Information Counter: US$3 per day, US$15 per week
Hotel Ubud: US$3 per day

WHERE TO STAY

Places to stay in Ubud may be roughly divided into three categories, distinguished not so much by their rates as by the overall comfort and condition of the rooms. What were once, only ten years ago, top-of-the-line hostelries, are now often run-down and poorly managed. New places are constantly being built to meet the demands of an expanding tourist trade, so rest assured that you will be able find a place to suit both your tastes and your budget.

Note, however, that most rooms have cold water only, and none have air-conditioning. Though the days can be warm, the evenings in Ubud are cool and no one has thought it necessary yet to install such expensive systems. You will find that the natural beauty and charm of Ubud more than make up for its lack of modern amenities.

To make advance reservations (necessary only during the peak tourist seasons, in August and around Christmas/New Year), simply address your letters to the hotel, Ubud, Bali, Indonesia. There are no street names or numbers, nor are their telephones. On short notice, send a telex or telegram.

First Class
(US$15 a night and up)

Each of these hostelries is like a little haven, tucked away from the main road and providing the traveller with respite from the aggravations of the outside world. Smaller than any of the hotels found in the beach areas, they offer an intimate and peaceful atmosphere conducive to contemplation and relaxation. It is no wonder that visitors to Ubud often stay for weeks at a time.

Ananda Cottages (10 bungalows, one family-size with 6 beds) Restaurant adjacent. On the road between Campuan and Sanggingan, and only minutes from the stunning Museum Neka. Surrounded by rice paddies, and away from the mainstream. US$15-25 a night.

Munut Bungalows (9 bungalows) Just after the Campuan bridge, turn a sharp left and climb the hill. Price includes a delicious breakfast of eggs, black rice pudding and fresh fruit. This delightful establishment is run by a local painter and his charming wife, Candri, who have previously operated two other hotels, and are planning to open a new one in the house once owned by European painter Rudolph Bonnet (near the bridge below the Campuan Hotel). Some rooms are up on the second story, and have traditional high, thatched roofs. Others are set in a garden surrounded by lily ponds. US$7-25 per night.

Murni's Bungalows (3 houses, each with 2 bedrooms, 2 baths, kitchen, living room, and veranda) with hot water, and fans. Operated by the owner of Murni's Warung, on the main road just before the bridge in Campuan. Looking out over rice paddies, and yet close to the center of town. US$60 a night.

Hans Snel's Bungalows (5 bungalows, the largest of which has hot water from a solar heater: "No sun, no hot!") You will know when you are on the right path to this well-kept and private setting, which is owned and operated by the Dutch-born painter, for it is paved in concrete and bears the names of friends and frequent visitors. The garden itself is a work of art in stone and flower, and surrounds a central area with bar and restaurant. An art gallery displays a retrospective of the owner's work. US$25-35 per night, including breakfast. (Best to book in advance.)

Hotel Tjampuhan (30 bungalows) natural swimming pool, tennis and badminton court, restaurant, bar, laundry service and hot water. Located on a hillside overlooking the Ubud Valley and Campuhan River, this hotel is situated at the far end of the main road. The original bungalow was formerly the home of Walter Spies, and the hotel has been kept up and cared for in the past several decades. Car tours around the island can be arranged (US$20 for 4 hours, $35 for 8 hours). US$20 a night, including breakfast.

Ubud Inn and Restaurant (10 bungalows) located on the main road to the Monkey Forest, this lovely and peaceful inn was a rice paddy until its owner and manager, Gusti Nyoman Berata, converted it into a "great escape" in 1979. Surrounded by rice paddies, this is one of the most serene places in Ubud. US$14 to $18 a night, including breakfast.

Intermediate Range
(US$7 to $15 a night)

This category includes places that, while not top-of-the-line, are still very comfortable for the majority of visitors. A few were once first-class and have fallen into the moderate price range.

Ardjuna's Inn (10 bungalows). Owned and operated since 1983 by the American artist, Antonio Blanco, and his wife, who live below in their palatial home. Turn left just after the Campuan bridge across the street from the Beggar's Bush, and at the top of the hill (opposite Munut's) you will find this quiet, modest inn. US$3.50-6 including breakfast.

Menara Lodge Restaurant (4 bungalows)

Operated as much for friends of the owner, Cokorda Agung Mas, as for the traveller, this hotel serves as a center for the arts and letters of Ubud. Cokorda taught ethno-musicology (Music and Dance documentation) at UCLA for two years in the 60s, and keeps alive an awareness and appreciation of these traditional arts, as well as his contacts with western scholars. Offers a library, an art gallery, dance concerts and gamelan lessons. US$5 a night, including breakfast.

Monkey Forest Hideaway (8 rooms, one with a veranda overlooking the river of natural spring water) on the main road to the Monkey Forest. Restaurant with Balinese, Indonesian, and European food, gift shop, small library. Nestled in the trees, and featuring large tile bathtubs. Owned by friendly and helpful Atjin who sees large parties off with an authentic Balinese meal in his own home across the way. Rooms are between US$10-12 a night.

Puri Saraswati Bungalows (4 suites with hot water, 7 bungalows, and 10 rooms in losmen) Once the playground of the royal palace, this elaborate garden setting offers a quiet oasis in the center of town. Suites are furnished with lace-draped beds, and overlook the palace lake gardens next door. Laundry service provided. US$25-30 for a suite, $12-20 for a bungalow, $10-12 for rooms, including continental breakfast.

Puri Saren Agung (16 bungalows with hot water) Still owned and operated by a member of Ubud's royal family, T'jokorda Gde Putra Sukawati, this hotel is located on the royal palace grounds. Many famous people, including Charlie Chaplin and President Kennedy, have passed through the palace gates. Rooms are in elaborate structures around a central courtyard, and are furnished with Balinese antiques. Classes in dance, carving and painting are offered to visitors, and performances of music and dance are held on Mondays. Large bathrooms with showers and tubs. US$24 a night, plus 15 per cent tax.

Hotel Ubud (18 bungalows) The owner of this old Balinese home, Raka Jhonny, has studied Hotel Management in Belgium, and treats his guests to fresh towels, mosquito coils, boiled water, and money changing. The larger rooms include hot water for bathing, and a fan. Bicycle, motorcyle and minibus rentals available. US$9 to $35 a night.

Budget lodging in Ubud is plentiful, but the foreign traveler may have difficulty feeling completely comfortable in these modest, often dirty, and poorly tended losmen. If you are on a short shoestring budget, take a look around town where "Homestay" and "Losmen" signs are hanging, and make your own choice. Each one is located on the map, and you will see with a quick glance

that there are many from which to choose. The main road to the Monkey Forest, and the road between Campuhan and Sanggingan are not to be missed for the most idyllic of the budget class lodgings. US$2 to $5 a night.

WHERE TO EAT

The food in Ubud ranges from excellent to acceptable, with everything from European cuisine to simply prepared local dishes.

Beggar's Bush (just beyond the Campuan Bridge) is in an attractive building perched over the Campuan River, housing the first and only pub in Ubud. Here you can get Western and Balinese food, including a special spiced, smoked duck. The pub upstairs has beer on tap, and is frequented by local youth.

Cafe Lotus (on the main road, right across the street from the Tourist Information Center) offers a regular menu of delicious Western and European fare such as fresh pastas (fettucine carbonara and neopolitan), chicken kiev, and fruit crepes. In addition, the chef produces daily specials, all of which are imaginative and nicely prepared. Deserts are a house specialty. Try the strawberry tart for a real lift.

Griya Barbeque Restaurant received the government's Food Award in 1982 for their barbecued chicken, beef, pork, and tuna. "Griya" means "house of a Brahmin," and the food is first class.

Murni's Warung (on the main road beside the Campuan Bridge) is an Ubud institution. Serving many excellent items such as "Murni's Original Upper Elk Valley Authentic American Hamburger" and a special Balinese meal of smoked duck, vegetable *lawah* and yellow saffron rice, this clean and comfortable cafe is a hang-out for the foreigner who wishes to meet fellow travelers or capture a feeling of "home away from home." Murni has been here for years, and she knows what westerners want. Check out the freshly-baked cookies and cakes, the superb fish dishes and the fresh fruit salad. There is an adjacent shop where you can buy antiques, jewelry, terra cotta and wood carvings. A selection of postcards, books and film is available in the restaurant.

Hans Snel's Garden Restaurant (in the center of town, one block north of the Puri Saren) serves both Western and Indonesian food in a lovely garden setting. Try the spring chicken and sweet and sour fish, or the curry wonton appetizer. Moderately expensive, but worth it.

Nomad's Restaurant (on main road, in the center of town) serves daily specials in addition to Indonesian and Western dishes. A popular place for diners who don't want to pay high prices, or trek down to Murni's.

Ubud Restaurant (on the main road to the Monkey Forest) is situated in the rice paddies, and is peaceful unless the store next door is playing rock and roll music. Offering Chinese, Balinese, and Western cuisine, this mid-priced restaurant is a great place to stop for lunch while strolling to the Monkey Forest.

Hotel Tjampuhan (to the right, across the Campuan Bridge) serves a different set meal every night:
Sunday: Balinese roast suckling pig
Monday: Sate
Tuesday: Rijsttafel
Wednesday: Specially made chicken
Friday: Balinese smoked duckling
Saturday: Frog's legs

Wayan's Warung (on the main road to the Monkey Forest) is a spanking new place, serving light meals for the day-tripper. Spaghetti neopolitana, sandwiches, Swiss *roesti*, German potatoes, and homemade bread are the house specialties in the medium price range.

There are many lower-priced warung in Ubud. Two of the most popular are:
Ary's (on the main road, next to the Tourist Information Center) is busy all day and night, serving inexpensive Indonesian nasi goreng and sate, omelettes, spaghetti, and sandwiches.

Harry Chew's (on the main road to the Monkey Forest) has an extensive menu of good food at cheap prices. You may have Chinese, Indonesian, or vegetarian meals here, or order one day in advance for smoked duck or rijsttafel.

MUSEUMS AND GALLERIES

There are numerous galleries in Ubud where you may see and purchase many styles of local paintings. They are all indicated on the Ubud map available at the Tourist Information Center. Several of the more well-known painters have galleries in their homes. You may also wish to visit the museums which house hundreds of paintings, dating back to the pre-1930's when local artists had not yet absorbed western techniques from their resident European painters.

Museum Puri Lukisan (on the main road, near the center of town) was built in 1954 by the late Tjorkorda Gde Agung Sukawati, Prince of Ubud. It houses a large collection of paintings and early sculpture by artists who lived in or around Ubud. A gallery adjoins the original collection, and here you will find paintings for sale. Once a magnificent edifice, this museum has sadly become run-down from lack of maintenance. Open 8-4 daily. Rp200 entrance fee.

Neka Museum (in Singgingan, north of Campuhan) was founded by Suteja Neka in 1982, and is owned and managed by the "Dharma Seni" Foundation.

Set overlooking fields of rice paddies, this exquisite group of buildings affords the visitor a peaceful viewing environment. The collection comprises works by a number of artists, all of whom used Bali for their subject matter. An adjacent gallery houses paintings for sale. Open 8 a.m.-4 p.m. daily. Rp200 etrance fee.

Neka Art Gallery (on the main road, at the eastern edge of Ubud). Owned by Suteja Neka, son of a famous local woodcarver. Neka collects and sells Balinese paintings in Malaysia, Thailand, Japan, Singapore, Europe and America. The gallery houses a collection of contemporary works for sale.

Antonio Maria Blanco (up the hill to the left, just over the Campuan Bridge) is an American-born artist who came to Ubud in the 50s, fell in love with a beautiful Balinese dancer, and decided to stay. He and his wife live in a magnificent and well-preserved house representative of old Balinese architecture, and donated by the Indonesian government. Blanco has a gallery here where he displays his work of the last 30 years. Conceptual and erotic painting and collage are his forte.

Hans Snel Gallery (a block north of Saraswati palace). In the home and hotel/restaurant of Dutch painter. A retrospective collection of his work from the 50s to present is on display in a beautiful showroom.

I Gusti Nyoman Lempad Museum and Gallery (on the main road, near the center of Ubud) is the home of the late painter who was active in the Pitha Maha, a society of artists founded with the help of Europeans Walter Spies and Rudolph Bonnet in the 30s. Lempad created a distinctive style of sparse, elongated composition, and painted until he was 104 years old. Ask to see the artist's original works inside the garden court that are not, however, for sale.

Excursions: **Dance Performances** abound in and about Ubud. You can see local dancers perform at the Puri Saren on Mondays at 6:30 pm for US$2.

Just a 10-minute walk down the road from Ubud is **Peliatan** where the world-travelled Classical Dance Company performs every Saturday at 6:30 p.m. Tickets may be purchased from young boys who prowl the main street of Ubud on the day of the performance, or at the door for US$2.50. A typical program includes the following dance styles:

Gabor/Pendet (an offering dance)
Baris (a warrior dance)
Kebyar Terompong (a solo dance in which the dancer plays the kettle drums).
Legong Kraton (a dance/drama for young girls)
Oleg Tambulilingan (a contemporary dance created by the late, great Mario)

Tours are also available to Bona where a small, professional company entertains with Kecak and Fire Dances. Organized by Bali Dewata and Golden Kuta Tours, these dances are performed nightly during the tourist season, Monday, Wednesday, and Friday at other times. You may buy tickets from the bus driver who waits outside the palace gates in Ubud at 7 p.m, or at the Tourist Information Center for Rp2500 on the day of the performance.

Island Tours to all parts of Bali are available at the office next to the Museum Puri Lukisan, or at the Tourist Information Center. Sample excursions:

Volcano and Lake	Rp 5000
Besakih	Rp 5000
Karangasen	Rp 7500
Tanah Lot	Rp 5000

Local Excursions can be made on foot, or by bicycle, motorbike, or car. Going by foot affords the most pleasure, and gives you the feeling of really being in Ubud. Three places are especially pleasant to visit:

The Monkey Forest is south of the main road, and can be reached by taking the road that runs alongside the Marketplace. Galleries, stalls, warungs, and shops are scattered along this quiet country road which takes you directly to a heavily-forested templeground where monkeys hang out in the trees, or come down to eat peanuts from your hand.

Penestanan is the home

of the "Young Artists," so called because they were younger than those first trained by the European painters. Watch for the signs at Campuhan that take you to a secluded community graced with occasional art galleries.

Sanggingan is north of Campuhan, and if you are not staying in this part of town, you simply must not miss it before leaving Ubud. There are a number of art galleries here in addition to the spectacular Neka Museum, but the main attraction is a peaceful jaunt through the beautiful countryside.

LOVINA BEACH

A northern beachfront alternative to Kuta and Sanur, this is a serene and infrequently visited vacation spot located just nine kilometers to the west of Bali's original capital and bustling port, Singaraja. One of the most beautiful and restful places to stay in Bali, Lovina Beach was first established nine years ago when the son of the prevailing King of Singaraja, Auak Agung Panji Tisna, built what is now the Tasik Madu Hotel as a lovetoken for his wife. It is for this romantic reason that many local inhabitants like to play on the word, Lovina, mixing English ("love") with Indonesian ("inap" means to spend the night). Whatever the linguistic interpretation is, this quiet "heaven on Earth" is for many travelers the "lovely" Bali that they came to see, but sadly missed in the southern part of the island.

Black sand beaches and quiet waters nestled inside of extensive coral reefs distinguish this idyllic beach. Snorkeling is superb here, as hundreds of fish and other forms of sealife inhabit the shallow waters surrounding the reefs. Tranquil sailboats dot the waters, but there is no proliferation of the high-speed watersports frequently encountered in the southern seas. You will not find any trinkets or tinsel for sale along the roadside, nor pushy vendors on the beach carrying sarongs filled with useless paraphenalia. Best news is that the local government has passed a moratorium on building, thus preventing any new hotel development along the non-ocean side of the main road, and limiting building on the oceanside. Rice paddies that currently separate the accommodations into three major sections are required by law to stay put, insuring an open and uncluttered beachfront for the future.

The only place in Bali that is predominantly Muslim, the northern island areas have also retained the local dialect. You will find that the residents speak *Bahasa Indonesia* as well as some English, but they are not as comfortable in conversation as in the southern spots.

GETTING THERE

Lovina is within an easy three-hour drive from Denpasar, and only 10 minutes west of Singaraja. Take either of the two major inland highways for what may be your most spectacular road trips in Bali, depending upon whether or not there is fog or rain over the mountains. The eastern inland route through Gianyar and Bangli gives an incredible view of G. Batur from Kintamani, while the more direct western route passes by Lake Bratan and the volcanic highlands. Approaching Lovina from the East takes you around the dry, desert-like side of the island where you will be astonished by the sharp contrast in geography and botanical species. Only three hours from the small beach of Candi Dasa, this route is both interesting and facile. The Western approach is long and requires several days, but many find the excellent snorkeling and skin diving at Pulau Menjangan a sufficient reason to travel to this side of the island. Or you may have already arrived via the Bali Strait to Gilimanuk.

GETTING ACQUAINTED

Lovina Beach is characterized by its relative lack of commercialism. When you first drive into town, you will be amazed at the emptiness of the main road. The town is divided into three major areas, separated by rice paddies. Everything you need is readily available in nearby Singaraja. It is Lovina Beach where you will go to rid yourself of earthly attachments. Prices for everything are low in comparison to southern tourist spots.

If you do have the aggravating need to change money, there is an authorized money changer on the south side of town about two-thirds of the way to the end. Postal service is available at Badai Restaurant, also on the south side. If you wish to rent a bicycle, go to the Nirwana Seaside Cottages on the north side, near the beach. Snorkeling equipment and advice is available at Aditya Bungalows and at the Kalibukbuk Inn, or at any of the beachside homestays.

WHERE TO STAY

Lodgings in Lovina Beach are inexpensive and quite comfortable. Roughly divided into three categories, there are many places for travelers of any sized pocketbook to stay. The main road in Lovina Beach runs closer to the ocean the further west one travels. Thus, the lodgings which are the most secluded and peaceful are the ones furthest east. All listings below are presented in order of location, East to West, just as you would encounter them if driving from Singaraja. Do not be swayed by the condition of the signs you see on the road, for the quality and upkeep of an establishment often has little to do with its advertising skills.

First Class accommodation is located on the ocean-side of the main road, and consists of private bath with shower, Western toilet, and electricity. All of these are characterized by good management, cleanliness, and adjoining restaurants that feature substantial menus.

Prices quoted below are for double occupancy, and do not reflect government tax or service charges.

Baruna Beach Inn (24) Tel: 41252. Built in 1981, and showing signs of moderate wear and tear. On the beach at the beginning of the strip. Class III: (17) Rooms in the back, no carpet, upstairs or downstairs. US$7. Class II: (4) Twin beds, breakfast. US$8. Class I: (3) Double bed, breakfast. US$10.

Suci Jati (12) Tel: 21952. Built in 1983. Owned and lovingly managed by Simon (of Simon's Seaside Cottages) with thoughtful touches such as outdoor shower, safety deposit lockers, laundry service, towel, soap, and daily sheet changes. Three buildings with four fan-cooled units in each, tiled floors, large garden bathrooms, thatched roofs, ideal location behind rice paddies and close to the beach. Price does not include

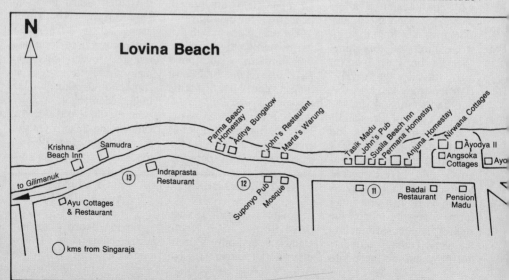

breakfast, but tea and coffee are free. A unique and special place to stay. US$10 for doubles; $8 for singles.

Banualit Beach Inn (14) Tel: (0362) 41889. On the beach, isolated, quiet, and exquisitely managed. Truly a little paradise. Advance reservations for Class I and II lodgings recommended. Class IV: (2) Small room. US$3.50. Class III: (8) Fancooled. Includes breakfast. US$7.50. Class II: (2) Airconditioned, double bed. US$8. Class I: (2) Upstairs, private veranda overlooking sea, air-conditioned, intercom, large garden bathroom with shower. US$12.50.

Nirwana Seaside Cottages (20) Close to a popular section of the beach, yet also far from the road. Has its own restaurant and bar. Bicycle rental, snorkel equipment and guide, tours to Kintamani available. Tea and fruit served in the morning. Class III: (12) Share shower. US$3.

Class II: (5) Double occupancy. US$6

Class I: (3) Occupancy for four, upstairs or down. US$11.

Aditya Bungalows (30) P.O. Box 35, Singaraja, 81101, tlx: 35261 STAR DPR ADT. Large, ·well-managed, and comfortable. On the beach, but also close to the road. Restaurant, art and clothing shop, snorkeling equipment, and Friday night Legong dancing. Price does not include breakfast. Class IV: US$3.50. Class III: Upstairs, thatched roof. US$5. Class II: Garden setting, no sink. US$6. Class I: Beachfront. US$8.

Intermediate Range lodgings are the most plentiful in Lovina Beach. All have shower and private bathroom, and are quite sufficient for the experienced traveler.

Mandara Cottages (6) On the beach, center of town.

Class II: Share shower. US$2.50. Class I: Private shower, Western toilet. Includes breakfast. US$8.

Perama Beach Inn (11) Right on the main road, 50 meters from the beach. In clean and neat garden setting. Snorkeling available. Class II: (9) Share bath. Inclusive of breakfast. US$3.50. Class I: (2) Private bath with shower. US$4.50.

Lila Cita Beach Inn (21) On the beach in an isolated field. An excellent value. Class III: (7) Share bath. US$2.50. Class II: (8) Private bath. US$3.50. Class I: (6) Western toilet downstairs, bedroom upstairs. Tea and fruit. US$4.

Kalibukbuk Beach Inn (6) On the beach behind tobacco fields, near a stream. Quiet and clean. Shower, Western toilet, snorkel equipment. Not including breakfast. Restaurant serves special barbecue every Friday night. US$3.

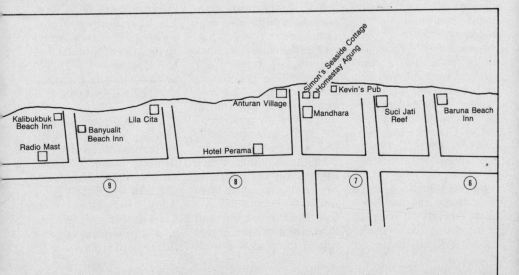

Ayodya Accommodation. On the main road, in a private home. Once very popular, but traffic has built up recently, making it a noisy location. US$2.50.

Astina Seaside Cottages (11) Built in 1984, a remote hideaway, favored by contemplative travelers. Unmarked with a sign, it is nestled behind several fields just off the beach. Turn into the dirt road across the street from Khi Khi Restaurant (where a sign indicates: "The Beach 400m") and drive to the end. Class III: (4) Shared bath. Indonesian toilet. US$2.50. Class II: (3) Private bath, no basin. US$3.50. Class I: (4) Bungalow, with Western toilet, shower. US$4.50.

Angsoka Cottages. Close to the beach, yet centrally located. Private shower, breakfast not included. This is "luxury on a shoestring." Class II: (4) US$2.50. Class I: (8) US$4.50.

Tasik Madu. The hotel that put Lovina Beach on the map. Literally meaning "Sea of Honey," this was a gift from the King of Singaraja to his wife in 1977. Now operated by a relative, and sadly run-down, it is still a bargain for the budget traveler who wants to be part of history. Class II: Share bath. US$3.50. Class I: Private bath with shower. US$4.50.

Budget Range lodging is basic, but clean and adequate, especially if you plan to spend your days outside. Usually a shared shower and Indonesian toilet. Not nearly as plentiful as in Kuta or Sanur because here there are no highrise hotels to offset the other end of the scale.

Wisata Jaya (formerly Pension Madi) is right on the road, but otherwise an excellent choice for the low budget traveler. Eight clean and comfortable rooms with private bath. Price includes breakfast. US$2.50.

Arjuna Homestay, on the road. Share shower, Indonesian toilet. Price includes breakfast. US$1.50.

Susila Beach Inn is not on the beach, but, rather, on the main road. Private bath. US$1.50.

WHAT TO EAT

Fresh seafood is the culinary specialty of Lovina Beach. Most restaurants offer a variety of Indonesian dishes, but the food here is like the life: simple and satisfying. One of the most popular tourist hang-outs is **Badai Restaurant**, right over a river on the main road. Here you can find inexpensive yet delicious fish dishes. Try the fish battered and deep-fried, or grilled with garlic and butter. Vegetarian dishes are also available, as well as a handy postal service. Write postcards while you wait for your dinner. Both the **Banualit Beach Inn** and **Aditya Bungalows** have restaurants that serve fresh prawns, calamari, and fish. The **Dayana Bar and Restaurant** on the oceanside of the road is a well-managed place that offers home-cooked food. The mixed seafood grill and yogurt lassies are house specialties. And if looking for a great thirst-quencher, try the fruit drink at **Adi Rama Restaurant.** Waffles, omelettes, soup, and lobster are well-prepared and delicious.

Meals for the budget traveler can be found at **Khi Khi Restaurant,** or **Yellow Coconut.** There seems to be some kind of "fried rice contest" going on in Lovina Beach, with **Marta's Warung** offering 13 kinds. First runner-up is **John's Restaurant** with seven. If you want any kind of meat at John's, you must order one day in advance. (Perhaps this is the reason why he is only first runner-up.) And at the **Srikandi Hotel** you can get Hungarian goulash and other European favorites.

Nightlife in Lovina Beach is limited to a few pubs and bars. One of the most active is the **Bali Bintang Pub** it is quickly turning into the "Blue Ocean" of Lovina Beach with its aggressive crowd of young "individualists." If you just want a beer, try the quieter bars at Aditya Bungalows or Nirwana Seaside Cottages.

EXCURSIONS

You will need a motor vehicle to get around, so take a drive up to the one and only Balinese Buddhist temple. To get to this extraordinary site, turn south just west of Aditya Bungalows. Here you will find pools to bathe in, and panoramic vistas of unsurpassed beauty.

CANDI DASA

Until recently, this two kilometer strip of exquisite beachfront was a quiet stretch of untouched paradise. A temple, **Pura Pengumuman**, was the only man made fixture for miles around before an Ashram was built on these shores in 1983. It was then that the tourists who were fed up with the growing commercialism of the South Bali area began to wander east and north for a more restful vacation. A string of small bungalow-type hotels and a few restaurants that serve excellent local seafood dishes have since cropped up, making Candi Dasa a veritable "tourist spot," but luckily, one with a low profile. It remains in a class by itself, far away from the high-rise hotels and extravagant prices of the more popular sites, yet it is only within a two to three-hour drive from Bali's capital, Denpasar.

A perfect place for quiet strolls on the beach, refreshing dips in the gentle waters, and friendly conversation, Candi Dasa has no gawking shopsellers, discos, or frantic traffic snarls. The beach is encompassed by a coral reef, making the waves tame and, therefore, unappealing to the surfers. Though the lack of indigenous village life lends a sort of open-ended, unrooted ambiance to this community, it also keeps the clutter of arts and crafts down to a minimum. In short, the entire town of Candi Dasa exists for the sake of the tourist alone, and you will be treated here with the utmost of graceful service. The lifestyle here is basic, relaxed, and close to the natural elements. If you are looking for an oceanside, low-budget alternative to South Bali's traffic and overpopulation, this is an excellent, no-frills choice.

GETTING THERE

Candi Dasa is located on the Southeast coast of Bali, just north of Padang Bai and approximately 80 kilometers from Denpasar on the main highway. Padang Bai is reknown for its excellent snorkeling and skin diving spots, and also as the place to catch a boat to neighboring island Lombok. You may rent a car, or motorcycle and drive yourself, or easily take public transport. The drive takes you through the towns of Celuk and Batubulan where you may wish to hop out and do some shopping. This is the center of silvermaking and woodcarving, and it is here where you will not only find some of the most beautiful and plentiful examples of Bali's fine craftwork, but also the best prices.

GETTING ACQUAINTED

The town of Candi Dasa consists of a two kilometer strip right of the main road by which you arrive. Accommodation is more plentiful on the oceanside, while restaurants are more frequently found on the non-oceanside of the road. You will see immediately that there are many places to stay, and a quick drive through town will acquaint you with various landmarks. Upon first speaking to any of the local residents, you may feel that there is something wrong in your presentation, for they will not understand English, German, or Japanese as the "hipper" folks down on the southern shores. Out here in the country, high Balinese is the common language, and while *Bahasa Indonesia* is understood, your language may not be.

In the center of town on the oceanside, you will find the **Friendship Shop** where you can obtain information, and laundry service. You may also purchase tickets to island tours and dance performances, or take advantage of their airport shuttle service. Right next door is **MG P.T. Mahanta Express** which will rent a bike or motorcycle to you, take you for a tour, or help you with your ticket and cargo information.

Across the street from the Friendship Shop, on the non-oceanside, is an authorized money changer at the **Homestay Sasra Bahu**. A little further down, on the same side, at **Nakula Homestay**, is a teleTel office. For necessary purchases and amenities, there are the **Depot Sumber Rasa** (oceanside) and **Eddy Shop** (non-oceanside). Here you can buy toilet paper, soap, towels, bottled water, drug items, and candles (to enhance the low-voltage electricity of the town). At the north end of town, on the oceanside, **Kelapa Homestay** has a small library with French, German, and English paperbacks, guidebooks and postcards for sale, bicycle and motorcycle rentals, and massage.

WHERE TO STAY

Prices for everything in Candi Dasa are lower than in the larger, more heavily touristed areas. Accommodation can be had for as little as Rp 1,000/night or as much as Rp 17,000. There are no high class hotels here, no air-conditioning, nor swimming pools. But you may find very comfortable lodging at ridiculously low prices, and the ocean itself insures a more luxurious and refreshing swim than any swimming pool could possibly provide.

First Class refers to clean, new, ocean front bungalows set in beautifully manicured gardens. Most have traditional Balinese thatched roofs and tile floors. All have veranda, shower, Western toilet, electricity, and breakfast included. Double occupancy price quoted below. The low voltage electricity of the town gives warmly-lit fixtures a romantic appeal. Many of these accommodations will provide a lantern for your evening veranda tête-à-têtes.

Puri Pandan Bungalows (oceanside, close to center of town) has 10 bungalows, each with a garden bathroom that features a stone-lined shower, and two single beds. The "happening" place in Candi Dasa, with its spacious restaurant and bar, this is the most expensive of all lodgings in town. US$15 a night.

Candi Dasa Beach Inn (oceanside, West side of town) has 18 bungalows. Large rooms with double or twin beds, several opening onto the beach. Standard: Splash bath, shower, US$8. Deluxe: Shower-tub, US$13.50 a night.

Bambu Garden Bungalows (non-oceanside, right at West entrance) has seven bungalows with a panoramic view of Lombok to Padangbai, and fully tiled sleeping and bathing quarters. US$8-US$12.

Puri Amarta Beach Inn (oceanside, at East end of town) has 18 bungalows, ranging from small to large. Class III: no shower or tub, (9 total), US$4. Class II: Shower, double bed (6 total), US$8. Class I: Upstairs sleeping loft with double bed (3 total), US$13 a night.

Intermediate range lodgings are plentiful in Candi Dasa. Each of these has small bathrooms with splash baths and a shower head, Indonesian-style toilet, and electricity. All these located in pleasant garden surroundings.

Wiratha's Bungalows (oceanside, West end) has 10 bungalows in a varied price range. Breakfast is included. Class II: US$4. Class I: Larger, includes towel and blanket, Western toilet, US$8.

Rama Bungalows (oceanside, East end) has 12 bungalows in varied price range. Class II: Two beds, splash bath, no shower, US$3.50. Class I: Three beds, shower, breakfast, US$8.

Natia Homestay (oceanside, East end) has 13 bungalows in varied price range. Breakfast included. US$8.

Pandawa Bungalows (oceanside, on East end of lake) 10 bungalows, each with shower, breakfast, and coffee or tea all day. US$3.50.

Agung Homestay (oceanside, center of town) has only 2 rooms, each with shower. US$3.50.

. **Puri Bali** (oceanside, West end) has 9 bungalows with splash bath and shower. US$3.50.

Homestay Segara Wangi (oceanside, West

end) has 7 rooms with single beds. US$3.50.

Geringsing Homestay (oceanside, West end) has 7 rooms in an intimate garden with a well. US$3.50.

Sri Artha I (non-oceanside, West entrance) has 7 rooms from US$1.50 to $5.

Budget lodgings are the bare, essential places to catch a good night's sleep for a cheap price. Usually a shared shower and bath, Indonesian style toilet. US$1 to $2.50 a night, double occupancy.

Sasra Bahu Homestay (non-oceanside, center of town) Price includes breakfast. Shiatsu massage available. US$2.50

Sri Artha Inn (built in 1984, non-oceanside, West entrance) Shower. US$2.50.

Graha Cantiloka Beach Inn (non-oceanside, East end) US$1 to $2.50.

WHAT TO EAT

All restaurants in Candi Dasa feature local and fresh seafood that is delicious regardless of the manner of preparation. Fresh-water *gurami* fish, tuna, prawns, lobster, and crab are all available in addition to the usual Indonesian and European favorite dishes. Again, prices in Candi Dasa are very low, and do not necessarily reflect the quality of food. Be prepared to dine at your own leisure, for the facilities are usually humble, and the pace of life, relaxed. There are many places to eat, but few have more than six or seven tables in each, guaranteeing an intimate atmosphere despite the lack of fancy facilities.

For an extravagant meal in Candi Dasa, you will have to go to the **Puri Pandan Restaurant** where lobster à la Pandan, stir-fried with eggs and vegetables, is top on the menu. Here you can bask in the sun as you sit at the oceanfront tables, order a fruit flambé and sip a mixed cocktail. *Legong* dances with full *gamelan* orchestra are presented once a week to the guests of the hotel and restaurant. Or walk down the beach to the **Candi Dasa Beach Restaurant** which serves inexpensive sweet and sour prawns or grilled fish that are as good as anything you can get in Kuta Beach, for only half the price.

Across the street at the **Tunjung Bar & Restaurant**, a *rijstaffel* of fried rice, vegetable soup, pork satay, spring roll, *krupuk*, and hot tea can be yours for as little as US$0.75. The **Cumplung Restaurant** serves chili crab, guacamole, and curry dishes. On the same side of the street at **Astina Restaurant**, the cooking is just like home. Try the chicken/vegetable soup or the grilled chicken. Yogurt, so good for the traveler, is available at **Gusti Pub & Restaurant**. Here you can also find brochette fish and jaffles, but the portions are small, so order a second dish of something equally as delicious. (It's still a bargain.)

For the budget-wary traveler, **Ayu** and **Harry Chew** are good places to get lots of food for not a lot of money. **Ngandi Restaurant** is also always packed, and serves a wonderful meal for less than a dollar.

EXCURSIONS

Walking is the only way to see Candi Dasa. It is so small that if you travel too fast, you will miss it altogether. At the east end of town is the temple **Pura Pengumuman**, with its traditional "stairway to heaven" and splendid view of the town and ocean. The lake below is the gathering place of the townsfolk at sunset. Here you will find the mothers and children bathing while the older boys play soccer on the beach nearby. On the west end of town is a covered depot where you can look out to Lombok and Padangbai.

To the east and west of Candi Dasa are two of the most popular snorkeling and skin diving areas, Gili Toapekong and Padang Bai. You can either ask at the **Friendship Shop** or go to these towns yourself where you can easily find local dive shops with information, equipment, and boat rental.

SURVIVAL INDONESIAN

LANGUAGE

Indonesia's motto, *Bhinneka Tunggal Ika* ("unity in diversity") is seen in its most driving, potent form in the world of language. Although there are over 250 distinct languages and dialects spoken in the archipelago, the one national tongue, *Bahasa Indonesia,* will take you from the northernmost tip of Sumatra through Java and across the string of islands to Irian Jaya.

Bahasa Indonesia is both an old and new language. It is based on Malay, which has been the *lingua franca* throughout much of Southeast Asia for centuries. Sailors, traders and Islamic missionaries spoke what became known as marketplace or 'Bazaar' Malay, a simplified version of the sophisticated Malay spoken on the Malay Peninsula.

In 1929, while the country was still under colonial rule, the All Indonesia Youth Congress wisely urged the development of a single national language, based not upon colloquial Bazaar Malay but upon the pure classical Malay of the Peninsula. This language was admirably suited to Indonesia's needs, since it was the basis of many of the regional languages and, like them, contained many words of Sanskrit and Arabic origin. As a symbol of national pride and unity, *Bahasa Indonesia* spread rapidly, incorporat-ing many new words so that today, although similar, it is quite distinct from Malay.

The ancient Balinese language is quite complicated and far more difficult to learn than *Bahasa Indonesia.* Unless you get into remote areas far from the usual tourist track, *Bahasa Indonesia* is all you will need to know.

Although formal Indonesian is a complex language demanding serious study, the construction of basic Indonesian sentences is relatively simple. Indonesian is written in the Roman alphabet and, unlike some Asian languages, is not tonal. There are no articles in Indonesian: *rumah* means 'a house.' To make a plural, you simply double the noun: *rumah-rumah* means 'houses' and is normally written as *rumah 2.*

Another help for beginners is the lack of complicated verbal tenses. To denote time, a few key adverbs are used, the most useful being *sudah* (already), denoting the past, *belum* (not yet), flexibly indicating what is about to or never to happen, and *akan* (will), denoting the future.

When speaking *Bahasa Indonesia* you need to keep a few basic rules in mind. Adjectives always follow the noun: *rumah* (house) and *besar* (big) together are *rumah besar* meaning 'big house.' When constructing a sentence, the order is usually subject-verb-object: *saya* (I) *minum* (drink) *air* (water) *dingin* (cold);

The possessive is made by putting the personal pronoun after the noun: *rumah saya* means 'my house.'

Indonesians always use their language to show respect when addressing others, especially when a younger person speaks to his elders. The custom is to address an elder man as *bapak* or *pak* (father) and an elder woman as *ibu* (mother), and even in the case of slightly younger people who are obviously VIPS this form is suitable and correct. *Nyonya* is polite when speaking with a married woman, *nona* with an unmarried woman.

To achieve standardization of spelling in Malaysia and Indonesia, *ejaan baru* (new spelling) was introduced in both countries in August 1972. All publications printed since then use the new form, and many signs have been altered to conform to the new spelling, though you may still come across old spellings from time to time.

Listed below are a few guidelines on the pronunciation of *Bahasa Indonesia* which, with minor exceptions, is written phonetically with much the same sound values as Italian. The pre-1972 spellings, where applicable, are in brackets. The best way to acquire the correct pronunciation is of course, to listen to the way Indonesians speak. Once you start to use the language you will find that most people are eager to help.

a
short as in 'father'
(*apa* = what, *ada* = there is)

ai
rather like the 'i' in 'mine'
(*kain* = material, *sampai* = to arrive)

k
hard at the beginning of a word as in 'king,' hardly audible at the end of a word. (*kamus* = dictionary, *cantik* = beautiful)

kh (ch)
slightly aspirated as in 'khan' or the Scottish 'ch' in 'loch'
(*Khusus* = special, *khabar* = news)

ng
as in 'singer' never as in 'danger' or 'Ringo'
(*bunga* = flower, *penginapan* = cheap hotel)

ngg
like the 'ng' in 'Ringo'
(*minggu* = week, *tinggi* = high)

r
always rolled
(*rokok* = cigarette, *pertama* = first)

u (oe)
as in 'full', never as in 'bucket'
(*umum* = public, *belum* = not yet)

y (j)
as in 'you'
(*saya* = I, or me, *kaya* = rich)

c (tj)
like the 'ch' in 'church'

(*candi* = temple, *kacang* = nut)

e
I. often unstressed as the barely sounded 'e' in 'open' (*berapa*, sounded like *b'rapa* = how much?)
2. sometimes stressed, sounding somewhere between the 'e' in bed' and 'a' in 'bad' (*boleh* = may, *bebar* = wide)

g
hard as in 'golf' never as in 'ginger'
(*guntur* = thunder, *bagus* = very good)

h
generally lightly aspirated (*hitam* = black, *lihat* = to see)

i
either short as in 'pin' or a longer sound like 'ee' in 'meet'
(*minat* = to ask for, *ibu* = mother)

j (dj)
as in 'John'
(*jalan* = road or street, *jahit* = to sew)

Two minor points about spelling. Despite the new rules, you will find many instances where people's names continue to be spelled with the old 'oe' rather than the current 'u'; some may change, but most stick to their birthright, including the President whose name is Soeharto and only rarely used by the press as Suharto.

In airline offices, travel agencies, medium to large hotels, and major stores, you'll find that English is widely understood. Many Indonesians over the age of 35 also speak Dutch with arying degrees of excellence. Other European and Asian languages are less well served. Avoid slang or regional usages as far as possible, and unless your listener is obviously fluent in your language, speak slowly and clearly. Even a smattering of *Bahasa Indonesia* (the Indonesian language) is a help, and its use will be much appreciated.

Basic Guide To Bahasa Indonesia: This micro-dictionary has, as far as possible, been divided into practical groups of related words and actions. As your command of the language improves, and as you move from one part of the island to another, you'll discover certain differences in regional and colloquial usage which are beyond the scope of this short vocabulary, but the context will often explain the meaning of a new word or phrase.

Greetings and Civilities

thank you (very much)
terima kasih (banyak)

good morning
selamat pagi

good day (roughly 11 a.m. to 3 p.m.)
selamat siang

good afternoon, evening
selamat sore

good night
selamat malam

goodbye (to person going)
selamat jalan

goodbye (to person staying)
selamat tinggal

I'm sorry
ma'af

welcome
selamat datang

please come in
silakan masuk

please sit down
silakan duduk

what is your name?
siapa nama saudara?

my name is ...
nama saya ...

where do you come from?
saudara datang dari mana?
or *dari mana?*

I come from ...
saya datang dari ...

Pronouns and Forms of Address

I
saya

you (singular)
kamu (to children)
saudara, anda

he, she
dia

we
kami (not including the listener)

you (plural)
saudara-saudara, anda

they
mereka

Mr.
Pak/Bapak

Mrs.
Nyonya/Ibu

Miss
Nona

young boy/girl
adeh

Directions and Transport

left
kiri

right
kanan

straight
terus

near
dekat

far
jauh

from
dari

to
ke

inside
didalam

outside of
diluar

between
antara

under
dibawah

here
disini

there
disana

in front of
didepan, dimuka

at the back
dibelakang

next to
disebelah

to ascent
naik

to descend
turun

to walk
jalan

to drive
stir, bawa

pedicab
becak

car
mobil

bus
bis

train
kereta-api

airplane
kapal terbang

ship
kapal laut

bicycle
sepeda

motor cycle
sepeda motor

where do you want to go?
mau kemana?

I want to go to...
saya mau ke...

stop here
berhenti disini, stop disini

I'll be back in five minutes
saya akan kembali lima menit

turn right
belok kekanan

how many kilometers?
berapa kilometer jauhnya?

slowly, slow down
pelan-pelan/perlahan-lahan

Important Places

hotel
hotel, penginapan. losmen

shop
toko

train station
stasiun kereta-api

airport
lapangan terbang

cinema
bioskop

bookshop
toko buku

petrol station
pompa bensin

bank
bank

post office
kantar pos

swimming pool
tempat pemandian, kolam renáng

Immigration Dept.
Departemen Immigrasi

tourist office
kantor parawisata

embassy
kedutaan besar

Spending the Night

room
kamar

bed
tempat tidur

bedroom
kamar tidur

bathroom
kamar mandi

toilet
kamar kecil

towel
handuk

bedsheet
seprei

pillow
bantal

water
air

soap
sabun

fan
kipas angin

to bathe
mandi

hot water
air panas

cold water
air dingin

to wash
cuci

to iron
gosok

clothes
pakaian

shirt
kemeja

trousers
celana

dress
baju, rok

Where is a hotel?
Dimana ada hotel?

How much for one night?
Berapa harganya satu malam?

Please wash these clothes
Tolong cuci pakaian-pakaian ini

Eating

restaurant
restoran, rumah makan

dining room
kamar makan

food
makaan

drink
minuman

breakfast
makan pagi

lunch
makan siang

dinner
makan malam

boiled water
air putih, air matang

iced water
air es

ice *es*	brains *otak*	vinegar *cuka*
tea *teh*	fish *ikan*	sweet *manis*
coffee *kopi*	prawns *udang*	sour *asam*
cordial *stroop*	vegetables *sayur*	bitter (without sugar) *pahit*
beer *bir*	fruit *buah*	hot (temperature) *panas*
fresh orange juice *air jeruk*	banana *pisang*	hot (spicy) *pedis, pedas*
milk *susu*	pineapple *nanas*	cold *dingin*
bread *roti*	coconut *kelapa*	'supreme' *istimewa*
butter *mentega*	mango *mangga*	boiled *rebus*
rice *nasi*	egg *telur*	fried *goreng*
noodles *mie, bihun, bakmie*	soft-boiled egg *telur setengah matang*	served in stock *godok*
soup *soto*	fried egg *telur mata sapi*	sauce *kuah, saus*
chicken *ayam*	dumpling (small) *pangsit*	cup *cangkir*
beef *daging (sapi)*	dumpling (large) *bakpao*	plate *piring*
pork *babi, daging babi*	sugar *gula*	glass *gelas*
lamb *domba*	salt *garam*	spoon *sendok*
goat (also 'mutton') *kambing*	pepper *merica, lada*	knife *pisau*
liver *hati*	soya sauce *kecap*	fork *garpu*

Shopping

shop
toko

money
uang

change (of money)
uang kembali

to buy
beli

price
harga

expensive
mahal

cheap
murah

fixed price
harga pas

How much is it?
Berapa?/Berapa harganya?

It is too expensive
Itu terlalu mahal

Do you have a cheaper one?
Adakan yang lebih murah?

Can you reduce the price?
Bisa saudara kurangkan harganya?

What is this?
Apa ini?

I'll take it
Saya akan ambil ini

I don't want it
Saya tidak mau

I'll come back later
Saya akan kembali nanti

Time

day
hari

night
malam

today
hari ini

morning (to about 10:30)
pagi

noon (broadly 10:30-3 p.m.)
siang

evening (3 to 8 p.m.)
sore

now
sekarang

just now
baru saja

soon, presently
nanti

before
dahulu, dulu

when (= the time that)
waktu

when? (interrogative)
kapan?

tomorrow
besok

yesterday
kemarin

minute
menit

hour
jam

week
minggu

month
bulan

year
tahun

past (the hour)
liwat

to (before the hour)
kurang

What is the time?
Jam berapa sekarang?

Seven o'clock
Jam tujuh

Half-past seven
(i.e. half to eight)
Setengah delapan

It is 10 to eight
Jam delapan kurang sepuluh

It is 10 past eight
Jam Delapan liwat sepuluh

Numbers and Days of the Week

1. one
satu

2. two
dua

3. three
tiga

4. four
empat

5. five
lima

6. six
enam

7. seven
tujuh

8. eight *delapan*	263. two hundred and sixty- three *duaratus enampuluh tiga*	but *tetapi, tapi*
9. nine *sembilan*	1,000 one thousand *seribu*	if *jika, kalau*
10. ten *sepuluh*	Sunday *Hari Minggu*	with *dengan*
11. eleven *sebelas*	Monday *Hari Senin/Senen*	this *ini*
12. twelve *duabelas*	Tuesday *Hari Selasa*	that *itu*
13. thirteen *tigabelas*	Wednesday *Hari Rabu*	like this *begini*
14. fourteen *empatbelas*	Thursday *Hari Kamis*	like that *begitu*
15. fifteen *limabelas*	Friday *Hari Jum'at/Juma'at*	similar to *seperti*
16. sixteen *enambelas*	Saturday *Hari Sabtu*	here *sini, disini*
17. seventeen *tujuhbelas*		there *sana, disana*
18. eighteen *delapanbelas*	**Handy Words and Phrases**	very nice *bagus*
19. nineteen *sembilanbelas*	yes *ya/ia*	more *lebih*
20. twenty *duapuluh*	no *tidak. tak* (also *nggak*)	less *kurang*
21. twenty-one *duapuluh satu*	(that's) correct *betul*	because *karena*
30. thirty *tiga puluh*	(that's) wrong *salah*	perhaps *barangkali, mungkin*
40. forty *empatpuluh*	much, many *banyak*	about (approximately) *kira-kira*
58. fifty-eight *limapuluh delapan*	very much, very many *banyak sekali*	then *kemudian, lalu*
100. one hundred *seratus*	and *dan*	good, alright *baik*

Some Verbs

There are several verbal prefixes such as *me-, mem-, men-, meng-, and ber-*. They can be confusing. You will be understood if you just use the root of the verb.

bring
bawa

carry
angkat

take
ambil

give
kasi, beri

buy
beli

sell
jual

ask/ask for
tanya/minta

speak
bicara

see
lihat

try
coba

look for
cari

wash
cuci

want
mau

can (permission)
boleh

can (possible, though commonly signifying permis-
sion as well)
bisa

speak
bicara

tell/say
bilang/berkata

I don't understand
Saya tidak mengerti

I don't speak Indonesian
*Saya tidak bisa bicara Ba-
hasa Indonesia*

I speak only a little Indone-
sian
*Saya bisa bicara sedikit saja
Bahasa*

Please speak slowly
Tolong bicara pelan-pelan

Interrogatives

who
siapa

what
apa

when
kapan

where (location)
dimana

where (direction)
kemana

why
kenapa, mengapa

how
bagaimana

how much, how many
berapa

which, which one
yang mana

A Few More Nouns

cigarette/clove cigarette
matches
korek api

train (railway)
kereta-api

house
rumah

paper
kertas

newspaper
surat khabar, koran

hair
rambut

map
peta

place
tempat

stamp (postage)
prangko, perangko

electricity
listrik

foreigner
orang asing

tourist
turis, wisatawan

Useful Adjectives

big
besar

small
kecil

young
muda

old (person)
tua

old (thing)
lama

new
baru

beautiful
cantik

good
baik

no good
tidak baik

hot
panas

cold
dingin

delicious
enak

clean
bersih

dirty
kotor

red
merah

white
putih

blue
biru

black
hitam

green
hijau

yellow
kuning

gold
mas

silver
perak

Understanding Signs

Many Indonesians words have been borrowed from other languages, and quickly reveal their meanings: *sekolah, universitas, mobil, bis, akademi, sektor, proklamasi* and *polisi*. Other important signs leave you guessing; the following short list may help you.

open
buka, dibuka

closed
tutup, ditutup

entrance
masuk

exit
keluar

don't touch
jangan pegang

no smoking
jangang merokok

push
tolak

pull
tarik

gate
pintu

ticket window
loket

information
keterangan

public
umum

hospital
rumah sakit

pharmacy
apotik

ticket
karcis

house
(institutional sense)
wisma

central
pusat

city
kota

district
daerah

zoo
kebun binatang

market
pasar

church
gereja

golf course
lapangan golf

customs
bea dan cukai

Filling in Forms

Forms are an unvoidable part of travel. Within Indonesia few forms carry translations into other languages, so here are a few key words and phrases to help you out.

name
nama

address
alamat

full address
alamat lengkap

male, female *laki-laki, perempuan*	*berangkat*	identification (passport, etc.) *surat keterangan*
	marital status *kawin*	
age *umur*		issued by *pembesar yang memberikan*
	religion *agama*	
date *tanggal (tgl)*		purpose of visit *maksud kunjungan*
	nationality *kebangsaan*	
time *jam*		signature *tanda tangan*
	profession *pekerjaan*	
departure		

LITERATURE

FURTHER READING

•Baum, Vicki. *A Tale of Bali* (novel). Oxford in Asia, paperback.

•Belo, Jane. *Trance in Bali*. New York: Columbia University Press, 1960. •A provocative and thorough study of the ritual of trance in Bali Hindu ceremonies, including photographs of trance mediums.

•Coast, John. *Dancing Out of Bali*. London: Faber and Faber Limited, 1954. A story of the author's experiences with the Peliatan dance and gamelan troup which he took on a highly successful tour through Europe and the United States in 1952.

•Covarrubias, Miguel. *Island of Bali*. New York: Alfred A. Knopf, 1936. Bali's classic. A wonderfully written book giving many insights to the Balinese, their outlook on life and their fascinating society.

•Drakulic, Nikola and Bajetto, Max. *Bali*. The Hague. W. Van Hoeve, 1952. A sensitive protrayal of Bali through the eyes of a photographer.

•Dutt, Romesh, C. (trans.) *The Ramayana and the Mahabharata*. London: J. M. Dent & Sons Ltd., 1910. A poetic translation of the two great Hindu epics.

•Friend, Donald. *The Cosmic Turtle*. Carroll's Australia and P. T. Bap Bali, 1976.

•Goris, Dr. R. *Bali: Cults and Customs*. Jakarta: The Government of the Republic of Indonesia. A book by a leading archaeologist exploring Bali's culture from ancient times to modern movements in art and music.

•Hanna, W. A. *Bali Profile: People, Events, Circumstances (1001-1976)*. American Universities Field Staff, 1976.

•Hiss, Philip Hanson. *Bali*. New York: Duell, Sloan and Pearce, 1941. A well integrated text and photo book by a photographer who sees the Balinese as the happiest people in the world.

•Holt, Claire. *Art in Indonesia: Continuities and Change*. Ithaca: Cornell University Press, 1967. A penetrating study of the variety of arts in Indonesia, featuring a chapter on Bali's artists and dynamic art styles.

•Kempers, A. J. Bernet. *Monumental Bali: Introduction to Balinese Archaeology and Guide to Monuments*. Den Haag: Van Goor Zonen, 1977.

•K'Tut Tantri. *Revolt in Paradise*. New York: Harper and Row, 1960. A fascinating autobiography of an American woman who came to Bali and was adopted by a Radja. Later she joined the Indonesian revolution to fight with the people she was devoted to.

•Mason, Victor. *Silih Dali Tale of Bali*. Hong Kong: South China Morning Post, 1975. Another delightful combination of humorous verse from the author of *The*

Haughty Toad with pictures from artist Dewah Putu Mokoh. The story of Silih Dali is told here for all children-at-heart, and especially for those who love animals, birds and bees, as well as Oliphaunts and Heffalumps.

•Mathews, Anna. *The Night of Prunama*. London: Joanthan Cape, 1965. A tale of the disastrous eruption of Gunung Agung, Bali's sacred volcano.

•McKie, Ronald and Bernay, Beryl. *Bali*. Sydney: Angus & Robertson Ltd., 1969. An enjoyable book on the author's travels in Bali, the people he meets and the stories he hears.

•McPhee, Colin. *Music in Bali*. New Haven, Conn" Yale University Press, 1966.

•Moebirman. *Wayang Parwa. The Shadow Play of Indonesia*. The Hague: Van Deventer-Maasstiching, 1960. An indonesian scholar's observations of the shadow theater in Bali and Java.

•Raffles, Sir Thomas Stamford. *The History of Java*. Two volumes. London: The Hon. East-India Company, 1817. A rare book on Java's past, with revealing references to Bali with many fine etchings.

•Ramseyer, Urs. *The Art and Culture of Bali*. Oxford: Oxford University Press, 1977.

•Rhodius, Hans. *Walter Spies (Maler and Musiker auf Bali 1895-1942): Schonheit und Reichtum des Lebens*. Den Haag: L. J. C. Boucher, 1964. A collection of paintings, letters and notes by Walter Spies, the German painter and musician who loved Bali and lived here for ten years.

•*Tanah Air Kita*. The Hague and Bandung: W. Van Hoeve N. V. The most inclusive photographic and descriptive book on the Indonesian islands.

•Shadeg, N. *A Basic Balinese Vocabulary*. Denpasar: 1977.

•Wagner, Frits A. *"Bali," Indonesia: The Art of an Island Group*. Art of the World Series. New York: Crown Publishers, Inc., 1959. An illustrated survey of the arts of Bali within the context of Indonesian art.

•Wertheim, W. F. (ed) *Bali: Studies in Life. Thought and Ritual*. Amsterdam: The Royal Tropical Institute, 1960, Also, *Bali: Further Studies in Life, Thought and Ritual*. The Hague: W. Van Hoeve, 1969. An informative series of essays by leading Dutch scholars who researched on Bali, its religion, temples, festivals and villages. de Zoete, Beryl and Spies, Walter. *Dance and Drama in Bali*. London: Faber and Faber Ltd., 1938. One of the most beautiful books written on Bali, relating its dances, legends and mythology with deep understanding for the Balinese people and their dramatic arts.

ART/PHOTO CREDITS

360

362